COSTA BLANCA
MOUNTAIN WALKS

volume 2: east

ABOUT THE AUTHOR

After wartime service in the navy, Bob Stansfield had a career in the police force, becoming superintendent, then lecturing in law in East Anglia. Bob is a lifelong mountain lover, and has walked, climbed and skied in most of the high places of Britain and in many parts of the Alps. He was a part-time instructor with Outward Bound and a voluntary warden in the Lake District, and also founded the first police climbing club.

Bob and his wife, Kathy, retired to the Costa Blanca in 1986. There they helped to found the Costa Blanca Mountain Walkers, a group which went on to thoroughly explore the walking possibilities of the region. Bob has written walking articles in local newspapers and published a series of walking guides locally. A selection was published by Cicerone in 1995 as *Mountain Walks on the Costa Blanca*. In this new edition, in two volumes, Bob has updated and expanded the scope of the first edition to give unrivalled comprehensive coverage of the area.

ADVICE TO READERS

Readers are advised that whilst every effort is taken by the author to ensure the accuracy of this guidebook, changes can occur which may affect the contents. A book of this nature with detailed descriptions and detailed maps is more prone to change than a more general guide. New fences appear, waymarking alters, there may be new buildings or eradication of old buildings. It is advisable to check locally on transport, accommodation, shops, etc., but even rights of way can be altered, and paths can be eradicated by fire, landslip, forest clearances or changes of ownership. The publisher would welcome notes of any such changes. Costa Blanca Mountain Walkers issue a twice-yearly newsletter with route updates, and the Publications Secretary will also supply an addendum to this book on request.

Costa Blanca
Mountain Walks

volume 2: east

Bob Stansfield

2 POLICE SQUARE, MILNTHORPE, CUMBRIA, LA7 7PY
www.cicerone.co.uk

Acknowledgements

Like the first edition, these walks represent a selection of the results of exploratory work done by the leaders of the Costa Blanca Mountain Walkers, and I am again glad to acknowledge their help and generosity in allowing me to chronicle their discoveries. Whilst I have received unstinted help and encouragement from a legion of fellow walkers, especially in bringing my walks up to date, some need a special mention here.

I wish to record my gratitude to the following: Kees Andriessen, Bill Assheton, Derrik Ayrton, Clive Axford, Chris Batnick, Malcolm Blakeney, Jack and Anita Bremner, Gladys Brettal, Jenny Carter, Vicky Carter, Brian and Aileen Evans, Peter Fallows, Maurice and Eunice Gibbs, George and Betty Goddard, Kaithe Greene, Roy and Sharon Hancliff, John Hemmons, Jim Johnston, Roger Massingham, Alan Myerscough, Peter Reason, Jean Ryan, Maurice Scholer, Vincent and Elena Schultz, and Eric Taylor.

Finally I am pleased to be able to record my gratitude to those readers who took the trouble to let me have suggestions for improving the book, and I have thanked them individually.

My dear wife Kathy, my most constant mountain companion for more years than we both care to remember, can no longer walk, but I am grateful for her unstinted collaboration in the preparation of this edition.

I take the greatest of pleasure in dedicating my work to her with love and gratitude.

Bob Stansfield
CALPE 2001

CONTENTS

SIERRA BERNIA

CALPE AREA – SIERRA TOIX/SIERRA OLTA

VAL DE JALÓN

Foreword to 2nd edition

There have been many changes since the first edition was published: mountain walking has become a major attraction, and accommodation, waymarkings and facilities for camping have improved.

This edition not only provides an update but also adds further day walks and two extended walks in the area. The biggest problem has been achieving a balanced selection, and sadly some favourite walks have had to be left out. Those keen to find their own walks need have no fear: there is an almost unlimited scope for further exploration by future generations of walkers.

It is very bad form to say farewell a second time, a bit like a Maria Callas's last performance or Hitler's last territorial claim in Europe. My desk is, however, quite clear, and although one or two more strolls may be lurking somewhere, I have said my goodbyes to the high ridges and to the summits that have given me so many happy memories.

Bob Stansfield
Calpe, August 2001

Olta Summit, walk 14

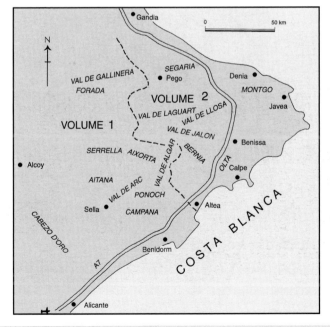

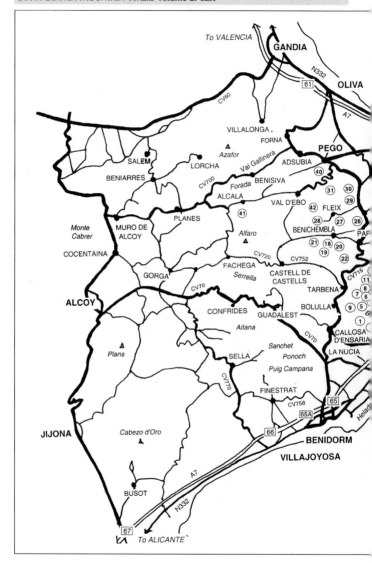

STARTING POINTS FOR THE WALKS

Numbers in circles show
approximate starting points of the walks

Numbers in boxes show
autoroute junctions

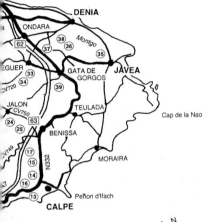

INTRODUCTION

The rugged mountains of the Costa Blanca offer wonderful walking in a landscape of pinnacled ridges, enormous crags, and shady pines. Orange and almond groves enhance the valleys, whilst attractive mountain villages provide hospitality, offering a taste of the real Spain, far removed in character from the developed coastal strip.

Mountain Walks on the Costa Blanca volumes 1 and 2 are simple, easily understood guidebooks, written to enable both visiting and resident mountain walkers to share the delights of ascending and traversing this most satisfying and picturesque mountain area of the Costa Blanca. The two volumes divide the region roughly into west and east. Volume 1 covers the area north and west of Benidorm, while volume 2 covers the area to the north of Calpe.

The guide is not offered in any way as a manual for mountain walking. Readers are assumed to have acquired these skills elsewhere. Some modest strolls are included, which are suitable for walkers of any age or ability, and the guide also offers advice on the differences between walking in these mountains and those of Britain.

Costa Blanca

The region known as the Levant, bordering the Mediterranean, includes the Costa Blanca, which runs from Denia in the north to Torrevieja in the south. The walks in this book fall within Alicante, part of the Costa Blanca and one of the three provinces of Valencia, an ancient kingdom with its own language, customs and flag. Spanish kings, and more recently a dictator, have tried hard to prohibit such manifestations of local pride, and until the recent restoration of the monarchy and the move towards democracy, the language, local costumes and fiestas were prohibited by law. Now there is a spirited revival, Valencia is a region with autonomy and its own government, and the flag proudly flies alongside the national one. Don't be at all surprised to hear country folk speaking Valenciano or a mixture of both languages, and nearly all notices, including road signs, are in Valenciano.

Spain, like France, has now named all its coasts in the interest, no doubt, of tourism. Luckily, the development of tourism has largely been confined to the coastal strip, where vines and oranges have given way to villas, apartments and the major resort of Benidorm. Inland, however, the countryside remains (with one or two exceptions) unspoiled, with the country people still making a living from agriculture. It is not many years ago that Benidorm was a poor fishing village, and women walked barefoot to Callosa de Ensarria to sell fish in the more prosperous inland town.

With the exception of Switzerland, Spain is the most mountainous country in Europe, and the Costa Blanca is no exception, with the mountains coming right down to the sea. By far the greatest concentration of mountain scenery is to be found in the north of the Costa, in the district known as Las Marinas, and these are the mountains traversed by the Costa Blanca Mountain Way (see 'The Costa Blanca Mountain Way' section of volume 1).

The Costa has excellent communications, and on the coast accommodation is lavish. Inland, over the past years hotels and accommodation have improved greatly and there are now good hotels in most of the valleys.

The climate is typically Mediterranean, the rain falling mainly in spring and autumn in heavy downpours. This gives the region over 300 glorious mountain days, although not everyone will want to be on the hills in the middle of a hot August day, when even at 1000m it can be 98°F (37°C).

The Area Covered by the Guide

This comprises mainly two *comarcas* (local authorities) of the province of Alicante, La Marina Baja and La Marina Alta (lower and higher). The area is easily identifiable on maps as the large promontory between Valencia and Alicante.

The ridges and valleys of the mountains radiate roughly from the city of Alcoy, 50km from the coast, like the fingers of a hand. The most northerly valley is that of the Rio Serpis, and is actually in the comarca of Safor. Next comes the beautiful Val de Gallinera, famous for castles and cherries. Further south, is the remote Val d'Ebo and the Val d'Alcala, accessible only by negotiating the acute hair-pin bends on the most difficult, but most picturesque, road in the area. Then there is the Val Laguart, a lovely unspoiled valley, with a road which leads right to its head and continues across the Caballo Verde Ridge at Col de Garga. The road continues, again with many a hair-pin, down into the next valley, that of the Rio Jalon, probably one of the most attractive valleys for tourists due to the picturesque situation, ringed by high mountains, with the broad lower valley ablaze with the blossom of thousands of almond trees in the spring (February). It is the only mountain valley which has been granted appellation status for the wines it produces. Further south, another tortuous mountain road negotiates the side of the Pinos Valley to reach the high plateau of the Bernia. The next valley, that of the Rios Guadalest and Algar, is without doubt the most popular with tourists, and the road has been improved to accommodate the many coaches which bring them daily from Benidorm. Despite this the valley remains unspoiled. Set amongst the highest peaks of the region, with the added attraction of the only large stretch of open water, the Embalse de Guadalest, justifies its reputation as the most beautiful of valleys. The final valley is that of the Rio Sella, which leads inland from Villajoyosa to cross the Aitana Ridge at Paso de Tudons.

The Mountains

It is a mistake to classify a mountain solely by its height – its form is much more important. The mountains of the area are modest in height – 1000m (3300ft) on average. Some, however, reach 1558m (5000ft). But they all have the true characteristics of a mountain – rocky summits, sheer crags, deep gullies and ravines, exciting ridges and pinnacles, and, above all, magnificent views. In addition they have the distinct advantage of accessibility with good approaches by road to the high plateaux or passes, and can all be climbed comfortably in a day, many in a few hours. No need here for cable-cars, mountain huts or a long walk in before you can even set foot on the mountain.

Geology

'The Alpine structures of Southern Spain, south of the MESETA, are divided into three units of BETICS (sensu stricto), SUB-BETICS and PRE-BETICS' (C.B. Mosley, *Field Guide to the Costa Blanca*). For those like me, ignorant of the finer points of geology, this means limestone with some nostalgic intrusions of gabbro. The limestone, a sedimentary rock, is easily eroded by the chemical action of the rain, and rivers soon disappear underground, forming a network of shafts and caverns beloved of the potholer. There are many areas of limestone pavement, with their fissures (grykes), which make for difficult walking. Much of the rock is friable, and on some of the ridges 'jug handles' are liable to come away in your hand. Despite this, there are a lot of difficult climbs put up on great walls of solid rock, particularly on Puig Campaña, Peñon d'Ifach, Toix and Altea Hills, the Sella area and Monte Ponoch.

Travel To and Around Costa Blanca

By Air

There is an international airport at Valencia, which is sometimes used by those visiting the north of the Costa Blanca, but by far the most popular is the airport at Alicante, El Altet, which is much used by package tour operators. There are taxis (rather expensive) and a bus service to Alicante Bus Station from the airport. All tour operators provide coach transport from the airport, and hire cars are available here, but it is better to hire your car in advance.

By Road

The main trunk road, CN332, runs down the coast, giving access to all the resorts. Only Benidorm, however, is so far by-passed, so at peak times there can be delays in passing through the towns.

The A7 autopista (motorway) is superb except for the fact that you have to pay rather dearly for this service. As a result of this toll charge you will find it uncrowded, even in the height of summer.

Minor roads may be narrow by British standards, but have an excellent surface. Caminos rural, even narrower, will take you high into the mountains, and usually have a good surface. Forestry roads give access, even to the summit of some mountains, but are only really suitable for four-wheel drive vehicles due to the variable surface, steep gradients and the tendency to disappear after a storm.

Roads often have kilometre marker stones, and these are a useful reference.

Bus Services

The service from Alicante city is extensive, and operated by Alcoyana.

Ubesa (Union Benissa) operate a service from Alicante to Valencia, with links to other towns along the route. Benidorm has a municipal service, including a service in the tourist season to Algar and Guadalest. Other resorts along the coast have a limited service solely to satisfy local needs.

The bus service to mountain villages is either non-existent or extremely poor, and this means of transport is virtually useless for those who wish to engage in mountain walking.

Information from Central Bus Station, Plaza de Seneca, Alicante (Tel: 522 0700).

Trains

Alicante has main-line connections with the rest of Spain and Europe. The main line runs inland to Valencia via Alcoy.

El Trenet, a narrow-gauge, single-track railway owned by the provincial government of Alicante runs daily services from Alicante to Denia. This line is extremely picturesque, especially between Benidorm and Benissa, where the track runs close to the Corniche. This is not a speedy service, as the train stops at every station, and some trains do not run from Altea to Denia, turning back at Altea del Olla.

With the exception possibly of Calpe, and the halt of Ferrandet, the line is of little use to mountain walkers. From Calpe station there is a bus service to the base of the Peñon d'Ifach, and from Ferrandet you can step out onto the Olta route. The railway company has commissioned a local mountaineer to survey a number of walks from stations along the route.

For train information contact:

> R.E.N.F.E. (Main Line),
> Avenida de Salamanca,
> Alicante
>
> F.G.V. (Coastal),
> Ferrocarriles de la Generalitat,
> Avenida de Villajoyosa, 2
> Alicante.

Taxis

Taxis are identifiable by the green light fitted to their roof. Costa Blanca taxis are far more expensive than those in Madrid and Barcelona. They are certainly not an option for the walker wanting a day out in the mountains.

Car Hire

This is by far the best option for the visiting mountain walker. The smaller cars are very reasonable to hire, sturdy and reliable. They can be booked in Britain as part of a package, available at the airport or at your hotel. For pre-booking in England a recommended firm, which has proved reliable and gives good value for money, is Premier Car Hire (Tel: 01279 641040). A current British (EEC) driving licence is generally acceptable. There are even small four-wheel drive vehicles available for hire, but be sure to book in advance for this type of vehicle.

Accommodation

There is plenty of accommodation of every description to be found on the Costa Blanca. Hotels, hostels and apartments abound. There are also casas de huespedes (boarding houses), pensiones (guest houses), fondas (inns) and casas de labranzas (farm houses) to be had, and the Provincial Tourist Board (Patronata Provincial de Turismo), at Esplanada de Espana, 2 Alicante, will supply a list of accommodation. Hospitality can be found, however rudimentary, even in the remote villages.

Package Holidays

These are very good value, especially if you take a 'special offer', which allows the tour operator to choose your hotel and resort within the Costa Blanca.

Hotels

Benidorm has more hotel beds than any other resort in Europe, so it is more than likely to be offered by your travel agent. There are also good hotels at all other resorts, and an excellent parador (state-run luxury hotel) in Javea. There are motels alongside the CN332 at Gata le Gorgos, Oliva, Vergel and Calpe.

Apartments

There are hundreds of these at the main resorts, and are extremely popular with the Spaniards as well as other nationalities. Apartments usually have minimal cooking facilities. Shopping in the popular resorts is easy and food is reasonably priced. Unlike France, shops do not open very early; they close for an early afternoon siesta, and stay open in the early evening. The largest supermarkets open longer, some even on Sunday. Self-catering is not a problem, due to the relatively cheap menus available in bars and restaurants.

Villas

Most letting agents can supply a list of villas for rent, to suit individual needs, and most include the use of a private swimming pool. These are very good value, especially for a large party.

Youth Hostels

Youth Hostel Aubergue La Marina is situated next to La Comita Campsite: take the first turning right leaving Moraira towards Calpe. The director is Amparo Franqueza, and the hostel offers accommodation for 130 in 2-, 4- and 6-bedded rooms. Usual activities including mountaineering (opened September 1994).

Camping

Many mountain villages have now established campsites. Notable campsites ideal for walkers are at Calpe (Camping Municipal, high on the flank of Olta), Campell in Val Laguart, Finestrat and at Alcala de la Jovada. The Provincial Tourist Board produces a list of the commercial coastal sites – but these are expensive and far from ideal for walkers. General information is available from:

Agrupacion Nacional de Camping de Espana
Duque de Medinaceli 2, Madrid

Oficina de Turismo Tourist – Info
Explanada de España 2, 03002 Alicante   (Tel: 521 22 85 & 520 00 00)

Oficinas Municipales de InformacionTuristica
Avda. Europa, 03500 Benidorm   (Tel: 586 00 95)

Oficinas Municipales de InformacionTuristica
Avda Ejércitos Españoies 66, 03710 Calpe.

In England a list of camp sites and information is available from
Spanish National Tourist Office
57-58 St James's Court
London SW1   (Tel: 0171 499 0901).

There is no need for a Camping Carnet in Spain. Camping libre, or camping off-site, is popular with the Spaniards. The advice of the tourist board is to ask the Ayuntamiento (Town Hall) in the villages for permission and advice. Camping Libre may be restricted in certain areas which are vulnerable to forest fires.

Accommodation Inland

There are two mountain huts that provide accommodation.

- Refugio La Figuera on the Col de Molinos, Km.18, on the CV721, Pego to Val de Ebo Road. Enquiries Town Hall (Ajuntamiento), Pego.
- Casa Refugio Font de L Arc, Camino de Val, Sella 03579, Tel 96 587 2102 or 96 594 1019. 4km from Sella at the end of the surfaced section of the road leading to Paso de los Contadores and Benimantell. Sleeping accommodation and rock climbing guides. For directions see Route No. 12 in volume 1.

Where to Stay

This is very much an individual choice depending on the area in which you intend to walk, but Calpe is considered to be the central point on the coast. From Calpe, in 15min, you can be across the Pass of the Windmills, ready to start your exploration of the beautiful Jalon Valley. In 30min, you can enter the Val Laguart, which will take you high into the mountains, or explore the Pinos Valley, which will take you to the high plateau of the Sierre Bernia, or go south to the thriving inland town of Callosa d'Ensarria, through extensive groves of citrus fruits. From Callosa d'Ensarria, you have to decide whether to visit the Algar Valley with its attractive waterfalls, or to head into the Guadalest Valley, without doubt the most beautiful and picturesque valley of them all.

In 45min, you can be in the interesting town of Pego, ready to explore the unspoiled valley of the Gallinera, with its four castles, six typical Spanish villages, all with Moorish names and, at the head of the valley, lies the beautiful Barranca Encantada (Enchanted Valley). Just a kilometre before you reach Pego, you might be tempted to turn off with the signs for Val d'Ebo, and climb, for 9km on the steepest, most dramatic, but definitely the most scenic road on the Costa (count the alpine bends, if you can drag your eyes away from the views).

Going south, in one hour you can be in Finestrat, a beautiful village, built on top of high cliffs, with casas colgadas (hanging houses) on the south side, pretty Hermita, set in beautiful gardens, on the highest point. From here, you get fantastic views of Alicante's second-highest mountain. Puig Campaña. In a further 15min, you can be in the mountain village of Sella.

This itinerary may be of some use in deciding where to stay on the Costa Blanca, but wherever you stay on the coast, you will have easy access to the mountains. All the times refer to leisurely driving on provincial roads. For those in a hurry, and with unlimited funds, the A7 autopista will reduce the times given considerably.

Communications

Telephones

Telephone kiosks are not always reliable. Although they look modern and efficient, they can gobble up your small change and still not connect you. Often you will find that the machine will not operate because the cash container is full. A much more sensible idea is to use the facilities of a Locutorio, a manned kiosk, where the operator will connect your call for you. They are more expensive but efficient. Most bars have pay phones which always seem to work, but the problem is the noise of the TV. Using the phone in your hotel bedroom may be efficient, but the charge can be excessive.

Fax

There are facilities in most hotels, and public facilities (commercial) at all the resorts.

Village sign

NOTES FOR WALKERS

Rights of Way

The Spanish law of trespass would seem to be basically the reverse of the English common law, where there is no general right of access to land, even common land, without statutory or common law rights. I am advised that in Spain you may wander at will, providing that you obey a few sensible rules. You should not commit damage, hunt, light fires, and so on, and you should not enter private land by climbing walls or fences. Where land is plainly private or the owner has given notice of privacy, you should respect his wishes. Many unsurfaced roads can be chained with a notice 'Camino Privado' or 'Camino Particular', but these notices are to restrict access by motor vehicles and do not normally affect walkers. In addition the Spanish civil codes give many absolute rights of access which can only be removed by statute. These include all riverbanks, lakes and the coast, access to the top of mountains and to historical sites, castles, *ermitas*, sanctuaries and springs and wells.

Waymarkings

Encouraged by the provincial government, some local authorities are designating their footpaths, known as Pequeno Recorridos (Short Distance Paths), giving them numbers and issuing leaflets showing the routes, but with no descriptions. The official markings are in white and yellow.

The same system of waymarkings is used on the Gran Recorridos (Long Distance Paths) only in red and white. The only GR in Alicante province is the GR7, which starts at the French border and finishes at the border with Murcia. It crosses only Benicadell and Monte Cabrer near Alcoy.

Weekends, Fiestas and Hunting

At weekends and fiestas you can expect the countryside, with its narrow roads, to be crowded, especially the picnic spots. Another hazard, which needs to be taken seriously, are the hunters. Spain's hunting seasons vary according to the prey, but generally extend from October to January. Game (rabbits, hares, pheasants, partridge, thrushes, etc.) can only be slaughtered on Sundays and fiestas. Wild boar are no luckier, they may be done to death on Thursdays and fiestas. This means that the frustrated hunters bang away at everything that moves on the few days when they can use their hunting licences, and a prudent mountaineer leaves them to it, unless he wishes to have his head mounted on a hunter's wall as a trophy!

Route-finding

In the mountains, due to the *garigue* (spiky vegetation), you cannot enjoy true cross-country walking as you can in Britain and the Alps. Here, I am afraid, there is no such thing as walking from peak to peak on a carpet of heather. Pursuing a direct route can be time-consuming, wearisome, painful and sometimes dangerous. The relief felt on reaching a rough but reasonable path is a joy to be savoured after this type of experience.

All the screes I have found so far will not 'run', and progress down them is painful, slow and dreary, with the possible exception of the north scree on Puig Campaña (see Route 7 in volume 1).

Mule tracks between villages seem to follow the easiest line, along a valley bottom or over a col, and there are still tracks to most of the castles and fuentes. If you are forced to climb terraces, try to look for the access provided for the mule at the end of a section. It may take a little more time, but it is easier. Trails made by hunters are well waymarked by empty cartridge cases and empty tins of seafood (I wonder if fishermen eat tinned rabbit?).

Country Code

- Respect all property – if you shelter in an abandoned *finca*, do no damage and leave no litter. Remember that many apparently unoccupied dwellings are used by the farmer at certain times of the year.
- Prevent fires; do not leave broken glass around; do not light fires. If you smoke, make sure that cigarettes are extinguished.
- Leave no litter – take it home with you.
- Make sure that you do not damage growing crops or pick fruit – it is the farmer's livelihood.
- Do not pick wild flowers – if you must, collect seeds.

- Keep dogs under strict control at all times and especially near livestock. Bulls are particularly attracted by dogs, which could have serious consequences.
- When you pass through farmyards or close to habitation show that you respect the occupiers' privacy and give no offence.

Forest Fires

Every summer, many hectares of forest are destroyed by forest fires, as it only takes a spark to ignite the tinder-dry scrub. There is no doubt that some fires are caused deliberately, either by arsonists or by the owners in order to gain permission to develop the land. Most, however, are due to carelessness, either by the farmers themselves, a cigarette end thrown from a vehicle, or by the townspeople having a traditional Sunday paella in the country. Campers, probably the most careful people, can suffer when the local government imposes a ban on camping during high fire-risk periods.

La Conselleria de Medio Ambiente (Council for the Environment) has laid down new procedures for dealing with forest fires. Especially when the dreaded Poniente wind blows like a gale from the west, the Met Office will update the following gradings for seven areas within Valencia every 48 hours:

- **prealerta** – all services on stand-by
- **alarma** – mobilisation of all forces at disposal of the *conselleria*, the civil governor and the forestry brigades
- **alarma extrema** – notification of all police, fire, Guardia Civil and mayors of all towns and villages in the area.

During alarms traffic will be checked, and restricted in the mountain areas affected. Walking and camping may be banned or restricted by police and Guardia.

Water

In the Costa Blanca, all public water supplies are fairly reliable and drinkable, but it is advisable to check locally. In the mountains there is normally no surface water, and the streams, running underground, are not subject to pollution. There is hardly any use of chemical fertilisers. Wherever there is an old *finca*, there will be a well, but unless there is evidence of recent use it is advisable to treat it with caution. If in doubt, use sterilising tablets as a safeguard.

Clothing and Equipment

It is assumed that readers are experienced in mountain walking, hence this section can be kept short. Although very heavy clothing is not needed, do make sure that especially in winter you have reserves of warm clothing, including a windproof anorak and trousers. Shorts cannot be recommended in the mountains as they do not protect you from the spiky vegetation, nor do they conserve core heat in an emergency. If walking in summer, always have a long-sleeved shirt and a hat, and carry barrier cream to protect you from the sun. You also need lots of water and some salt tablets. Any comfortable ankle boot with a good cleated sole will suffice.

Emergencies and Medical Care

It is advisable that at least one member of the party has basic first aid training, and that each member has a small simple first aid kit for their own use.

There is no volunteer mountain rescue organisation in Valencia; each incident is dealt with on an ad hoc basis by the Guardia Civil (Tel: 522 11 00), who will organise the rescue in conjunction with the Cruz Roja (Red Cross), which is organised on a local basis and is manned by young conscientious objectors as an alternative to doing military service. There is no official ambulance service either, and private ambulances are expensive. In addition, the Guardia Civil or the Cruz Roja will probably make a charge for their services, especially if a helicopter has to be brought in. It is, therefore, essential that adequate medical insurance cover is taken out.

Most large towns now have Insalud (National Health) Medical Centres, which are staffed 24 hours a day. At Denia and Villajoyosa there are excellent hospitals with full facilities. Denia hospital is on the southern edge of the town (under Montgo mountain), and the one at Villajoyosa is on the northern outskirts on the CN332. Both are well signposted.

Membership of the Federacion Espanola De Deportes De Montana y Escalada, Calle Alberto Aguilers, 3 – 4 o, izda, 2815, Madrid confers the usual services of mountain organisations, including full medical, recovery and the like in case of a mountain accident or illness.

Farmacias (Chemists)

Spanish pharmacists are most reliable. Many Spaniards seek their advice, and in the villages they often carry out first aid treatment. Remember, however, that in the villages their opening hours are restricted, and even in the towns they close for the siesta.

At night, on Fiestas and Sundays, there is always a Farmacia Guardia open, but you may have to go to the nearest large town. Information may be obtained from the local police or posted on the pharmacy shops.

Maps

The official Mapas Militar are at 1:50,000, the nearest thing to the UK Ordnance Survey maps. The detail and printing, however, are far from OS standard, and buying a new edition does not guarantee an updated map. I find that it pays to keep old maps. They are often more reliable, as the editor of the series is capricious, to say the least, in removing information from new editions. It also takes a very long time before new roads are shown on the maps, and the vast network of forestry and rural roads remains unmarked. There are also the 1:25,000 Ministry of Public Works (M.O.P.U.) maps, produced by the Institutio Georgrafico Nacional, who produce the Mapas Militar. These maps are still based on the old 1:50,000 grid system, with four sheets to the area covered. The printing is better and new roads are shown (still not the rural and forestry), but on some sheets important detail is missing which appeared on old smaller-scale maps. The contours and the spot heights on some sheets of Mapas Militar are questionable

Maps Required For Las Marinas

1:50,000 Mapas Militar

Jativa	29–31	(795)
Alcoy	29–32	(821)
Benisa	30–32	(822)
Villajoyosa	29–33	(847)
Altea	30–33	(848)

1:25,000 M.O.P.U.

796	I Gandia	III Oliva IV Denia
795	Jativa	Sheets I – IV (Xativa, Real de Gandea & Albaida, Villalonga)
822	Benisa	Sheets I, II & III (Orba, Benisa & Tarbena)

823	Javea	Sheets 1 & 3 (Javea & Benitachell)
847	Villajoyosa	Sheets II & IV (Relliu & Villajoyosa)
821	Alcoy	Sheets I – IV (Muro, Alcoy, Planes, Alcoy and Castell de Castells)
848	Altea	Sheets 1, 2 & 3 (Altea, Calpe & Benidorm)

Road Maps

These are quite good, but are at times misleading to say the least. They have the annoying habit of not showing road numbers for provincial and minor roads, which walkers use a lot. And there are glaring mistakes on some, such as showing a dam which failed 20 years ago and the wetlands below Pego as a vast lake. Some roads which were completed years ago and now have an official number are shown as mule tracks.

Michelin	1:400,000	Central/Eastern Spain 445
Firestone	1:200,000	Costa Blanca T28
M.O.P.U.	1:200,000	Province of Alicante (based on Mapas Militar)

Map Suppliers

Many newsagents and bookshops now display a sign showing that they supply Mapas Militar, but don't get excited – their stock-keeping is atrocious. I list suppliers who are (more or less) reliable.

Altea	Newsagent near Supermarket Pepe Clara, Calle Ingen Munoz, in centre of town
Alicante	Librea International, Altmir 6, near Town Hall
Benidorm	Librier Atlas, Calle Valencia
Calpe	Papeleria Vasquez, Av. Gabriel Miro and other branches
Jalon	The Sweetie Shop, on main road just before you reach the river (English)
Valencia	Papeleria Regolf, Mar2, side street near Cathedral and Zaragoza Gardens
In England	Stanfords
	27A Floral Street, London WC2E 9LP
	The Map Shop
	15 High Street
	Upton-upon-Severn, Worcs WR8 OHJ

Both stock the military maps plus smaller scale tourist maps of the area.

Place Names

In this text I have endeavoured to keep to Castilian Spanish when recording place and feature names. There is, however, a spirited revival of the use of Valenciano (similar to Catalan), the old language of the province. The older Mapas Militar always use Castilian, but all the new editions of Mapas Militar, and the new 1:25,000 edition, use Valenciano exclusively for place names and mountain features. This could cause some confusion to those familiar with the Castilian names. Appendix 3 contains a glossary of Valenciano terms for most mountain features.

When to Walk?

The Weather

Residents on the Costa do not, generally, walk in the mountains when it is raining, nor do they do so until the tracks have dried out. This may have British walkers rolling on the floor, but there are 300 plus dry days in this idyllic climate, and to cancel a walk now and again because of the weather is no great loss.

The climate on the mountains closest to the sea is much the same as on the coast, with two exceptions. The coast, under the maritime influence of the Mediterranean, does not suffer from frost at all, whereas inland, and over 300m, you will get regular frosts in winter, and even some snow higher up on Aitana and Serrella. The dry conditions on the coast are not reflected in the mountains, which get a slightly higher rainfall and much mist in winter, when the coast is clear.

But the region's 16in of annual rain has to fall some time, and generally the spring and autumn months can include short periods of wet, unsettled weather. The end of the year, Christmas, then New Year are normally settled and sunny, but generally the unsettled periods are short and clear up quickly. Probably the only safe prediction as to the weather is that from mid-June to mid-September you will be extremely unlucky if you get a wet day, as drought is the general rule throughout this period. Some time during September/October, the Gota Fria arrives. This consists of tempests and torrential rain which occur when the cold moist air stream from the north meets the overheated Mediterranean at the end of the summer. There is very heavy rain for many continuous days, resulting in landslides, floods and general devastation, much to the 'surprise' of the local authorities – it has only been happening since the Carthaginians were here! The only conditions really to be avoided are torrential rain during the Gota Fria. For the rest of the year, as long as you avoid unsettled conditions and are well equipped, walks can be attempted in comfort.

All village bars have TV and a copy of the local paper, Informacion, on whose penultimate page is a detailed weather forecast for the day. Be prepared for snow on the ridge tops of Serrella and Aitana.

The Costa does not have the same variation in daylight hours as Britain. At the summer solstice (June 22nd), there are sixteen hours of daylight, and at the winter solstice (Dec 22nd) ten hours. There is a slightly shorter twilight period than in Britain. The months from May to July give the greatest flexibility in planning your walks in daylight; a winter walk needs very careful planning.

Temperature

Winter temperatures are not to be compared with those encountered when hill-walking in Britain, but on the highest mountains windproof clothing is required, as on exposed ridges the wind can bite deeply. The generally sunny conditions give moderate temperatures during the day even in winter, but when the sun goes in the drop in temperature, added to the wind-chill factor, can be dramatic.

From mid-June to early September, the sun is very high in the sky, and temperatures often rise to over 90°F (over 35°C), with no appreciable drop due to altitude. Precautions against sunstroke, sunburn, heat exhaustion and cramps (this last is due to lack of salts) should be taken seriously.

Temperature Chart (°C)

	max	min	average
Jan	16	7	12
Feb	17	6	10
March	20	8	14
April	22	10	15
May	26	13	18
June	29	15	23
July	32	19	26
Aug	32	20	28
Sept	30	18	22
Oct	25	15	18
Nov	21	10	14
Dec	17	7	11

Dogs

Dogs merit this special note because of the many problems encountered in Spain. Dog owners must hold a current inoculation certificate against rabies, and a colour coded tag must be worn by the dog. Generally, for dogs over 30kg in weight, the dog needs to wear a muzzle in public places. During the hunting season, only licensed hunting dogs (usually very friendly) can roam at will; others need to be on a lead in the mountains (they might otherwise be shot in mistake for a fat fox). Letting a dog roam is not a good idea because of other hazards. The undergrowth hides fissures, pot-holes and abandoned wells, which could prove fatal if a dog falls down them. During the spring, hunters put down poisoned bait to try to get rid of foxes, wild cats, etc., and so protect the game. The law requires that the poison be put out only at dusk, and removed at dawn, but like many Spanish laws it is hardly ever able to be enforced.

There are natural hazards, too, for an inquisitive hound. Both viper and scorpion wounds can cause the death of a dog unless promptly treated by a vet, and the processional caterpillar can also poison a dog. If eaten or taken in the mouth, the swelling can cause asphyxiation. Finally, there is the sand fly, which comes out at night, and whose bite can carry Leishmaniosis, a very dangerous disease. So, if camping, take a pup tent as well! Ticks are a special problem in this area because the winters are not cold enough to control them. If they bite humans there is the possible risk of catching Lymes Disease, which will require prompt medical treatment.

Flora

The botanist calls the region's dry, rocky terrain *maquis* or *garigue*, and the plants which prosper through the long hot summer are tough and spiky. Cross-country walking is, therefore, quite painful, and can be dangerous as the undergrowth can hide fissures.

The vast variety of wild flowers, however, add to the enjoyment of walking, and tends to make botanists of us all. Of course, only those species tolerant of lime flourish, but throughout the year there is always some joy to be discovered by the wayside or clothing the slopes of the mountains. The most impressive display is in the early spring, when the valleys are filled with almond and orange blossom. The slopes become clothed in the pink and white of the Mediterranean heath mixed with the yellow of anthyllis, and later, the broom and gorse.

Giant asphodels and fennels, and verbascums, add to the display. Many cultivated species such as phlomis (yellow and purple), antirrhinum and gladioli grow wild here, and underfoot are grape hyacinth, miniature iris, crocus and an orange tulip (Tulipa Australis), and blue flax makes the slopes of Montgo look like a garden. Flora unique to this area include the rusty foxglove (Digitalis obscura) and, usually on some of the scree, the tiny rush-leaved daffodil (Narcissus requienii). In the woods the orchids flourish: venus, bee, spider and purple pyramid. On the tops the unusual hedgehog broom (Erinacea anthyllis) is to be admired. Even in July, the beautiful pink centaury (Centaurium erythraea) still blooms along with the red valerian (Centranthus ruber), and on the shady side of a crag or a bridge blue throatwort (Trachelium caeruleum) flourishes. Rock roses, cistus and potentilla still bloom on the high ground.

Summer heat and lack of water reduces the display, but those plants that have adapted to these conditions continue to bloom. Be prepared to walk on a carpet of herbs, lavender, sages, thyme, rue, curry plant and cotton lavender, which succeed in the high places. In autumn, once the Gota Fria is over, there is another surge of bloom, but not as dramatic as in the spring, and shade and moisture-loving plants take advantage of the autumn season to bloom – pennywort, hart's-tongue fern and violets, for example, which cannot tolerate the rest of the year's harsh conditions. Wild roses and blackthorn bloom again on the high slopes.

Wildlife

The wild flowers are a joy, but the wildlife of this area is a disappointment, due to over-hunting. Spaniards are inveterate hunters, but do not restrict themselves to game. Any wild bird (except the hoopoe, whose killing is said to bring bad luck) is a prime target, and it is said that in certain areas even large dragon-flies are not safe! Birds are still indiscriminately shot for food and netted, using water as a bait or by employing a bird-lime made of boiled wine. The more colourful specimens are trapped, using a captive bird as a lure, then sold in small cages as song birds to end their days on a town balcony.

The ornithologist needs luck and patience, but there are eagles to be seen, most harriers, many warblers and, on the crags, choughs, but quite naturally they avoid man like the plague. The most colourful birds, hoopoe, roller and bee-eater, are not mountain birds, but may be seen in the valleys. Such pheasant and partridge which have escaped the gun may also be seen. There is, however, compensation for the keen twitcher in the wetlands of La Albufera and the Marjal Mayor near the coast.

Wild boar, foxes, lynx (a protected species), hares and rabbits still roam the high places, but are rarely seen. Lizards and snakes are common in summer, and the dear little geckos come out at night to hunt mosquitoes, moths and so on. Toads (Bufo Bufo Sapo Comun) the size of your hand frequent the damp places of the Fuentes and wash-houses.

Flocks of sheep and goats are to be seen grazing under the watchful eye of the pastor (shepherd), with his motley collection of dogs, and in some valleys, where there is reliable water (like the Val de Infierno), bulls are grazed, always, thankfully, supervised by a herdsman.

The ancient, abandoned salinas (salt pans) under Peñon d'Ifach at Calpe are to be designated a Natural Park. The salinas attract a great variety of waders and water birds including the greater flamingo, which now winters here in flocks exceeding 100 birds.

Beware!

The only poisonous snakes found in Spain are the vipers, and of the three species only one, Vipera La Tast (*Vibora hocicuda*), is found in this region. It is very easy to recognise, with a triangular head, yellow-coloured, with a wavy line down the spine and dots on each flank. It can grow to 73cm, but more normally measures 60cm. It avoids man, but it may be found basking on a rock. The bite of a viper needs urgent medical attention, as does a scorpion sting. You are unlikely to meet a viper on your walks, but the following advice is useful.

- Remember that snakes are very active in warm weather especially the middle of the day.
- Be careful where you sit down. Do not move rocks (scorpions like the shade too) and remember that snakes live in walls.
- Wear breeches, gaiters or just tuck your pants into your socks. You cannot blame a snake for mistaking your trouser leg for a suitable bolt hole.
- Treat all snake bites as poisonous and get medical aid as soon as possible. Even non-poisonous snake bites could cause problems.

Bees are best avoided. You will find that the farmers move their small, wooden hives about the mountains to take advantage of the nectar which is available all the year round. The best advice is, of course, to leave the bees well alone to continue making their delicious honey, keep moving and carry some hydrocortisone.

The processional caterpillar (Thaumet opea pitycampa) is a menace in pine forests. This creature spins its nest in the pine trees, which defoliates the tree, and can kill small saplings. In the spring they form a chain to find a hole in the ground in which to pupate. Processions 2m long are not unusual. Every part of this creature is poisonous, especially the hairs which disintegrate to form a noxious powder, which causes severe skin rashes. Having unintentionally slept with two of these creatures, I cannot advocate too strongly that you shake out clothing and bedding. The most effective antidote for the rash is vinegar, although olive oil and lemon juice are also recommended. Hydrocortisone will not necessarily work.

Other Information

Food and Drink

These days there is not a lot of difference in shopping in Spain, compared to the UK, as even the smaller shops have adopted self-service, and those who are self-catering need only make a shopping list of the Spanish names and be able to convert euros to their sterling equivalent.

Bread: the standard white *barra* is regulated as to size and price by government decree. It is absolutely scrumptious when fresh, but within a short time becomes a lethal weapon. There is a vast variety of other bread, all of which are more expensive.

Fish: The Costa Blanca is awash with every conceivable variety of fish, from squid to lobsters, to sea bream, swordfish, fresh tuna and salmon. The Spaniards are addicted to the salted and dried cod, always traditionally brought to this region from Galicia in the north.

Meat: There are a lot of amateur butchers, so watch out for bone splinters. Mutton is extremely difficult to locate, and the lamb is slaughtered far too early, with the result that you do not get fine lamb chops or fillets. Pork, on the other hand, in any form, is absolutely delicious, as is the veal.

Cheese: Foreign cheeses are now imported in great variety. Spanish cheeses from the north, especially La Mancha (Manchego), a mixture of goat and sheep cheese, are first class.

Fruit and vegetables: There is a bewildering variety available in the markets and shops, all of excellent quality, and the season extends well beyond that in Britain (e.g. strawberries from February to July). Oranges are available all the year round, and ridiculously cheap. There are many exotic varieties readily available: melons, artichokes, asparagus, avocados, kiwi fruit, figs, dates and lots of almonds.

Wine

In this bounteous land it is a tradition to make your own wine, and most farmers do so, but mostly only for their own use. Whilst the main wine-growing areas are to the south, near Alicante, which has its own *denominacion*, the Costa Blanca area still grows a lot of vines, and there are bodegas (wineries) at Gata le Gorgos, Teulada, Benissa, Denia, Javea and Jalon, the only mountain valley to produce wine commercially.

The land, climate and quality of the vines has meant that from early times this land has been a prolific producer of extremely drinkable wine, which has kept a great many people happy, despite lack of pedigree. If in doubt, drink red.

There is now the Cosejo Regulador de la Denominacion de Origen which grants appelacion status each year to those wines which reach a certain standard, and there are many excellent wines, of diverse variety, granted this status.

Sherry, Montilla (poor man's sherry) and Cava (not a champagne but most people are fooled), and the local Moscatel, a lovely sweet desert wine, are surely well known outside Spain already.

The 'Appelacion' is produced by the Bodega de la Pobre Virgin at Jalon (capacity 1,700,000 litres), where you can join the coachloads of tourists in tasting the wine (degustacion) and purchase some, from the vat, or in the bottle. For the expert, the whites are from Moscatel grapes and the reds and rosados from Gironet. Teulada holds a wine festival in October when you can join in the fun and sample the new vintage.

Most restaurants will supply a very drinkable wine with the menu. Valencian, Alicante, Jumilla and the wines of Murcia are the most popular. More select wines are available on the wine list. In the mountains you often receive a generous jug of home brew, but seldom a good white, due to the fact that there is little call for anything but red by the locals. If Tio Paco's brew proves a little daunting, mix a spritzer by adding a little soda water or lemonade.

Restaurants

As might be expected, the restaurants in the towns and on the coast are more sophisticated and expensive, but even here there are good inexpensive small restaurants. In addition, there are the ubiquitous oriental restaurants which are always excellent value. There is even a McDonalds in Benidorm and Denia, and take-aways are now quite common (por llevar).

One of the good things that Franco decreed was that all restaurants should provide a simple menu consisting of starter, main course, sweet, and bread and wine for a fixed price. This law has now lapsed, but a great many restaurants still offer a good meal at an attractive price. The Jalon Valley has over thirty excellent restaurants which cater for every taste and pocket. However, at weekends and fiestas you will be lucky to get a table unless you book well in advance. When the almond blossom is in bloom, the Jalon restaurants are full every day.

In the mountains, you must generally accept more spartan fare, provided mainly to the taste of the locals, not the tourists. Nevertheless, it is possible to dine cheaply and well in the most unlikely localities. In the mountain bars and restaurants, you can nearly always get salad and pork chops with wine and bread, accompanied by the ever-present patatas fritas (chips). The Marling Menu Master, published by William and Clare Marling has proved invaluable.

Tipping

Spaniards seldom tip anyone. Foreigners, it seems, are expected to do so according to most guidebooks. Only give a very modest one after a good meal with good, attentive service.

Village Bars

Most villages have at least one bar, and it serves as a social centre. Opening hours vary with the demands of customers. There is usually a corner reserved for the pensioners of the village, where they can talk and play cards and dominos. The bar will always have some food available, although it may only be an omelette or tapas (snacks), and there are TV, local papers and a telephone. Once open, the bar remains so until the last customer leaves at night. Dogs are generally not allowed in the bars.

One cannot really complain about the inflated prices for refreshment on the coast. Even in some Spanish bars just inland from the coast, there is a sliding scale of charges for drinks, despite the law that charges must be prominently displayed. The lowest price is for family, friends, and favoured customers, the middle price is for normal customers, and those foreigners who are regulars, the highest price is for foreigners, tourists, and anyone the patron takes a dislike to! Normally, country and mountain village bars will give you a friendly welcome, even though they may be curious about you, and like to know what you are doing in their village.

Costa Crime – A Warning

The crime rate on the Costa is no worse than in other European holiday resorts, but many holidays are marred or even ruined by ingenious, determined, charming thieves and fraudsters.

Be most vigilant when in crowded places, markets, airports, fiestas and even supermarkets of anyone who approaches you, however charming and genuine they may appear. Ploys such as offering you a carnation, begging, telling you that you have a stain on your jacket, that you have dropped some money or have a puncture are common. By all means watch the Trileros, who perform a three-card trick with a potato and a pea. It is quite an act, but never join in, and watch out for the pick-pockets who also join in the fun. On some motorways gangs stop tourists pretending that there is a fault in their vehicle, then rob them. At beauty spots thieves watch where you put your valuables as you leave your car on the car park, then break into it. Even in your villa, do not leave valuables on show. Anything that you can do to make life more difficult for the criminals will result in them looking for an easier victim. Happily the mountains are, at the moment, free from problems.

WALKING ROUTES

Gradings

Gradings, despite all efforts to be objective, are never entirely successful, and eventually each individual grades a walk subjectively. These grades always err on the side of caution. I hope that those younger and fitter walkers will not be too disappointed by finishing some of the walks a little earlier than the time given. There will be more time to spend in the local bar.

Timing

These allow for occasional short stops but not for longer breaks. Remember that the weather and temperature can considerably extend the time given if you are to enjoy the walk.

Route Grades

Scramble (Sc) Rock work below the rock climbing grades

Strenuous (S) Steep, rough, and require the ability to get your knee under your chin

Moderate (M) Good general standard of walking, with reasonable gradients

Easy (E) Exactly what it says, but remember that it is still a mountain walk

Stroll (St) A gentle amble of 2–3 hours in majestic scenery, with a handy restaurant at the end.

If two grades are used, the first grade takes priority over the second (ie. moderate/strenuous means a moderate walk with some strenuous sections).

List of Walks

	Grade	Km	Walking time (h)	Ascent (m)	Alt. (m)	Start
1	M/S	7	4	1030	1129	Altea la Vieja
2	M/S	7	3h30	447	989	Altea la Vieja
3	Sc	7	5	480	1129	Casas de Bernia
4	Sc	6	6	560	989	Pinos
5	M	14	4h30	300	900	Casas de Bernia
6	M	6	2h45	147	900	Casas de Bernia
7	M	7	4h30	250	600	Casas de Bernia
8	M	9	4	330	880	Casas de Bernia
9	S	14	6	900	880	Fuentes de Algar
10	M	12	6	300	600	Pinos
11	M	6	4	400	859	Maserof
12	Sc	8.5	4h45	400	845	Maserof
13	Sc	8	4	320	320	Puerto Campomanes
14	M	10	4h45	500	591	Calpe
15	E	7.5	3h15	negligible	400	Calpe
16	St	14	5	negligible	300	Mascarat

	Grade	Km	Walking time (h)	Ascent (m)	Alt. (m)	Start
17	E	12	5h15	318	418	Pou Roig
18	M	17	5h30	700	800	Benichembla
19	M	15.5	7h30	679	979	Benichembla
20	M	9	4	479	695	Benichembla
21	E	15	5	486	866	Jalon Valley
22	M	15	6	690	958	Benichembla
23	M	9.5	4h	477	777	Jalón
24	M	10.5	5	410	598	Jalón
25	M	9	4h20	586	726	Paso de Molinos
26	M	6	3	100	419	Puerto de Orba
27	S	14	5hrs	450	842	Benimaurell
28	S	18	6h30	950/950	350	Benimaurell (descent)
29	E	9	3h30	negligible	200	Tormos
30	M	9	5h30	468	597	Tormos
31	M	9	5	286	786	Paso de Manzaneda
32	M	9	2h45	207	400	Benimeli
Var.	S/Sc	13	6	500	508	Benimeli
33	M	10	4	250	315	Llosa de Camacho
34	M	15	6	500	558	Pedreguer
35	M	12	6	571	752	Pla de Justa
36	S	12	7h30	593	752	Jesus Pobre
37	M	8	2h30	70	244	La Jara
38	M	2.75	1h45	160	201	La Jara
39	M	11.25	5	455	556	Pego
40	M	8.5	3h30	293	393	Gata de Gorgos
40a	M	14.5	6	423	428	Gata de Gorgos
41	M	13	5h30	200	752	Alcala
42	V.Diff (Grade 3)					Val de Ebo or Font de Jubias

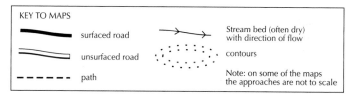

KEY TO MAPS

surfaced road

unsurfaced road

path

Stream bed (often dry) with direction of flow

contours

Note: on some of the maps the approaches are not to scale

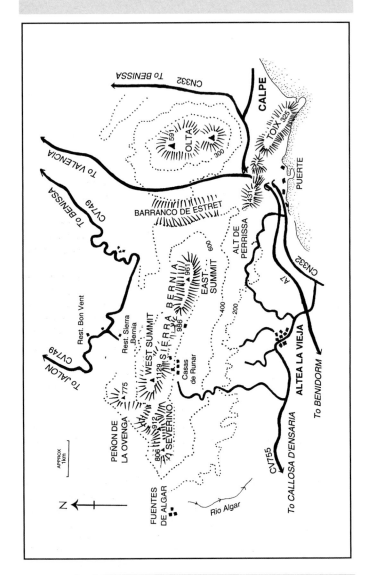

To BENISSA

CN332

CALPE

To VALENCIA

TOX 325

OLTA
▲ 591

▲ 300

PUERTE

CV49
To BENISSA

BARRANCO DE ESTRET

▲ 431

CN332

ALT DE PERRISSA

A7

Rest. Bon Vent

600

S I E R R A   B E R N I A

▲ 961
EAST
SUMMIT

400

200

Rest. Sierra
Bernia

▲ 986

WEST SUMMIT

To JALON
CV49

▲ 1129

Casas
de Runar

ALTEA LA VIEJA

To BENIDORM

▲ 775

PEÑON DE
LA OVENGA

▲ 912
SEVERINO

CV755

806

APPROX
1km

N ←

FUENTES
DE ALGAR

Rio Algar

To CALLOSA D'ENSARIA

Sierra Bernia

INTRODUCTION

The Cuillin of the Costa

Which is your favourite mountain? I find it almost impossible to select just one of the hundreds of mountains which I have climbed as a special favourite, although I admit that there have been peaks which I have sworn never to climb again and others where I was mightily relieved to see the bottom safely. Of course, some mountains offer only one or maybe two routes. Others boast of a number of them and other special features as well. One such mountain is the Sierra Bernia, and whilst I cannot claim to have uncovered all of its delights, I here offer some 12 walking and scrambling routes on it, along with descriptions of other features to be found either on or near it.

The Bernia was not the first mountain which I climbed on the Costa, but it was the first one I saw. We had driven from the airport to our friends' villa at Moraira, in the dark, enduring the tail end of the Gota Fria. The following morning dawned bright and sunny and, taking my first cup of coffee onto the terrace, I was met with a sight which I shall always remember: the Peñon de Ifach and beyond it the long jagged ridge of the Bernia, whose likeness to the Black Cuillin of Skye was unmistakable. On that first Spanish holiday, having only a road map, we just had to admire these majestic peaks without knowing their names. The following year we had the military maps and received some help from Roger Massingham's articles in a local magazine.

The 12km Gabbro rock ridge on the Scottish Isle of Skye is considered to be the nearest thing to an alpine ridge that Britain has to offer. I never fail to remember it when I see the Bernia. True, the rock is different and the Cuillin is much longer and more complicated, but they are both about the same height and both have a magnificent mixture of walking, scrambling and some very severe rock climbing.

The Bernia is a 4km limestone ridge, running west to east from the Fuentes de Algar to end at the sea at Calpe. It has always been one of my great ambitions to traverse the whole of that ridge and to produce a walker's/scrambler's guide. I fear that there is little hope of this being completed, as there are far too many gaps in it. Happily, walkers can still enjoy the thrill of the ridge, especially on the routes to the Eastern and Western summits and a small section above the *forat*. Climbers usually bivouac at Col de Fachuch to set off at dawn and are able to complete even the difficult sections by dusk, with either another camp at Casas de Bernia or a long walk back to Benissa.

The Bernia Ridge is the boundary between the Marina Alta and the Marina Baja. There are no roads across it, and from ancient times it has presented a formidable barrier to communications between Alicante and Valencia. Apart from the daunting mule track through the Mascarat under Calpe Castle, the only route north was via the Algar Valley and the Col de Rates to Pego. In the 19th century the new bridges and tunnel (still to be seen beside the modern road and now used by foolish folk to *puente* on elastic ropes above the gorge) provided a more direct route north. In 1915 there followed a narrow-gauge railway, El Trenet, to Gandia. Today there are modern road tunnels on the N332 and in recent years an autopista, making the final breach of the Bernia. Above them, dedicated rock gymnasts do it the hard way on the many severe rock routes developed in the gorge.

A few metres on the Altea side of the road tunnels, the extensive concrete revêtments mark the latest attempt to tame the most notoriously unstable feature of the mountain, the Galera Fault. It slipped in 1989, blocking the road and rail routes for many months.

As will be seen from the guide, there is much to see: a number of *fuentes*, many with picnic sites, an ancient ermita (chapel), the remains of a 16th-century castle, an old *nevera* (ice pit) and the *forat* (hole) in the crest, used to allow flocks of sheep to pass from side to side of the mountain and now favoured by walkers who are following the popular circuit route.

Getting to know the Bernia

There is a great contrast between the northern and southern slopes of the mountain. The former remains totally unspoilt – in fact, in a time warp – whilst the southern flanks have been sacrificed to building developers who have converted the lower slopes from orange groves to villas and even large urbanisations, especially near Altea La Vieja. At the very eastern end, the development road of a prestigious estate rises to the very crest of the ridge (appropriately named Calle Escocia). I really cannot see the Scots allowing their Cuillin to be so desecrated.

There are two minor bonuses for walkers, however. As long as the roads remain unsurfaced and this part of the site undeveloped, they provide good walking in magnificent surroundings, if you can ignore the pile drivers down in the valley and the sound of wealthy folk signing cheques. The second advantage is that lazy or impatient mountaineers can step out of their cars onto the ridge at Alt de Pedrissa (431m), a facility not available in Skye.

The Southern Aspect

I really do recommend, as a vantage point from which to study the mountain before committing yourself, an outside table at the bar in the Plaza del Banco, Altea La Vieja. The shapely peak on the extreme left is Peña Severino (800m), above Algar Falls, joined to its twin peak by a jagged ridge overlooking a col, Port del Fort, where the well-trodden routes from the north and the south join beneath the sheer crags of the main summit of the Bernia (1129m).

A few degrees to the right (east), note on a high shelf the few remains of the fort (see below). Below is the improbable collection of *casitas*, Casas de Ruñar, accessible, believe it or not, by car. The impressive crags of the Western Summit continue until they reach a col and the magnificent pinnacle of Risco del Portezuelo, which I have christened, in memory of a similar rock on the cuillin, the Basteir Tooth. Next there is another col with two small pinnacles, which I refer to as Rabbit's Ears, and the crags start to rise towards the Eastern Summit. If you know where to look, you can pick out the *forat*, the hole in the ridge, which on this side is marked by a large cave and, at the time of writing, two pine trees. Directly beneath the *forat*, you will be lucky if you can spot the few remaining stones of Ermita del Vicario.

From the highest point on the Eastern Summit, the ridge starts to descend towards the sea, ending in the small crag of Alt de Pedrissa (432m), and finally, continues over the Col del Fachuch with its transmitters to the dramatic drop (rock climbers only) into the Mascarat Gorge, through which the road, autopista and railway all run.

The Bernia continues on to the east as Sierra de Toix, dropping into the Mediterranean as Morro de Toix, at the southern end of Calpe's glorious beaches.

The Northern Aspect

The Pinos Valley, under the northern crags, is almost totally undeveloped, and the rock faces to me always seem more rugged than their southern counterparts. The valley's river, the Estret, runs underground today. Still the crops prosper, although most of the farmers – apart from a few ancient and determined residents at Casas de Berdiola, on a raised knoll in the middle of the valley – only come out at weekends and fiestas to tend them. You can study the mountain from the CV749 (formerly AV1425) which climbs steadily from Benissa, 15km to the tiny hamlet of Casas de Bernia, on the watershed at the junction of the Algar, Maserof and Pinos valleys.

The first feature to notice at the eastern end of the ridge is the deep Estret Gorge, where the river, in ancient times, carved a deep and neat slice through a spur of the Bernia on its way to create the even more dramatic defile of the Mascarat. To the right, look for a road across the slopes leading to an abandoned quarry, which is on the route to the Eastern Peak. If your eyesight is good, you may be able to follow a pencil-thin scree slope which issues from a gully spanned by two natural bridges on the ridge. The higher one is an artistically eroded natural rock archway. Below it, a giant rock slab which has fallen across the narrow cleft forms a second natural bridge.

Further to the right you might be lucky to pick out the *forat*, not easy to spot from this side, and the diagonal path which descends from it, passing some undercut strata used by shepherds as a corral, to the popular picnic spot of Fuente de Bernia, at the end of a rough road from the hamlet.

Pull off the road at Km 14 if you wish to savour the best view of the valley, with Casas de Berdiola below, the Rabbit's Ears and Risco de Portezuelo easily identifiable above on the ridge. To the right of the 'tooth' try to spot the three diagonal rakes which lead up from the scree slopes to the last section of the Western Ridge, used in a route to the main summit.

At the end of the ascent you reach the hamlet. Three of the farms have been turned into restaurants, which have variable opening hours. The old Casa Concepción is now the popular Restaurant Sierra Bernia, at the end of a side road, from the junction of your road with the one down to Jalón (formerly AV1424). Near this same junction, an old *casita* is now the Restaurant Refugio Bernia, and a short distance farther along the road leading towards Jalón is the Bon Vent, my personal favourite, open Wednesdays to Sundays, where Juan Manuel and Antonia serve a very good garlic chicken.

From the watershed you can admire the distant giants of Aitana and Serrella. In the foreground is the detached peak of Penyal de Ovenga (760m), with its two crosses, overlooking the deep gorge of Paso de los Bandoleros, which leads down to the Algar Valley. There are excellent views of the tortured strata of the western buttress of Sierra Ferrer on the other side of the gorge.

To the north-west can be seen the twin peaks of Peña Severino, with the joining narrow arête presenting a daunting sight from this angle.

From the east and from the west (ie. from Toix or Peñon de Ifach and from Algar and Guadalest), the ridge, seen end on, presents a dramatic sight as the pinnacles merge to form a good imitation of the Matterhorn's elegant conical summit.

The West Summit of the Bernia

The Fuentes

Fuente Bernia: picnic site on the north side, accessible by car from Casa Concepción (Restaurante Bernia)

Fuente del Fuerte: near the ruins on the south side

Fuente Ruñal: near Casas de Ruñal, on south side. The actual spring can only be reached on foot, but a picnic site is now accessible by car from CV755 (formerly AV150)

Fuente Santa Anna: just outside Altea La Vieja, access by car to picnic site

Ermita Del Vicario: walk on good tracks from Fuente Ruñal for half an hour.

The Nevera: traverse across the northern slopes, east for about 30 minutes, no track.

The Fort: whilst there are plenty of small castles on these mountains, this is the only fort that I know of and it is probably the largest defensive construction in these mountains. It was built by Giovanni Battista Antonelli (the same engineer who built the Tibi dam) for Felipe II, in 1562, at an altitude of 850m. The construction took only four months, and there are reports that it proved difficult to maintain the fabric, whether due to shoddy construction or its exposed position, I know not. There were also attempts to conceal the construction (how they hoped to achieve this I cannot think). Instead of using the local port at Altea, materials were landed at Moraira and brought by mule up from Jalón. According to ancient records the fort was built as a measure to control the activities of the North African corsairs, who were quite a nuisance at the time. The design was obviously 'state of the art' in the 16th century, as its plans look more like some 18th-century forts.

Fifty years later the fortification become redundant, and after being used as a refuge by Moors who were avoiding deportation it was demolished. The ruins make a very interesting site to explore. There are said to be plans to restore parts of the fort to be used as a refuge by local mountaineers.

1: BERNIA WEST SUMMIT FROM ALTEA LA VIEJA

Grade:	moderate/strenuous
Distance:	7km
Time:	4hrs
Ascent:	1030m
Maps:	Altea 848 (30–33)

This is one of the most popular routes for ascending the Bernia from the south and it is waymarked in yellow and white as PRV7 from Fuente Santa Ana (Font del Garrofet) as far as the fort.

To save walking the first 2.5km, which is very pleasant, and climbing some 150m, cars can be taken as far as the water tower at the end of the first section. For the 'peak bagger', the impatient, the old and infirm, and the bone idle, cars can also be taken, unbelievably up to 600m, at Casas Ruñar. You leave the CV755, Altea la Vieja to Callosa road, at Km.18.5 turn-off to the north for a climb of 5km alongside Barranco del Riquet.

Getting There

Leave the coastal road, CN332, at Km.161, just east of Olla de Altea, with a sign to the A7 Autopista and Callosa d'En Sarria, and join the CV755, signposted to Guadalest and Altea la Vieja. Enter the village and find parking as best you can, as near as possible to the Plaza del Banco. An outside table at the bar opposite the bank is as good a place as any to refresh yourself for the task ahead and to identify your objectives, over 1000m above you.

The two peaks on the left (western) end of this magnificent ridge are the Severinos (800m), then comes the main summit (1126m), with the ruins of the ancient fort immediately below it, and lower down the tiny white dots are the *casitas* of Casa Ruñar on a shelf at 600m. The next identifiable feature is a col at the eastern end of the summit ridge where there is an impressive pinnacle, Risco de Portezuelo (986m), which looks much like the Basteir Tooth on the Cuillin Ridge.

From here the Eastern Ridge starts, best left to the experienced and well-equipped rock cimbers, until the *forat* (the natural hole in the crest) and the Eastern Summit (961m), which are both accessible to walkers. If you are searching for two other features of the ridge, the rock arches, cease to search – they are hidden from view on the northern side.

Finally there is the end of the ridge at Collado de Fachuch (437m), overlooking the deep gorge of the Mascarat, on the coast and accessible by car via Urb. Altea Hills (housing estate).

To Fuente Santa Ana

Start by walking through this lovely little village, first walking back to the traffic lights, and turning left (north) to follow the main street, Calle Cura Llinaies. Pass the restaurants and shops, then go between old village houses and citrus groves until, as you gain height, the first views of Aitana and Aixorta appear to the west. On the left, turn round for a good view of Puig Campaña, Sanchet and Ponoch to the south. Make a detour to visit a small plaza and the ancient church of Santa Ana, now being restored and well worth a visit.

Back on the route you find that you are following a calvary, with its attractive Stations of the Cross adorned with ceramics, and the street starts to descend through the *huerto*, with good views of your objective, Sierra Bernia, ahead. This part of the walk has been well waymarked in yellow and white as PRV7, as you pass corrals for goats and walk through citrus groves. Above you on a shelf, beneath the summit, are the tiny white *casitas* of Casas Ruñar, at about 600m and on your route.

On the left-hand side of the track is a watercourse, the Barranco de los Peñas, as a surfaced road now leads us to Fuente Santa Ana, the old village water supply, decorated with ceramics and an old mill stone.

Upwards to the Water Tower

Continue for a very short while past the *fuente*, watching out for the waymarking on the left where you leave the road and take to a narrow path through pines (at times eroded) until you gain the surfaced estate road at an electric transformer.

Pass through villas, still waymarked, until the road deteriorates, passing a concrete water tank on the right, with a large stone-faced water tower ahead. There are views now of the Bernia again and wider views of the coast.   *1hr 2.5km*

To Fuente Ruñar

Pass the water tower and continue on the Mozarabic trail, which heads east for a while and then enters a deep ravine, Barranca de Las Peñas. As you gain height there are magnificent views of the coast, with the vast sweep of Altea Bay, Sierra Helada, Benidorm Bay and the little Cortina hills, with Puig Campaña, Sanchet and Ponoch towering over them.

As you enter the ravine, pause to marvel at the engineering skills of the ancient Moors, most of whose steps and *revêtements* survive, despite 400 years of neglect. At the head of the ravine, change sides and start to climb, in zig-zags, up the eastern side.

You keep left at a junction, with the waymarkings, so there is no route-finding required. This is perhaps as well, as for a short while you lose sight of your objective.

When the ridge does reappear, you find that the main summit is right ahead of you, with Casas Ruñar a little to the west. To the right of the hamlet, at the head of a shallow *barranco*, is a little stone *casita* which is your next objective. Pass a small almond grove with lots of waymarkings to ensure that you do not get lost to reach the *casita*, with its oven, well and pegs on the wall to hold water jars. From the corner of the *casita* move west along a good trail to reach the well-laid-out picnic area, where you can rest awhile, right under the pinnacle of Risco de Postezuelo. Two small flakes of rock mark the beginning of the Eastern Ridge leading to the Eastern Summit.

Piste Forestal, a broad track which heads east from the *fuente*, leads in 20 minutes to the ruins of Ermita Vicario and in 2 hours to Urb. Sierra Altea (see Walk 2).   *2hrs 15mins   5km*

To the Fort

Walk west along a good road until you meet the surfaced road coming up from the main road below, turn to the right, north, towards a stone water tank, and find behind a metal door fitted into the rock the original Fuente Ruñar.

Move slightly west (left) from the *fuente* and still follow the waymarkers until you meet another path, on the right, coming down from the *forat* (see Walk 6), and continue west towards the ruins of the old fort and its well, beneath the crags of the Bernia main summit. To the west the ridge continues as Severino (Walk 9). The yellow and white waymarkings continue west to a rock gateway and down to Casas Bernia (Walks 3 and 6) as you leave the PRV7.

To the Summit

There is still over 200m of stiff climbing ahead to reach your peak and you head generally north towards the large band of sheer crags, with a small stunted pine determinedly surviving in a cleft in the rocks.

First, head across scree in a north-easterly direction, heading for a prominent buttress. This is a much used route, but it is difficult to maintain on such a steep, loose surface and waymarkings soon disappear. When you reach a buttress and turn left, towards the west, a more reliable track is found contouring in the direction of the Western Arête. Waymarkings reappear as you reach the easy rock scramble onto the arête, just as it plunges down into the Algar Valley.

The route is easier to find now as you turn east, over rocks, with some interesting moves and a steep groove. Your views have now opened up of the northern mountains, notably Ferrer and Montgo, as well as the island of Ibiza, in clear weather, on the eastern horizon.

At one point, where there is a metal stake placed in the rock, take time to glance down on the northern side to what, I believe, is the only *nevera* (ice-pit) on the Bernia. All too soon this enjoyable traverse is over as you gain the trig point on the summit, with its record book in a box.

A few metres to the east are the remaining walls of an old look-out tower, believed to be Moorish and pre-dating the fort below. As befits its elevation, the views all round are spectacular, especially, I feel, those along the ridge, east to the sea and west along the Severino Arête.

Descents

In addition to reversing the ascent route, which I am sure you will find equally enjoyable, there are a number of alternatives, all of which, however, need careful planning and helpful family or friends.

From the fort follow the waymarkings west to the rock gateway and then down the well-worn track to Casa Bernia in 45 minutes (Walk 3). From Casas Ruñar there are two routes in addition to the ascent route.

- Follow the surfaced road to the right (west) and, near a cave house, take off to the right on a track to Corral de Severino and the path down to Fuentes de Algar (Walk 9).   *2hrs*
- From the picnic area at Fuente Ruñar, follow the broad forestry road for half an hour to Ermita Vicario and pick up the route to Urb. Sierra Altea (Walk 2).   *1hr 30mins*

The luckiest of walkers will be those with helpful friends who have brought up cars and set up a barbecue at Fuente Ruñar. With the wind in the right direction, wafting the smell of roasting meat upwards, it should inspire the walkers and, if not careful, attract a few uninvited guests.

Peña Severino (Walk 8) from the West ridge of the Bernia

2: BERNIA EASTERN SUMMIT FROM ALTEA LA VIEJA

Grade:	**moderate/strenuous**
Distance:	**7km**
Time:	**3hrs 30mins**
Ascent:	**447m**
Maps:	**Altea 848 (30–33)**

The ascent of the Eastern Summit (961m) from Pinos is described as Walk 4. This route is a popular alternative ascent from the south.

Getting There

Leave the CN332 at Km.161, with signs for the motorway A7, and take the first turning to the right, the CV755 with signs to Altea la Vieja and Callosa de Ensarria. In 1.7km turn off to the right with signs for Don Cao Golf Club. The road to the club breaks off to the right in 1.5km and you continue to climb to the north through attractive villas, along Avinida Principal, until the road swings right to the east, with lots of side roads named after flowers and shrubs. Above you on the left is a Moorish-type development and the road Calle Costa Azahar. As the villas end you negotiate a *barranca*. After this the villas start again, and at Km.4.2 turn off to the left on Calle Costa Azul, parking your car at the first junction, where an unsurfaced road leads north towards the Bernia Ridge high above you.

An alternative, for those coming from the north, is to leave the CN332 at Km.163, with signs for Altea Hills, driving for 2.8km to Calle Costa Azul, passing the opulent development on your right as you climb.

Making a Start – to the Shelf

Your first objective is to climb above the lower band of cliffs to gain a broad shelf which runs the entire length of the ridge (nearly 10km) under the base of the southern crags (see Walk 1).

Start by following a broad, unsurfaced road which climbs north-east to reach a large stone-faced water tank, which you pass on the right. In a few minutes the road levels out and you turn off to the left on a narrow path at a smaller tank with a waymarker (a blue cupola placed by Altea Mountaineering Club).

It seems possible that this part of the route follows an ancient Mozarabic trail, but it is much decayed. The trail zig-zags upwards until it has gained sufficient height, then moves to the left (west) along the top of the lower band of cliffs. In windy weather be very careful near the edge, as not many years ago a young girl, admiring the view, was blown off the rocks to her death.

A variety of waymarkings now adorn the rocks on this section – red ones, blue cupolas and even black ones – and on this section too there are magnificent views already of the coastal plain, with Sierra Helada and the distant peaks of Puig Campaña and Ponoch towering over the vast *huertos* of the Guadalest and Algar valleys. At a junction (The Triangle), another path joins from the right.   1hr   2km

As the ascent steepens, the path climbs through decayed terraces to gain a broader track, which you follow to the left (west) to gain a very small well or *nevera* on the right of the path. I have put a cairn at the point where your route joins the broad track to help you on the return journey (as I once lost the route here for a short time).

In this area there are a number of tiny terraces which have been sown with cereals, for which there seemed, at first, to be no valid explanation. All was to be made clear, however, when we found feeding buckets (with a hole in the bottom) suspended from a tree, and realised that the local hunters were doing their best to encourage game birds, just as the gamekeepers did in Suffolk.

To the Lower Casita

A few paces beyond the *nevera*, a waymarker indicates a narrow path on the right-hand side, which is the old route to the lower *casita*. The path is still there, but after a recent fire a number of fallen trees have blocked the first section. An easier route is to continue west along the broad road until you reach a junction with a large rock pinnacle. The road ahead will take you to the ruins of the tiny Ermita Vicario and on to Fuente Ruñar in about 45 minutes (see Walk 1).

Double back to the right, in an easterly direction and on an equally good road, and pass through pines to arive at the lower *casita*, with its well, oven and *era* (threshing floor), complete with stone roller. The *casita* is being restored, and one can speculate on who the owner might be, perhaps a successful local business man who in his spare time, perhaps, likes to get back to his roots for a fiesta or to hunt. I am sure that he will not mind you resting on his *era* to admire the view.

1hr 40mins   3.5km

To the Upper Casita

Leave the *casita* and follow a good path to the east, passing a blue *deposito* and a *fuente* with drinking troughs. The views ahead now extend through the pines towards the last eastern crags of the ridge and to the final summit of Alt de la Pedrissa (431m), then to the Col de Fachuch with its transmitters. Finally the dramatic Mascarat Gorge, the remaining wall of Calpe castle and Sierra del Toix come into sight. Climb a short gully to reach the upper *casita*, complete with a corral for animals. Above you, to the north, is your next objective, the ridge of the Bernia and the Eastern Summit.

Up the Scree

Your route, which follows Walk 4 to the Eastern Summit, runs under the yellow-coloured crags of the Eastern Ridge, and you now follow a well-marked trail, north-east, until you reach the base of a steep scree run.

2hrs   4km

Scree-running, if you are wearing an old pair of boots, can be quite enjoyable and a swift way of descending mountains. Climbing up steep scree is never enjoyable, especially in Spain, and I confess that I have only descended this section, so my timing is provided by others.

2hrs 30mins

West to the Belvedere

Your first objective is a small ledge beneath a rock wall, and to get there keep first to the base of the crags on the southern side of the ridge and move west, descending a little before climbing up to it.

Your route now follows a broad groove in some smooth rock as you surmount an easy 5m wall. Above the wall scramble up some steep rocks to one of the impressive natural features of this ridge, the Rock Bridge, formed by a neat slab of rock breaking away and falling across a narrow fissure. Lower down, on the northern side of the ridge, is a yet more artistic feature, the delicate natural arch spanning a thin, steep scree chute, the last remnants of a decayed cave.

There are other interesting natural caves and fissures hereabout which are worth exploring by those equipped to do so. Move on to the west, climbing up to reach a small belvedere, with good views now to the west of Sierra Aitana and the Guadalest Valley.   *3hrs 15mins*

Arête and Summit

As you face the pinnacle, on the north side of the belvedere, you can see your route to the summit to the left of it, a traverse of the final arête. First tackle the pinnacle by turning it on the right and climbing a short, easy rock pitch, then address yourself to an easy rock staircase which leads to the crest of the arête. Make a mental note of the point at which you will leave the arête on your return from the summit. Ahead of you is a sheer rock wall on the southern side, with at least a 5 degree overhang and an impressive drop to the screes far below. We call this wall The Billboard: it can easily be identified from Altea la Vieja and pinpoints the Eastern Summit. The northern side of the ridge is less precipitious but is composed of sharp, upended flakes of limestone, which are not very pleasant to walk on. Traverse just below the crest, but do not forget to pop up now and then to savour the terrific drop on the south side.

In 5 minutes of easy walking you arrive at the summit cairn.
                                              3hrs 30mins   7km

The Summit

The views in all directions are magnificent, especially those along the ridge. To the west, impressive arêtes and pinnacles lead towards the massive pinnacle of Risco del Portezuelo and on to the main summit. To the east, the ridge continues, dropping eventually to the sea at Morro del Toix, with the Peñon de Ifach and the attractive resort of Calpe between them. A little to the north-west is the modest peak of Peña Ovenga, overlooking the Paso de los Bandoleros, whilst to the south-west are the twin summits of Peña Severino, joined by a sharp arête. You can see the whole of the Aitana range, from Puig Campaña, with its attendant Cortinas, to the summit itself, the highest peak in Alicante province. There are also extensive views of extensive views of the Guadalest and Algar valleys.

Sadly, it is time for walkers to turn back. Although some parts of the next section of the ridge to Risco del Portezuelo can be explored by surefooted scramblers, the full traverse is reserved for well-equipped rock climbers.

On the northern side of the ridge, below you, the undercut cliffs which form the shepherds' shelter, close to the path from the Fuente de Bernia, can be seen, but the *forat* itself is hidden from view.

Descents

Any alternative to retracing your steps needs careful planning, either by meeting up with another party or arranging for transport home.

To Pinos

From the summit, reverse Walk 4 to the hamlet of Pinos on the Benissa to Jalón road.

To Col De Fachuch

From the col where Walk 4 leaves the ridge, there is a natural line down the ridge to Col de Fachuch, where you will find yourself on Calle Escotia, of the exclusive Altea Hills Estate. There are some waymarkings at the start of this route, but I have not walked it so far.

To Fuente Ruñar

Reverse the ascent route by turning off to the right (west) at the junction with a rock pinnacle. In 30 minutes you can visit the ruins of Ermita Vicario and continue on a nice level road to reach the picnic area at Fuente Ruñar, at the end of a motor road from the valley.   *1hr*

To Alhama Springs

Finally, from Fuente Ruñar you can reverse the route to the main summit from Alhama Springs (Walk 1).

3: BERNIA WEST SUMMIT
VIA WEST RIDGE FROM CASAS DE BERNIA

Grade:	scramble
Distance:	7km
Time:	5hrs
Ascent:	480m
Maps:	Altea 848 (30–33), Benisa 822 (30–32)

Making a Start

Leave the car park at Bernia (near to the Restaurant Sierra Bernia) and walk towards the ridge (south) for a few minutes until the road forks. Take the left-hand road (east) towards the *fuente*; the other track can be seen zig-zagging up to the western col, and is your return route. After passing two *casitas* on the right you see another house higher up the slope, and your road enters a shallow *barranco*, where you leave it, as a narrow path ascends the steep slope (due south) towards the ridge. *10 mins*

For the first 1 hour 30 minutes, in classical style, the route heads straight for the ridge over very steep and rocky ground. It will be 4 hours 30 minutes before you tread a good path again!

Getting to Grips with the Mountain

The path soon disappears but there are red waymarks as far as the ramp. There is nothing for it but to use your mountain skills to find the easiest way through the boulders, rocks and vegetation, always going as directly upwards as possible, towards a group of white boulders which will be reached in about 10 minutes. Another 10 minutes will bring you to the top of this shoulder and a welcome rest at some larger rocks with a red marker. *30 mins*

Now you can see clearly your route on to the ridge (due south). Your markers for the first stage are three huge boulders on a steep scree slope. You head for the gap between some small crags and the right-hand boulder, where the vegetation is less troublesome. Immediately above is a band of small crags, and once these are reached, move right (west) for a short time to climb up a rake (sloping terrace), then back

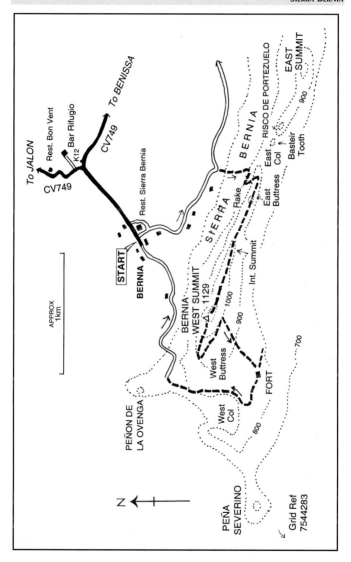

left to gain the top of East Buttress. You can see in all three rakes, dropping from left to right across the buttress wall. The lower one is only a narrow groove, the middle one is yours, and the upper one is a difficult rock climb.

To the Rock Wall

Cross a little terrace and another knoll, and start the steep climb through broken rock and scree (no path) heading for the boulders, which can be reached in 20 minutes. I'm sure you will now need another breather, which will enable you to enjoy the extensive views to the north. You can also contemplate the steep scree which leads upwards to the base of the band of crags (as long as it continues to flourish, there is a good guide – a crack filled with ivy), and in another 20 minutes you will be there.   *1hr*

On to the North Rake

Now, at last, you have a goat track to follow along the base of the crags (west) until a red marker shows the start of your rake. On the way, you can look up to see the first rake. Your rake is broad and firm, but take care, as it is exposed if you venture to the outer edge. In all too short a time you leave it to climb a path up the slope to the main ridge.

1hr 22mins

On to the Ridge

The markers going left (east) descend to the Eastern Col beneath the Tooth and to the *fuente*. From the ridge you can now admire the magnificent view of the whole ridge east, right down to Mascarat, Toix and Peñon d'Ifach. To the west, the twin summits of Bernia are now visible, with the white triangulation post on the main (western) summit. You can also see a small intermediate summit between them.

The Summit Ridge

Now all the effort to reach the ridge is rewarded in full as you start your traverse to the summit. Obviously you will choose a route to suit your capabilities. Wherever possible, the ridge rocks are the normal line for the expert, but for others there is marked a safer and easier route, avoiding some of the more difficult pinnacles.

Get onto the ridge, keeping first to the left (south) side, but in 5 minutes cross over to the north side and a short rock climb.

2hrs 5mins

Fig Tree Groove to Eastern Buttress

Go up a groove with chockstones and pass behind the fig tree, then ascend a broad gully to gain the Eastern Buttress.   *2hrs 35mins*

To Main Peak Summit

Descend as best you can on the ridge rocks to Intermediate Summit, which you pass on the left (south) side, and go down a very sporting arête into a small gap, from which you escape up a short rock groove on the north side to see the Main (West) Summit ahead. Pass the last remains of a 14th-century watchtower on the left to gain the main summit and the triangulation pillar (installed by helicopter in 1988).

3hrs

The views, as might be expected, are extensive, and especially beautiful is the eastern aspect down the ridge to the sea.

Traverse of West Summit Ridge

Leave the summit and start by descending a rough arête which has a metal stake fixed to the rock. Making sure that you are on a good stance, look down over the precipitous north side to see the only *nevera* (ice-pit) on the Bernia. This is a lovely traverse, as the ridge descends quite sharply, ending in a boulder-filled groove. On to another delightful rocky arête, which you leave at its end by climbing down the left (south) side on to easier ground. Your time on the ridge is now limited, so enjoy every last moment, as all too soon twin cairns and red markers remind us to find a way off the ridge on the left (south) side.   *3hrs 25mins*

You now join a rough rake across the base of the crags of Holly Oak Wall (the tree is high up in a crack). There are some red markers, but you are crossing scree, and you should aim for a crag on the farthest side. When you are nearly there, look out for a very indistinct track going back right, aiming for the castle ruins below. If you are lucky, you will join a good marked track and arrive at the ruins of Fort Bernia.

4hrs

A Good Path at Last!

Say goodbye to rough walking now, as you join a well-trodden path west to a rock gateway, and go round the end of the Bernia summit's western crag as you descend the dramatic valley to Broad Col and Peña Ovenga.   *4hrs 15mins*

Go east now onto a broad forestry road, which will lead you back to Bernia village after what must be the most rewarding ridge walk in the region.   *5hrs*

There are three restaurants available (see map). Refugio opens most days, and Sierra Bernia too, but Bon Vent is open only Wednesday to Sunday.

Approaching the West Summit, Sierra Bernia

4: BERNIA EAST SUMMIT FROM PINOS

Grade:	scramble
Distance:	6km
Time:	6hrs
Ascent:	560m
Maps:	Altea 848 (30–33), Benisa 822 (30–32)

The Bernia Ridge, at its eastern end, can be approached from a number of directions. From the east, where the rocks give out, at Collado de Fachuch, above the Mascarat Gorge, there is an easy approach by car right to the ridge itself, due to the construction of an urban road (Altea Hills). From the south, you can again take your car high on the mountain, through developed areas (Urb. Sierra Altea), from Altea la Vieja, leaving your car near the big water tank at the top of the development and striking off on a reasonable path to the col. This route approaches the mountain from the north.

Getting There

Leave the main trunk road (CN332) just south of Benissa and turn off on the CV750, signposted Jalón, and in a few metres fork left on the CV749, signposted Pinos. At Km.18 you will pass the Pinos Restaurant and, below on the left, the tiny church and the scattered hamlet of Pinos. At Km.14 turn off left (south) and park your car where the road splits. This is an excellent place to examine your route before setting off and to identify the main features you will pass on the walk. Below, to the west, gathered together on a small piece of high ground, are a number of farms which go under the name of Casas Berdiola. Across the valley, you can study the whole of the Bernia Ridge from Collado de Fachuch to the main Western Summit. The main forestry road, which traverses beneath the crags towards the prominent band of rocks which drop down from the ridge towards the Estret Gorge, can clearly be identified. Finding the natural bridge and stone arch up on the ridge is a more difficult task. The key is the very narrow scree run just to the left (east) of the Eastern Summit, the final objective of this walk.

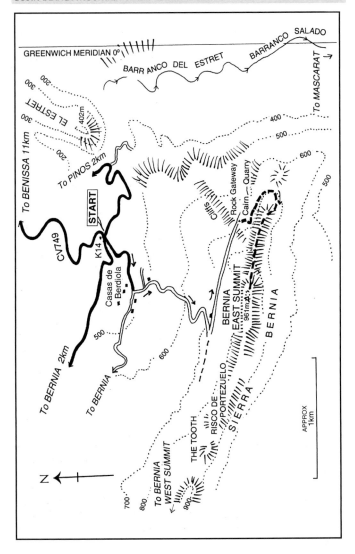

Down into the Pinos Valley

Those of you who are in a hurry can take your cars for another 2km to the bottom of the valley, but the walk down the right-hand road (south-west) is so pleasant an introduction to the walk that I strongly recommend that you walk this first 2km, anticipating as you go the delights of the ridge across the valley bottom, and, on your right, passing the chained drive of a little villa, Casa Dolores. The road now starts to climb gently towards Casas Berdiola (Walk 10), and in a few minutes your road forks off left (chained to prevent use by cars). *30mins*

Towards the Rock Gateway

Follow a good unsurfaced forestry road as it climbs directly towards the ridge, and in a few minutes ignore a road which goes down left (Walk 7). You pass a little *casita* on the left (east), and then you go through other *casitas* as the road moves west for a short time. At an old *finca*, join a good forestry road, and turn left on an eastern track towards a quarry and the rock gateway in the band of crags. You can now see ahead the deep cleft of the Estret Gorge, which leads down to the dramatic Mascarat Gorge on the coast. There are now extensive views of the whole Pinos Valley, with Casas Berdiola to the north and Pinos to the north-east. In the distance to the north-east, the great bulk of Mongto appears, and a little to the south is the gorge of La Garganta (The Throat) near Gata de Gorgos and, on the coast, the hill of Isidoro, with its radio antennae, near the village of Benitachell. You now cross the band of rocks at the rock gateway and seek out on the right-hand side a cairn which marks a vague track which climbs to the col.

1hr 15mins

To the Col

The track zig-zags and disappears once or twice, but cairns have been placed to help you as you climb basically south-east to reach the col between two prominent buttresses. As you climb note how, to the south-east, Olta first appears, followed eventually by the Peñon d'Ifach and, finally, Sierra Toix. Once you have gained the ridge you can appreciate the extensive views of the coast, including Sierra Helada, the Cortinas, Puig Campaña and even the provincial capital of Alicante with, perched high on a rocky prominence, the castle of Santa Barbara. At this point, another approach route, previously described, joins the ridge (Walk 2). *2hrs*

To the Belvedere

Your first objective is a small ledge beneath a yellow rock wall, and to get there you keep to the base of the crags on the south side of the ridge, descending a little before climbing to the wall itself and then traversing to the ledge.   *2hrs 30mins*

The route now follows a broad groove in smooth rocks and surmounts an easy 5m wall. Above the wall, scramble up some steep rocks to one of the great natural features of the Bernia Ridge – the Rock Bridge. The bridge is made up of a great slab of rock which has fallen across a chasm. Beneath it is another marvel of nature, the Rock Archway, which spans the narrow scree chute that descends precipitously to the valley floor.

There are some interesting natural caves and fissures hereabouts, but you must press on to the west to reach a reasonably broad belvedere. Views are now opening up to the south and south-west of Aitana and the Guadalest Valley.   *2hrs 45mins*

On to the Arête

You must now take to the rocks for the final climb to the Eastern Peak, which can be seen above you. First, tackle the pinnacle above the belvedere by going right up a short, easy rock pitch and, once round the back of the pinnacle, addressing yourself to an easy rock staircase which will lead you onto the crest of the arête. Ahead, to the west, can be seen a sheer rock wall on the south side, with about a 5 degree overhang, above a steep drop of at least 50m onto the scree below. This feature is called The Billboard, and it can be clearly identified from Altea la Vieja. The northern side of this wall is less precipitous, but is made up of sharp flakes of limestone, which is not the easiest terrain to negotiate. I recommend that you traverse for only about 5 minutes, just below the crest, popping up now and then to peep over the edge to relish the sheer drop on the southern side. After crossing the arête in about 5 minutes of easy walking, you reach your ultimate objective, the East Summit of Sierra Bernia.   *3hrs*

The Summit

Once more, the views are truly magnificent. To the west, the ridge continues with impressive pinnacles and arêtes to the buttress which leads on to the main (western) summit of the Sierra Bernia. To the right (north) of the ridge is little Peña Ovenga, and to the left (south) the

The track from Fuente Ruñar, below the Bernia Ridge (Walk 1)

Almond blossom near Casa de Bernia, with Bernia ridge behind (Walk 6)

The Bernia Ridge from the Pinos Valley (Walk 10)

twin summits of Peña Severino, joined by a razor-sharp arête. You can see the whole of the Aitana Ridge, from Puig Campaña, with its attendant Cortinas, to the great summit of Aitana itself, the highest peak in Alicante province. There are extensive views of the Guadalest and Algar valleys. In the foreground, down below you, on the right-hand side of the ridge, you can identify the undercut crags which the shepherds once used as a shelter; you pass these on the way up from the Fuente Bernia to the *forat* (the hole which pierces the ridge). The *forat* itself is hidden from view. I am particularly impressed with the view down the ridge to the east as the crags fall away, ultimately dropping into the Mediterranean as Moro del Toix, and of the monolith of Peñon d'Ifach, with the attractive little resort of Calpe nestling between them.

Further West?

Sadly, at present, there is no walking route beyond the Eastern Peak, as further exploration is restricted to well-equipped rock climbers.

Descent

I strongly recommend reversing the ascent route, and have always been able to resist the temptation to climb down, through the arch, and run down the steep, rough scree. There is a route from the arch which climbs a 10m wall on the northern side of the ridge to the crest and then down the north side back to the col. The going is very rough and I prefer the southern route.   *6hrs*

Refreshments are available at the Pinos Restaurant, but be careful if you are ordering the 'Menu del Dia', as the first course is always sardines (the speciality of the house). A visiting friend, a devotee of the sardine, ordered them as his main course, and subsequently had to eat them as starter and main course, some twenty sardines in all. Fortunately, this did not extend to the dessert!

5: BERNIA FORT AND CIRCUIT

Grade: moderate

Distance: 14km

Time: 4hrs 30mins

Ascent   300m

Maps: Altea 848 (30–33), Benisa 822 (30–32)

This fort (built for a Spanish king in 1565) was used as a last refuge by the Moors fleeing persecution and expulsion in the 17th century. The Moors were evicted and the fort demolished in 1612. Extensive ruins lie on the southern shoulder beneath the summit crags at the western end of the ridge.

The walk is about 14km, an anti-clockwise circuit of the ridge crossing south to north by means of a forat, or natural tunnel. Walking is often on good paths, but there is some scree and a little easy rock work. The ascent to the ridge itself starts with a short, easy rock climb.

Getting There

A start can be made by parking cars at the end of the short road leading from Km.12 on the CV749 from Benissa to Jalón, and walking west towards the ridge. Ahead are the zig-zags of an unsurfaced road which leads to a broad col between Bernia and Penon de la Ovenga, which can be reached in 30 minutes (some brave souls take cars as far as this col). A short diversion to the top of Penon de La Ovenga gives dramatic views down into the Paso de los Bandoleros (allow 40mins).

The Col

The track now turns left (south-west) to climb steadily along the flank of the Bernia to reach a rocky col between the mountain and Peña Severino. This is a good track, so take time to appreciate the great gully on your right which leads to the source of the Rio Algar. Tarbena can be seen perched high on a small plateau, with Bolulla below it. Behind you can see the tortured red strata of the Sierra Ferrer leading to Col de Rates. There is a small cave on the left and then you are at the col, with uninterrupted views to the south from Altea to Aitana.   *50mins*

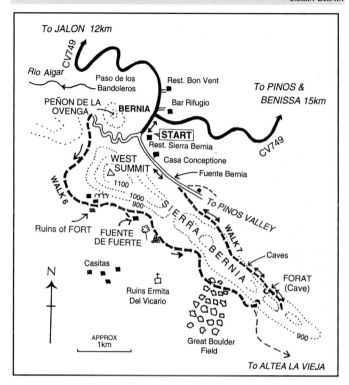

The Fort

This is reached by turning left (south-east) on well-defined paths for 10minutes. Although the fort was demolished, and has since suffered from the attentions of treasure hunters, the extent of this great fortification can still be seen.   *1hr*

From the fort maintain height and take a path going parallel to the ridge (south-east). You will first find a painted boulder, and then two squarish boulders on line. Near here, red markers will lead you in 1hr 30mins to the *forat*, high on the summit ridge near the eastern end. The track is good for 15 minutes, but then becomes rough with a number of scree chutes (loose rock) and a few rock scrambles.

The ruins of 16th-century Fort Bernia

The Route to the Forat

You have a clear view ahead to your next objective, which can be seen at the base of the bare crags with a few trees at its mouth, about four small buttresses from the eastern end of the ridge. The track will climb fairly steadily, keeping high but under the crags. There are a number of trees surviving on these high slopes, and one magnificent specimen is your first objective, marked by a rock cairn.

Follow the red markers, descend some rocks to a broad scree run, and immediately climb left up the scree. To continue ahead would lead to the *fuente*, and this route should only be used if you are in need of water. Below is a small settlement of *casitas* and orchards.

1hr 30mins

In 20 minutes the cairn under the large oak tree is reached, and then it is necessary to cross more scree and descend a little by a large juniper tree. You should now be directly beneath a small col on the main ridge, with two distinctive pinnacles, and directly above the ruins of the Ermita del Vicario.

2hrs

After another 15 minutes, you enter the great Boulder Field, which takes 15 minutes to cross and entails a little rock work.   *2hrs 30mins*

The path now starts to climb steadily towards the *forat*, which should now be clearly visible above. Cross some flat slabs, and in another 30 minutes you will reach the magnificent portals of the cave, and an excellent place for lunch. Note particularly the rock plants and trees which have colonised the rocks.   *3hrs*

The Forat (Cave)

It is now necessary to pass through this low cave in order to gain the northern side of the ridge and continue your circuit. (Sheep and goats sometimes use the cave for shelter, which can result in unpleasant consequences.) Some people crawl through on hands and knees, others try to maintain a more dignified posture, but unless you are particularly small you will have to bend very low to make this, thankfully, short traverse (5mins). On reaching the northern side you have equally extensive views The drop in temperature can be most noticeable. On your right-hand side, you will see red markers on the rocks, which lead, after a short and easy rock climb, to a path which gives access to the actual rock ridge of the mountain. Take care, however, as the gradient is steep, but the intimate views of this beautiful ridge make it well worth the effort.   *(Allow 45mins for this diversion.)*

Descent to the Bernia Plateau

A good path now moves left (north-west), keeping at first close to the crags and passing under some overhanging rocks (used as shelters by shepherds). In 20 minutes there is a short rock scramble to a good path leading in easy stages to a large *fuente* (spring), then along a broad track back to your starting point.   *4hrs 30mins*

6: BERNIA FUENTE, FORAT AND RIDGE FROM CASAS DE BERNIA

Grade:	moderate
Distance:	6km
Time:	2hrs 45mins
Ascent:	147m
Maps:	Altea 848 (30–33), Benisa 822 (30–32)

Getting There

Use the CV749, from Jalón to Benissa, to the hamlet of Casas Bernia on a side road at Km.12. Parking is at the end of this road near to Restaurant Sierra Bernia.

Stroll to the Fuente

Start by continuing along the road south towards the summit of the Bernia, and after 5 minutes bear to the left at a junction with waymarkers pointing to the route of PRV7 to the fort and to the *forat*. The times shown are somewhat optimistic, and you turn off to the left, heading east alongside the northern crags of the mountain through almond groves and passing a number of small *casitas*.

Ahead, the views down the Pinos Valley towards Benissa, with Montgo in the distance, are extensive. The road contours around the head of a *barranco*, where a route marker indicates the start of the traverse of the main summit (Walk 3), and you arrive at Fuente Bernia, with its running water, troughs and picnic area. The road ahead leads down the Pinos Valley (Walk 10). *30mins 1.5km*

To the Forat

This section of the route is a narrow, but well-waymarked track, which climbs steadily along the northern side of the mountain. Pass through a boulder field, which requires a little scrambling, until you reach the shallow caves once used as a corral for animals. Initial views are of the Ferrer Ridge, above the Paso de los Bandoleros, to the north and Tossal de Navarro, the end of the Loma Larga, to the north-east. Ahead to the east is Montgo and Isadoro on the coast.

As you gain height, Moraira headland, with its castle and the main summit of Olta, appear ahead, and there are more extensive views down the Pinos Valley to the tiny hamlets of Casas de Berdiola and Pinos with its little *ermita*. Above is the East Peak of the Bernia, and to its left, at the bottom of the valley, the gash of the Estret Gorge and, just to the right of a band of crags, the start of the route to the East Peak (Walk 4).   *1hr   1.75km*

Now the route leads over some flat slabs, needing care in greasy conditions, and then some rocky sections before reaching the *forat*, which is hidden right until the last moment, but can be identified by the small flake of rock above it.   *1hr 15mins   3km*

At the Forat on the Bernia,
looking west to Puig Campaña, Monte Ponoch and Sanchet

Through the Forat

The headroom in the *forat* varies, but if you are willing to soil your knees and take off your rucksack, you can crawl through easily. In winter especially, you will find the sunnier and warmer side of the mountain waiting for you, with a high cave festooned with tiny rock plants and ferns, protecting the entrance from the wind and weather. At times wild goats take advantage of this attractive belvedere, and can make a bit of a mess and (some say) leave ticks when they go, although I have no personal experience of these pests.

There is a lone pine tree clinging to the scree below on the circuit route to the fort (Walk 5), and you look out over the wide sweep of Altea Bay, with the mountains of Sierra Helada, the Cortinas, Puig Campaña, Ponoch, Sanchet and Aitana in the distance. Below are the urbanisations on the lower slopes, Altea La Vieja and the vast *huerto* of the Algar and Guadalest valleys, with Benidorm's tower blocks on the coast as well. Immediately below you are the ruins of Ermita Vicario, and to the west Callosa d'Ensarria, with Almedia (note the prominent ventilator chimney). At the end of the ridge are Peña Severino and the main summit of the Bernia, with the hamlet of Casas Ruñar below them.

To the Ridge

Return to the northern side of the *forat* and follow the red waymarkers on the right-hand side of the entrance (east), which necessitates a couple of interesting rock moves (which need care) to ascend in 20 minutes on a rough path (100m) to a col on the ridge itself (847m). If you are not a rock climber or properly equipped, you should not be tempted by the red waymarkers which indicate the climbers' traverse of the ridge.

If you are used to scrambling, then you can traverse to the west for about half an hour below the ridge rocks until you reach a narrow arête and some quite serious rock pitches.

Down to Casas Bernia

Retrace your steps to the Fuente Bernia and allow just a little more time for the descent, in the interests of safety, and take your refreshments at one of the three restaurants, but be prepared for disappointment, as rarely are the three of them open. Sierra Bernia (except Sunday) and Bon Vent (Km.11, Wed–Sun) are fairly reliable, and The Refugio, near the turn-off to the car park, rather less so.

2hrs 45mins   6km

7: PASO DE LOS BANDOLEROS

Grade:	moderate
Distance:	7km
Time:	4hrs 30mins
Ascent:	250m
Map:	Benisa 822 (30–32)

El Paso de los Bandoleros (the Pass of the Brigands) is a deep gully between two high sierras, the Bernia and the Ferrer, and some time long ago a substantial river flowed down this gully to join the Rio Algar. The river has long since gone underground, but the barranco remains and is the object of this walk. Like most other ravines in this part of the world, it is not possible to traverse the whole way down to the Algar Valley, due to the river having formed high waterfalls when it encountered strata of harder rock. The resulting drop of about 50m might be attractive to mountaineers using ropes, but not to walkers. Whilst this is a modest walk, you seldom have the benefit of good paths and there is quite a lot of very rough walking.

Getting There

The walk starts and ends at the Bon Vent Restaurant on the Bernia plateau, near to Km.12 on the CV749 from Jalón. From Benissa, you can take the CV749 via Pinos to reach the Bernia plateau. The Bon Vent is normally open from Wednesday to Sunday, when the proprietor, Juan Manuel, is in residence.

Making a Start

Leave the restaurant and walk along the road towards Jalón for about 2km, which gives you plenty of time to admire the majestic views of the Bernia and the Ferrer. Between these two is the Paso, and beyond, in the distance, Bolulla, Callosa d'Ensarria and the whole mountain range from Puig Campaña to Aitana. Overlooking the gorge, on the southern side, is the shapely peak of Peña Ovenga, behind which is the very end of the Bernia Ridge, Peña Severino. At the bottom of the

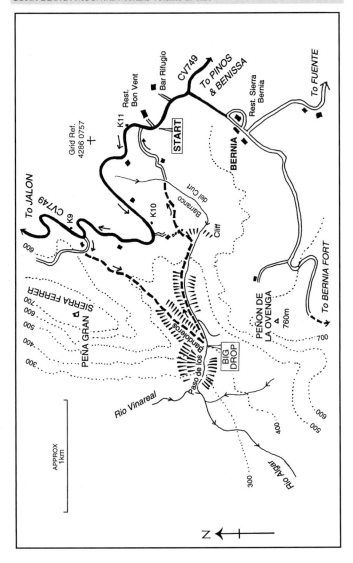

first major hairpin bend, near Km.9, an unsurfaced road leads off left (west) to an old *finca*. In 10 minutes, at the old *finca*, turn off left (south-west) towards Peña Severino and walk through almond groves until a good path appears (red markers). *1hr 40mins*

Into the Barranco

A reasonable track now follows the right-hand (west) side of a deep *barranco*, which will lead you directly down into the Paso. The track ends in about 30 minutes, and you take to flat slabs which lead down into the boulders of the old river bed, where the Barranco del Curt joins it from the north. *2hrs*

Above you, on the right-hand side of the gorge, is a cave which energetic folk have explored and emerged from the roof. Most of us, however, will enjoy a brief rest before exploring further down the gorge.

To the Old Waterfall

For some 10 minutes it is possible to follow the route of the old river, clambering between the large boulders, which make progress rather slow, before you are confronted with the impressive drop over what once was a waterfall. You now have good views down into the Algar Valley and upwards towards the crags through which the water once thundered. To continue down into the Algar Valley it is necessary to climb the scree leading to the crag on the left-hand side of the gorge. Circumvent it, and descend over very rough ground into the Algar Valley. To return to the Bernia plateau, however, retrace your steps upstream to the junction of the two *barrancos*. *2hrs 30mins*

Climbing the Barranco Del Curt

Walkers may wish to retrace their steps; others, prepared for a bit of rough walking, may prefer to make this a circular route and tackle another *barranco*. Now head north-east on a good path on the northern side of the *barranco* until there is a small rock scramble, and ahead can be seen a red-coloured crag, which overhangs some caves. This is another old waterfall. By all means explore the caves, but the best route upwards is to avoid the crag, keeping left (north) on easier ground. You climb up close to an outcrop of rock (thankfully on red markings) and head for the gap between two other outcrops on the skyline. *3hrs*

It is debatable whether there is really a path over this rough ground, but the markers should help you to reach the top, marked by a large cairn and a boundary wall (marked on the MOPU map).
3hrs 45mins

Back to the Bon Vent

Follow the line of the wall until an old ruined *finca* is reached and you have views to the north-east of the Bon Vent Restaurant.

Those who have tired of the rough walking can, quite justifiably, follow the unsurfaced road north for 5 minutes, join the road and turn right for just over 1km back to the restaurant. Other hardier souls (or masochists) can plot a course towards the Bon Vent, crossing some shallow terraces to a *casita* from which a broad unsurfaced road leads directly to the restaurant. *4hrs 30mins*

I have watched Juan Manuel and his wife Antonia struggle to improve the facilities at this idyllically placed little restaurant, but there is no need for any improvement in the quality of his food or his cheerful service.

8: PEÑA SEVERINO
(with Peña Ovenga) from Casas de Bernia

Grade:	moderate
Distance:	9km
Time:	4hrs
Ascent:	330m
Maps:	Altea 848 (30–33), Benisa 822 (30–32)

The attention of the legions who make the justifiably popular walk from Bernia village to the fort is, of course, claimed by the mighty peak of the Western Summit which soars to 1100m and then runs east as a dramatic jagged ridge for 4km to the sea. Ignored by most is a beautiful peak on the right of the path up to the fort. This is one of the objects of today's walk, the Eastern Peak of Peña Severino.

There are in fact two peaks, each over 800m, and between them a delightful arête. It has long been my ambition to achieve a

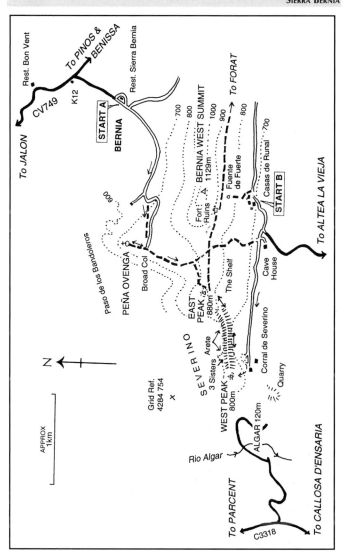

complete traverse of this arête, but whilst both peaks can be safely ascended by walkers, the traverse is sadly the province of a strong, well-equipped rock-climbing party, prepared to nail themselves to rotten rock! On this walk you will visit both of the peaks and enjoy the inspiring views along the arête without having to suffer the discomfort of the traverse itself. (Within a few metres of the Western Summit the way is blocked by sheer pinnacles.)

There are two alternative start points to the walk: Start A approaches from the north and Start B from the south.

Start A: Getting There

Leave your transport at the parking place near the Bernia Restaurant, Km.12 on the CV749 from Benissa to Jalón.

To the Broad Col and Peña Ovenga

Head south-west along a good road, and in a few minutes the road to the *fuente* forks off left. Keep straight on towards the Western Summit of Bernia to follow a well-engineered forestry road up to the col. People with sturdy cars can take them to the col in normal conditions. Near the last zig-zag there is a short-cut, marked in yellow and white. Use it by all means if you find the broad forestry road not to your liking. On arriving at the end of the road at Broad Col consider, if you will, an ascent of a minor rocky crest to the north, Peña Ovenga. The ascent will take you only 20 minutes, admittedly over very rough, broken limestone, but the sheer drop down into the Paso de los Bandoleros is worth the effort. The summit is crowned by a wooden cross, so someone must love this little peak. (Its name, I think, means forgotten peak.)   *30mins + 40mins for Ovenga*

To Peña Severina East Peak

Now you have a pleasant half hour, on a good track, with some sensational views down into a deep *barranco* which joins the Paso de los Bandoleros, with Tarbena perched on a shelf high above the valley and under the mountains. To your left there are intimate views of the crags of the Bernia and ahead the rock gateway leading to Bernia Fort, with your mountain on its right. Just as you make the final climb to the

rock gateway seek out another path going right (south-west) under
some crags.   *45mins*

There is a mini col to aim for near a prominent flake, then keep
traversing upwards to the skyline (there really is a path) but avoid tracks
going downhill. Keep left, under the crags (there is a pine tree to aim
for), and you will gain the shelf with views now to the south, Altea and
Benidorm. Take a breather and enjoy the view; you are only a few
minutes from the Eastern Summit.   *1hr 15mins*

There is a path up to the summit of the mountain which is a bit
rocky and moves out to the right a bit at the end to traverse over rocks
to a cairn.   *1hr 40mins*

The Eastern Summit

To the east the Bernia and the western end of its ridge present a
magnificent spectacle, but it is to the west that my eyes have always
been drawn, to the arête. Walkers, should they choose to do so, can
descend for about 20 minutes to the start of Pinnacle Arête for
sensational views of an overhanging north wall which looks pretty
rotten, and a ridge which has held together only because it never
freezes. (One Pennine winter and most of it would fall off!) Below can
be seen a good track which leads to an abandoned *finca*, Corral de
Severino. The views of the tortured strata of the end of Sierra Ferrer
(beloved of geology tutors) are an attraction to the north. There is more
to see, but I leave it to you to check your map whilst you enjoy a rest
on this lovely summit.

The Western Summit

It is possible for experienced mountaineers to drop down (not literally)
from Pinnacle Ridge to the track below. Others should reverse the route
to the rock gateway or take a direct route, east, across the shelf to reach
the track to Bernia Fort. From the gateway keep a look out for a track
descending south which will join the next described route. (Allow 1h
15mins from summit to lower path.)

Start B: Approach from Altea la Vieja

Leave Altea la Vieja and head towards Callosa D'Ensarria on the CV755
Km.18.5 for 2km (since the road was upgraded there are no kilometre
posts!). There is a prominent round-headed pine on your left, and you
pass through a gateway on to a narrow but well-surfaced road which

will take you in about 5km to the unbelievable hamlet of Casas de Ruñar, perched on a level bit of ground right under the fort at an elevation of 700m. At 4km from the main road, note a house built into a cliff on the left-hand side and a chained track also on your left. This is the start of your walk, with parking for a few cars only.

To Corral De Severino

Turn off the surfaced road onto an unsurfaced one, which is chained, and zig-zag upwards, passing the Cave House, someone's weekend home. Now settle down to an easy walk along a contour, slightly north of west, and at a wider point note a waymarked Mozarabic trail heading upwards (north) to near the Bernia Fort. On this lovely traverse you get extensive views and can inspect the arête, which looks benign from this side. Ahead is the Western Peak. In half an hour you will pass a depression on the right-hand side which has in the past been cultivated just before you arrive at the ruined *finca* Corral de Severino.

45mins

Ascent of Western Peak

Unlike its sister this peak has no path to help you, and the only advice is to head for the skyline from the *finca*. If you head for the crags which join the peak to the Three Sisters (the pinnacles which join the peak to the arête) you will have to do some easy rock scrambling. The safest route is to keep over to the left (west) where the ground is still steep but less complicated. In about 45 minutes you should be on the summit with its cairn.

1hr 30mins

In all directions the views are sensational, and I find it difficult to mention any particular one. The view along the arête, of course, is favourite. Below is Algar and the Aixorta, with Callosa and the whole of the Guadalest Valley. Cocoll, with its new air-strip, and Col de Rates with Tarbena and Bollula, and even the Segaria Ridge near Orba can be identified.

At present there is no alternative return route surveyed, but there is the possibility of descending to Algar from the *finca*, to the quarry or even of leaving the summit and following a faint path which heads down into the Paso de los Bandoleros. (We still have to look at these routes. If, meanwhile, you should manage to find them, please let us know.)

9: PEÑA SEVERINO FROM FUENTES DE ALGAR

Grade:	strenuous
Distance:	14km
Time:	6hrs
Ascent:	900m
Maps:	Altea 848 (30–33), Benisa 822 (30–32)

Peña Severino is a shapely peak, and is the true western end of the better known Sierra Bernia. It is made up of two summits of 800m with a rocky arête between them, and the western peak forms an attractive backdrop to the tiny but popular hamlet of Algar and dominates the skyline as you approach from Callosa de Ensarria on the CV715 road. There are two walks described here: the first is a modest one to ascend the Western Summit from the Algar Valley (5hrs, 11.5km), and the second, for those with the stamina, is a circular route back down into the Algar Valley, via the upper col of the Bernia and a very demanding gully (at least 6hrs, 14km).

Getting There

The well-watered and fruitful Algar Valley, ringed by high peaks, has many attractions (see volume 1). Leave the CV715 at Km.2 to descend through the hamlet with its numerous car parks (there is a charge), and follow my route from the river bridge to free parking higher up the road.

Making a Start to the Quarry

From the river bridge continue north-west, passing the Restaurant Don Juan on the right, and climb up until the entrance to the falls is passed on the left and the road swings right in a north-eastern direction, passing the entrance to the Museum Media Ambiente on the left. Continue until, just before the public car park, a road leads off to the left, with a yellow and white marker board 'Fonts de Algar PRG 38 Route 5'. Follow this surfaced road as it climbs through nisperus groves. The road loses its surface after about a kilometre and you reach a quarry on the right-hand side. Already, as you have gained height, you are treated to excellent views to the south of Puig Campaña, Ponoch, Sanchet and the Aitana Ridge.   *1hr   2.5km*

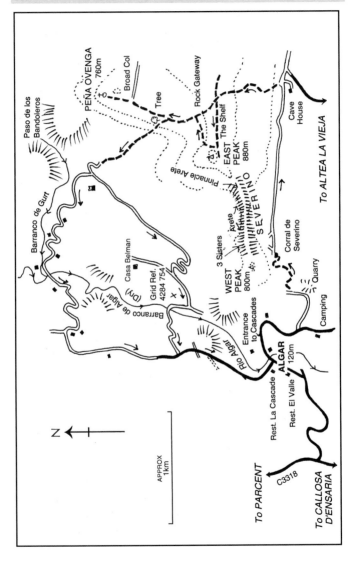

To Corral De Severino

After a few minutes there is a fork, and you go right uphill until, just before the road ends, a path leads off on the right-hand side with some yellow and white markers, first along the top of a terrace, passing a well. Now head basically south-east, as the steep track zig-zags to gain height. You are now high above the Algar Valley with more extensive views. Above can be seen some scree, which you have to cross. Pass an old ruin, and there are now views of Bolulla village to the west.

1hr 30mins   4.5km

There is a well-trodden track across the scree, beneath the crags of Severino, to gain a reasonable track and head for the skyline. First to appear above to the left is the West Summit, and then, straight ahead, the Main (Western) summit of the Bernia and the Eastern Summit of Severino. Finally the fort below the Bernia summit appears, and you arrive at the collection of ruins which are Corral de Severino.

2hrs 5km

To the Western Summit

From the ruins you just go up north to gain the rocky summit. There is no path to help you, but the easier ground is to the left, whilst if you stray to the right you will find some rock scrambling to do.

2hrs 40mins   5.5km

To the south you now have most of the Algar Valley below you, from Col de Rates down to the coast. In the middle-distance is Callosa de Ensarria, the Guadalest Valley and, in the distance, the peaks of Puig Campaña, Ponoch, Sanchet and the Aitana Ridge. To the north-east is the Segaria Ridge near Tormos. Most dramatic is the view along the arête towards the Eastern Summit.

Return the same way to the Corral and then follow the same path down to Algar, watching out, as you leave the ruins, to take the right-hand path at a junction.

5hrs 30mins   11km

The Circuit Route

From the ruins there is a good unsurfaced road which heads east under the southern crags of the arête, which are much more benign than the sheer cliffs on the northern side. The large hollow on the left of the road has been used for cultivation and is probably a depression in the limestone known as a *polje*. Just as the road starts to drop a little, look out for the start of an old mule trail on the left-hand side, with some red markers, and start your climb up to the Puerto de Bernia.

2hrs 30mins   6.5km

The track is at times much eroded and zig-zags steeply until you meet the main track, which leads right to the Bernia Fort and left to the Puerto and the hamlet of Bernia. Turn left and in half an hour reach the rock gateway at the col.

3hrs   8km

Peña Severino from the Algar Valley

Optional Ascent of the Eastern Summit

For fit peak baggers, an ascent of this summit can be made by climbing a rocky groove on the left just before you reach the rock gateway. From a level area, make your way west until you find a mule track leading up to the rocky summit with its cairn. The views of the sheer northern wall of the arête and of the tortured stratum of the end of the Ferrer Ridge, as it plunges into the gorge, are the most impressive. Descend by the same route until the trail ends, then take a short cut down to the left, northern side, where an indistinct path descends and traverses east, under some crags, to join the good trail below the rock gateway on the northern side of the col. *Add 1 hr walking and 1.5km to route.*

The well-trodden path now descends gently to the north-east, with dramatic views down left to a deep gully with some lovely crags and pinnacles under Severino, and views of Paso De Los Bandoleros in the upper Algar Valley. The mountain village of Tarbena can be seen on a shelf above the valley. In about 5 minutes you reach an old pine tree, which, until some fool lit a barbecue under it, provided welcome shade, and at this point you leave the path to descend to the Algar.

3hrs 20mins   9km

Descent to the Algar Valley

There is now no path to help you, only some embryo cairns and a few red markers to show you where someone else has gone before you. Keep to the left of the gully and at all costs do not descend into it – it is inhabited by man-eating brambles! Eventually, after descending about 600m, a faint track appears with some markers, crosses over the gully and reaches a broad forestry road near to the extensive ruins of an old *finca*, in a beautiful position, on a knoll overlooking the valley near to the rocky cleft of the Paso De Los Bandoleros.

4hrs 30mins   11km

Back to Algar

You are now on the Algar Valley Walk (described in Volume 1, Walk 25), and all you have to do is to decide whether to turn left or right. If you turn right, east, towards the Paso, you have 2 hours 30 minutes and 8km to walk; if you turn left, west, only 1 hour 30 minutes and 4 km before you reach the hospitality of the village.

Shorter route 6 hrs   14km

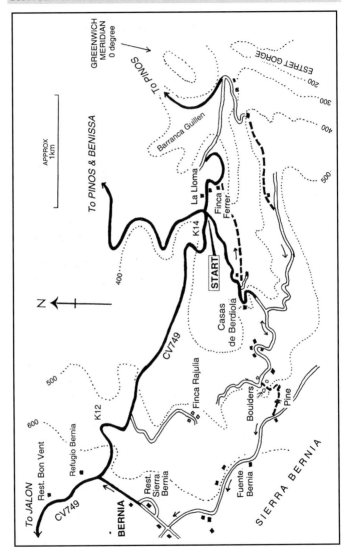

10: PINOS VALLEY FROM PINOS

Grade:	moderate
Distance:	12km
Time:	6hrs
Ascent:	300m
Maps:	Altea 30–33 (898), Benisa 30–32 (822)

This valley runs alongside and below the jagged crags of Bernia Ridge from the dramatic Estret Gorge (which continues to become the even more dramatic Mascarat Gorge on the coast between Altea and Calpe) to the high plateau of the Bernia. There is, however, no river (on the surface at least) in the valley, but it contains many small farms which benefit from its sheltered position. Many of the farms are only occupied during the weekends and at fiestas, when the owners come out from the town to tend their crops. A few, however, are still occupied, even though they have none of the benefits of modern living. Unlike most of the other walks, which end on top of a mountain, this one is spent ascending the valley to the Bernia, and throughout the rather long day you will have the chance to admire the northern crags of the Bernia and the distant views of the coast.

Mostly on very good tracks, there is one short section of an old Mozarabic trail on the ascent. It is a walk which most walkers can enjoy, and if you are sure that one of the restaurants will be open, you can travel very light. It is unusual on my walks to pass through farmyards, but on this one you pass through a number of them. Please respect the owners' property and privacy.

Making a Start

Leave the CV749 (Benissa to Jalón) road at Km.14, and park in clearing where two metalled roads lead down into the valley. Get your bearings, and you will see Pinos's little church on a ridge to the north-east and, to the south-east, the small hamlet of Casas Berdiolas, which is the halfway point of your walk. Take the left-hand road east towards the jaws of the Estret Gorge and Olta, passing two white *fincas* with the same name, La Lloma (the Hill), and in 10 minutes a *finca* with a palm tree, Finca de Francisco Ferrer, which you will again pass at the end of the day. As you walk downwards the surfaced road ends and you turn off right on a rather rougher road for a short while to rejoin the surfaced road, which comes down from Pinos village, at the bottom of the valley.

15mins

Cross the dry, stony river bed as it enters the gorge, and turn away from it (north-west) on a good road parallel with the Bernia Ridge. Go through the stone gate posts, and start to climb under two *casitas* as the track zig-zags upwards to a third *finca* with unusual stucco work on its wall. It is necessary to go behind this *finca* to find a mule track (if the *finca* is occupied, seek permission; in any case, you can climb the two terraces just before reaching it) which traverses gently at first and then zig-zags upwards. In 10 minutes (marker) leave the track and walk along the almond terraces to another occupied *finca*, where you cross the farmyard to gain a good road going north-west.   *1hr*

To Casas Berdiola

As you walk this section, you can admire the steep crags of the Bernia and try to identify the rock bridge on the very crest, with a beautiful natural arch below it (these are directly above a long, narrow scree run). Also in the distance, just below the crags, can be seen a small white *casita* which you will pass in about one and a half hours' time, and at the head of the valley is the hamlet of Bernia, which is your lunch stop. Another road joins from the left and the tiny hamlet of Casas Berdiola appears ahead. Glance backwards for a lovely view of Moraira Castle, framed in the jaws of the Estret. You now join a good road coming up from the valley bottom. Turn left, and in 15 minutes you will pass through the hamlet of Casas Berdiola. Continue upwards.

1hr 40mins

To Bernia Village

As you climb, look for a very unusual *finca* built against a massive boulder on your left under the ridge, and you get a clear view of your next objective, a small white *casita* higher up the valley. Pass a ruined *casita*, then some flat, exposed slabs and enter a shallow *barranca* with some large boulders.   *2hrs 10mins*

The Bernia Ridge from the Pinos Valley (photo Maurice Gibbs)

This is where you leave the good road and move left towards the ridge on a badly eroded track. Follow the markers to find an old Mozarabic trail which you follow upwards until the little white *casita* comes into view. Head directly for the *casita* – the path has been cleared and waymarked to avoid it. Once at the *casita*, with its stone seat around a tree, you can take a break to admire the extensive views, with the Ferrer Ridge seen to the north and the hamlet of Bernia ahead. Now join a good road (north-west) under the ridge and pass the *fuente* (spring) which flows all the year round. This is the starting point for the ascent to the ridge and to the *forat*, the hole in the rock which gives access to the southern side of the ridge. (This is another route which will take about an hour.) Carry on past the *fuente* and in half an hour reach the junction with the track coming down from the West Col and the fort. Turn right, passing the Sierra Bernia Restaurant, onto a surfaced road and the junction of the Jalón and Benissa roads. Near the junction is the Refugio Restaurant, and about a kilometre along on the road to Jalón the Bon Vent Restaurant, which has never refused me refreshment.

3hrs 20mins

Down Into the Valley Again

There once was a nice alternative descent back down to Casas Berdiola, but, sadly, this is no longer available. You can, if you choose, make a pleasant descent by the motor road 2km back to your cars, or return the way you came back to Casas de Berdiola.   *4hrs 30mins*

Retrace the route to the Casas Berdiola, and in another 10 minutes arrive at the junction with your morning's route, where you keep left, passing under a small villa, Casa Dolores, to reach the valley bottom. Here join a surfaced road which climbs up to your starting point in half an hour. A much more attractive route is to seek out the narrow path which starts just above a concrete road, on the right-hand side. There are red markers to help you keep on course as you walk high above a gorge, with a lovely little *finca* below you, until you reach Finca Francisco Ferrer. Join the surfaced road and turn left, up the hill, back to your starting point. Refreshments are on hand 3km along the road to Benissa at the Pinos Restaurant.   *6hrs*

11: PIC DEL FERRER

Grade:	moderate
Distance:	6km
Time:	4hrs
Ascent:	400m
Maps:	Benisa 822 (30–32)

The ridge of Sierra Ferrer is a rocky arête, 4km long, which runs from near Jalón south to the Bernia, where its stratum plunge dramatically into the defile of the Paso de los Bandoleros. It divides the Maserof and upper Algar Valley, and a traverse of the northern arête is described in Walk 12.

This route is much less demanding and, after the first hour's slog up to the col, becomes a lovely gentle walk along the ridge.

Getting There

The easiest approach is to turn south in Jalón village onto the CV749, signposted to Bernia. The alternative approach, from Benissa via Pinos on the same road, is a little longer and slower. Park your cars near the extensive *finca* of Maserof at Km.5. This is a bodega where clients can buy vines, which will be looked after by the owner, harvested and bottled for collection by the client at the end of the *vendimia*.

Towards the Col

With your back to the *finca* you can admire the rocky northern arête, divided by a col from the first summit of the southern one, Penyes de l'Umbria, with a broad road leading upwards from the motor road, a few metres south of the bodega. This is the first stage of your ascent.

Keep climbing upwards, west, passing an old ruin on the left and the well, Pou de Pastor, used to water the herds of cattle which are grazed on the slopes of the Ferrer. The road now steepens and then descends a little (note your onward path which branches left just above the dip) before the final climb to the col. Views ahead are of the northern crags and then the Penyes de l'Umbria, whilst behind can be seen the Maserof Valley and a large walled residence, reputed to be

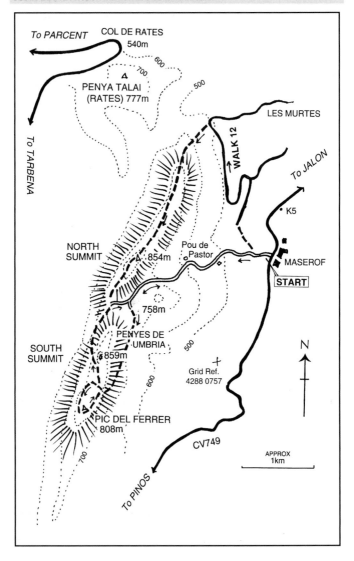

To PARCENT   COL DE RATES
540m

700   600

PENYA TALAI
(RATES) 777m

500

To TARBENA

LES MURTES

WALK 12

To JALON

K5

NORTH
SUMMIT   854m   Pou de
Pastor   MASEROF

START

758m

PENYES DE
UMBRIA

SOUTH
SUMMIT   859m

500

N

PIC DEL FERRER
808m

600

Grid Ref.
4288 0757

700

CV749   APPROX
1km

To PINOS

the domain of a wealthy recluse, with the long ridge of the Loma Larga to the east. *1hr 2km*

To Pic Del Ferrer

Now leave the road to turn left, south-west, and walk along a narrow track which leads under a band of crags which guard the summit of Penyes de l'Umbria and then along the uppermost of a series of terraces, with the rocky summit of Pic del Ferrer ahead. When the terraces end, turn more to the west to climb up, through old terraces, to gain the col. As you climb, first the Eastern Ridge of the Bernia appears ahead, to the south-west, then the whole ridge and the main summit, followed by the Serrella in the distance. Finally, to the east Peñon d'Ifach, Toix and the Mediterranean come into view. Once on the col views open up to the west, with Peña Mulero, Aixorta, Aitana the skyline; the castles of Tarbena, Bolulla and Serrella in the middle-distance; and below, the upper Algar Valley. To the north at the head of the Algar Valley is Col de Rates and in the far distance Benicadell.

To the Summit of Pic Del Ferrer

Climb up a rough path on the western side of the northern crags to ascend a rake on the top of a vertical crag on bare rock, then scramble up through the rocks to gain the summit with magnificent views in all directions. *2hrs 3.5km*

To the south, there is an impressive detached flake of rock in the foreground, with ivy growing on the northern side, then the rocky ridge continues on to the last summit Penya Gran (772m), with Puig Campaña, Ponoch and Sanchet in the distance. To the north the arête, with its near vertical stratum, continues beyond Penyes de Umbria (note a track on the western side which is your return route) and the northern arête leading to Peña Talai, overlooking Col de Rates. Beyond, the Segaria rises from the *huerta*, with Denia and Montgo on the coast and the headland of Cabo Nao at Javea. If visibility is good you can pick out Ibiza, the nearest Balearic island to the east, across the Mediterranean.

Back to the Col and on to Penyes de Umbria

Leave the summit and descend over the rocks on the eastern side, heading north-west on an intermittent track, to regain the col. Then change sides to follow a good, if overgrown, path under the crags of

Penyes de Umbria to climb up to a spur and then descend by an eroded path to regain the broad road at the col which divides the northern and southern arêtes. The summit of Penyes de Umbria (859m), the true summit of Ferrer, can be gained by scrambling up the rocks from the spur.   *3hrs 15mins   3.75km*

Back Down to Maserof

All that remains now is to follow your ascent road back down to Maserof, but beware of the good broad road – it is steep and has a loose surface and usually claims at least one victim, especially after a wine and tapas party on the summit. Refreshments are, of course, near at hand, either at Jalón or on the Bernia (Wed to Sun) at Km.11, where the Bon Vent does a mean garlic chicken too.   *4hrs   6km*

12: FERRER NORTH RIDGE FROM MASEROF

Grade:	scramble
Distance:	8.5km
Time:	4hrs 45mins
Ascent:	400m
Maps:	Benisa 822 (30–32)

The Ferrer Ridge is a 4km sharp, rocky arête, which runs roughly north to south from above Jalón to the Paso De Los Bandoleros on the Bernia plateau. It is made up of bedded Oligocene limestone, which has been thrust and faulted to make the stratum rise almost to the vertical. Especially dramatic are the stratum on the western face, when seen from the Algar Valley. At the southern end of the ridge, the limestone is cut into a deep gorge, the Paso de los Bandoleros, which separates the Ferrer from an outcrop of the Bernia, Peña Ovenga (788m), from which the view of the tortured stratum of the southern buttress is quite sensational. (For geologists this is the Ferrer fault and thrust – see Excursion 7 in The Geological Field Guide to the Costa Blanca by C.B. Moseley). The ridge is split into two sections by a central col opposite Maserof, on the road from Jalón to Bernia, and it is the northern section which offers this challenging scramble, which, although quite exposed in parts, can be tackled by scramblers used to exposure, if they avoid extreme weather conditions and take care to look out for loose rock!

Getting There

The easiest approach is to turn south in Jalón village on the CV749 road, signposted Bernia. From this road, the ridge looks like a coxcomb of bare rock. The alternative approach from Benissa via Pinos on the same road is a little longer and a slower road. Park your vehicles near the extensive *finca* at Maserof, Km.5. This is a bodega where clients can buy vines, which will be looked after by the owner, harvested and bottled for collection by the client at the end of the *vendimia*. With your back to the bodega, you can see the broad unsurfaced road zig-zagging towards the central col and you can admire the whole of the northern traverse.

The Walk In

To start the walk, you need to traverse cross-country to the northern end of the ridge, and you first use the unsurfaced road which leads to the col, but only for a few minutes. You then continue by crossing trackless ground heading north of west to drop into a small *barranca*, following its eastern side until you can see a prominent road, which traverses beneath the ridge. Climbing out of the *barranca* towards a ruined *finca*, you will find that this road is surfaced, and you follow it basically north for a time. At a junction with a most unnecessary 'Stop' sign, turn left, as another road joins you from the valley bottom. There is a small *casita* on the left and the road now zig-zags, still heading mostly north-west. After passing the entrance to a new villa on the left, Rates Peak and the Sierra Bernia come into view, and eventually you will reach a ruined *finca* where the road starts to drop. Here, you leave the surfaced road to start the rough climb up to the rocks of the ridge, and it will be over 3 hours before you tread a reasonable road again.

30 mins   2km

To the Ridge

The northern buttress can now be seen above you, and you have good views of the deep ravine which separates your mountain from its neighbour, Rates Peak. As you climb, you get good views of Olta in the distance. As you try to follow an indistinct track, probably made by goats, at times, it might be easier to use the exposed rock strata, which, for a short while, goes in your direction. Keep heading for the skyline and the gap in the arête, which gives access to the crest.

1hr 15mins   3.5km

The Traverse

Those of you with rock-climbing skills will, of course, keep to the very edge of the crest throughout. The route described here is the easiest and safest for those with modest experience, but you need a good head for heights.

The first section follows easy ground for about 10 minutes, with views down into the Algar Valley on the right-hand side, until you reach the sheer crags on the eastern side, which force you to move right and start scrambling. First move onto a rock staircase, then into a groove (Greasy Gully) to reach the arête. Views are now more extensive – note particularly the Aixorta range, the Serrella with Serrella Castle, Tarbena Castle and, behind you, Alcalali and Jalón. The most impressive views, however, are those ahead of you of the jagged arête which leads to your objective, the northern summit.

Next, tackle another rocky arête which is quite exposed, but passable with care, by taking a line on firm rocks on the very edge of the exposed eastern face. After this, drop down to a ledge on the right (western side) just below the crest to reach the narrowest and most exposed section of the traverse. To the south, Penon de Ifach, Toix and Olta, near Calpe, come into view.

This most exposed and sharpest part of the ridge needs great care and should not be attempted in wet or windy conditions, as there is no alternative route but to keep to the crest of the rocks. Thankfully, this section is very short, and you descend on easy slabs on the right (western side) of the ridge, then climb back up to find a grassy belvedere, which makes an excellent halfway resting place.

As you leave the belvedere to rejoin the ridge, you get impressive views of the near vertical stratum of the northern summit. Looking back to the north-west, you can identify the Col de Rates, with its little restaurant, the Merendero and also Murla and Benichembla, sheltering under the rocky peak of Peña Roc. To the south are the Serrella Massif and in the distance Aitana itself. You should, from this position, be able to see the Balearic Islands, or at least Ibiza, if conditions are clear.

To your left, you can now identify the broad forestry road, your return route, as it twists and turns to reach the central col. Now move right into a small gap and climb through some pines just below the

Ferrer Ridge from Bernia, with Peña Ovenga in front (Walks 8, 9)

photo by Maurice Gibbs

The ruins of Calpe Castle, Peñon d'Ifach and Sierra Toix (Walk 13)

Sea cliffs at Toix (Walk 13)

crest of the ridge until you reach the base of a pinnacle. This pinnacle is avoided by moving right again around it to a spur of rock, from which there are dramatic views of the rocks and pinnacles of the Southern Ridge and the welcome sight of the road which terminates at the central col. *3.75hrs   6km*

Back Down to Maserof

Those of you of a sensitive or nervous disposition can now cease to dither, as the scrambling for the day is over and all that remains is a pleasant final stroll down into the valley again. You can still identify the town of Teulada, a long way away, just to the right of the prominent quarries in the gorge of La Garganta on the Benissa to Gata de Gorgos road. You can also enjoy good views of your ridge and relive your traverse of the crest. My own traverse was certainly a memorable scramble, due to the black ice which coated the rocks and which the December sun had difficulty in reaching. The day was also reminiscent of past alpine days because of the constant yet pleasant sound of cow-bells in the valley below, which persisted during the whole traverse and tempted some of the party to attempt to yodel. On the way down, we met the *vaquero* with his large herd of black cows, calves and one gigantic happy bull. The only time that you really need to worry about them is if you have a dog with you, as their eyesight, I am told, makes them mistake a dog for a calf. *4hrs 45mins   8.5km*

The nearest refreshments are in Jalón or, if you wish to proceed to the Bernia plateau, the restaurant Bon Vent will welcome you Wednesday to Sunday, at Km.12.

On the ridge of the Sierra Toix with the TV transmitters (Walk 13)

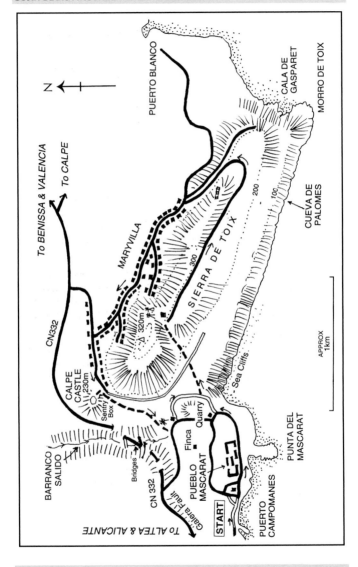

Calpe Area – Sierra Toix/Sierra Olta

13: SIERRA DE TOIX AND CALPE CASTLE

Grade:	scramble
Distance:	8km
Time:	4hrs
Ascent:	320m
Maps:	Altea 848 (30–33)

Sierra de Toix is one of the very few of mountains of the region whose summit may be attained in a motor vehicle. I am sure that my readers would not wish to do this and would much prefer to scramble straight up from sea level, over 1000ft, to the rugged summit ridge from Punta Mascarat.

The sierra runs south-east from the gorge of Barranca Salido, which severs it from the rest of the Bernia Ridge, and ends in the sheer cliffs of Morro de Toix. It, together with Peñon De Ifach, forms the arms which enclose the Arenal Beach of Calpe.

This is a rough rock scramble up a gully, in classical style, straight for the summit, after which exercise there is a pleasant road walk around the mountain, with magnificent scenery, under the northern cliffs back to visit the scant remains of Calpe's Moorish Castle.

Getting There

Start by leaving the CN332 coastal road, north of Altea, at Km.163, following signs to Marina Luis Campomanes, and park in the main plaza, where there are plenty of bars and restaurants, including the Club Nautico, available for refreshments. Cars can now be taken as far as the new Pueblo Mascarat.

To Punta Del Mascarat

Right from the start of this walk there are lots of interesting things to see – the marina, for instance, is built right on the Greenwich meridian of longitude, dividing the eastern and western hemispheres, which is of course very important to navigators. If you were to follow the line north, you would finish up in Greenwich Park and the Royal Observatory.

Above us is a notorious geological feature, the unstable Galera Fault, where there is a crack in the stratum which from time to time can move. It last shifted in 1989, and as a result both the road and the railway line were closed for many months until impressive concrete supports, which can be seen above you, were installed to stabilise the mountain.

Leave the plaza and turn right, east, along a road, with the boatyard on your right, and when the road climbs up to the left of some flats under construction keep on along the coast and climb up to the road which runs on the seaward side of the development, Pueblo Mascarat. There are lovely little coves below you and the small headland is Punta Del Mascarat. When the buildings of the Pueblo end, keep on as the road curves to the left and you have your first clear view of the day's climb.

On the left, there are the road and rail bridges which span Barranco Salido, a great favourite with those who love to hurl themselves into an abyss, tied by the ankles to an elastic rope. A variation of this pastime is 'pendulating', where a rope is passed from one bridge to the other, and the enthusiast is thus able to jump off and swing through the arch of the bridge.

Then comes the small pass, Colado de Castelet, with the one remaining wall of Calpe's Moorish Castle on the left. An ancient mule track was the only access from the south to Calpe before the road tunnel was built at the turn of the century. Next there are the main western crags of Toix, with excellent rock climbs of up to 400ft on sound rock and now very popular with British climbers as well as the locals. To the right of these crags is a broad, rocky gully which is your route up the summit with its transmitters. Below these crags a track contours downwards from the villas in the col. The climbers use this track, and below the gully can be seen a very rough path which they have made to get down to the beach directly below you, where there are other climbing routes on the vertical sea cliffs. Further along this line of impressive cliffs there are underwater caves to attract divers.

20mins   1km

The infamous bridge jump in the Mascarat Gorge

The Ascent to the Summit

Follow the road as it swings to the left for a few metres until you can turn off right, towards the summit, on a rough road, which provides access to the quarry on your left. To find the easiest access to the gully and start your scramble, at a yellow marker find the most popular route up to the upper track and turn left along it until you are nearly at the first villa. The many paths worn by rock climbers will, I am sure, help you as you choose your own route upwards. These rock climbs are on crags, just a little less vertical than those on the other side of the crag, and are justly popular – being in the sun for most of the day. Sadly, most have no names and are known by the colour of the paint used to mark where the ring bolts have been fixed in the rock (strictly a Spanish custom). *40mins   2km*

After about half an hour pass a large cove in the rock, where some new climbing routes have been explored, and then the antennae on the summit ridge come into view ahead and you should follow any paths which head for them, or rather just a little to the right of them, as the road for which you are making ends at the transmitting station. Scramblers may be tempted to go straight up to the ridge, but beware of difficult rock on the approach to the summit (see below). Reach the road at the transmitter station and, if you wish, climb the rocks alongside the perimeter fence to gain the arête of the summit ridge and look down the sheer northern cliffs to the tiny villas below, each with its pretty blue pool. To the west the summit may tempt you to traverse further but, sadly, the last pitch, across a fairly straightforward but extremely exposed short arête, needs the protection of a rope for peace of mind, as a slip would mean either returning quickly to the bottom of the gully or landing on the terrace of one of the villas some 500ft below. *1.5hrs   3km*

To the south-west is Altea Bay with Sierra Helada, Benidorm and the Cortinas. Puig Campaña, Ponoch and Sanchet are to the west, whilst further north is the Aitana range. To the north-west are Aixorta and the Bernia, whilst to the north are Olta and Loma Larga, with the Greenwich meridian passing through the col between Tosal de Navarro and Cao. In the far distance Cabal, the gorge of Garganta at Gata de Gorgos and finally Montgo and Isadoro on the coast are visible. Below you the golden sands of Calpe's Arenal Beach lead from the tiny port of Puerto Blanco to the Peñon de Ifach. What a view indeed and well worth the effort.

Descent to Collado Del Castelet

Now all you have to do is to follow the service road, east just under the ridge, until a coloured wind sock indicates the point from which brave souls hurl themselves from the ridge to soar amongst the seagulls on their flimsy bit of nylon, and you round the end of Morro de Toix and start your downward traverse under the steep northern crags.

1hr 45mins   3.5km

You will first notice another road leading off to the right, which leads to a lower part of the cliffs, and then another road leads off right down to Puerto Blanco. Ignore the next two roads on the left, which lead only up to villas and to the start of rock climbs, and keep dropping gently, until in about half an hour you are right under the summit.

2hrs 10mins   4.5km

Finally, near villa 27L, turn left uphill for a short while (the road to the right leads to the CN332) and at a villa on the right, Casa Blanca, turn off the surfaced road (which will become the climbers' track) onto a rough track to pass a concrete water tank on the left and reach the col, Collado de Castelet, with a view of your next objective, the ruins of Calpe Castle above you.

2hrs 30mins   5.5km

Ascent of the Castle

If Calpe's Council keeps its promise, by the time you visit the ruins there will be a well-constructed path with hand rails, and my directions will be redundant.

In the col, start from the small Moorish 'sentry box' and ascend from the south, as the northern side of this crag drops vertically to the main road. The Moorish path has long since disappeared, and when you reach a low band of brown rock keep to the left of it and scramble up as best you can, passing a small pit on your right, to gain the top with its one remaining wall of the ancient castle.

There are now good views of the crags of Toix and into the depths of the Salido Gorge.

2hrs 45mins

Descent to Punta Del Mascarat

Whilst at the castle, you might want to decide which route to descend by – they are both clearly visible to you.

Via the Climbers' Track

Return to the surfaced road at Casa Blanca and turn right, noting at the last villa a polite notice requesting people to 'climb quietly', and return to the track under the crags to reverse your ascent route to Punta Mascarat.

Via the Old Road

The old road which connected Altea and Calpe via the col is clearly shown on the map, but is not very evident on the ground, mainly due to residents dumping garden refuse at the northern end of it, where it passes close to villas, and to the ravages of time.

Return to the water tank and turn off to the right, with the walls of some villas on your left. After a few metres you will have to leave the path to walk around the garden rubbish over rough ground and endeavour to regain the path again, heading always west of south. Thankfully you have some landmarks to follow when the villa walls end, and for a short stretch the road shows how wide and well constructed it must once have been. First walk alongside the power cables, keeping on a southern bearing, until you get good views of the road and rail bridges below you – at times you will have to push through the undergrowth. There is a deep gully on your left which you should not try to cross, then pass under the cables, seeking out an old ruined *finca* with a palm tree. Pass to the right of these ruins. There is a good path from them which joins the quarry road which leads to Punta del Mascarat. Be careful, the quarry is just beneath you.

3hrs 45mins   7km

Return by your approach route to the starting point, the marina and the welcome hospitality of its bars. *4hrs   8km*

14: SIERRA DE OLTA SUMMITS

Grade:	moderate
Distance:	10km
Time:	4hrs 45mins
Ascent:	500m
Map:	Altea 848 (30–33)

On this walk, you will discover that Olta, although perhaps insignificant in comparison with the giants further inland, is still a true mountain worthy of exploration. It has all the best characteristics of a mountain, rocky summits, all its flanks protected by sheer crags and an isolated position ensuring all-round views. Don't be deceived by its height (591m), as small coastal mountains rising directly from the sea can be almost as demanding as the Alps.

The Mountain

Olta is the mountain whose southern summit greets the motorist as he emerges from the tunnels of the Barranca de Mascarat on the CN332, and its eastern cliffs keep him company as he skirts Calpe towards Benissa. The northern summit seen from the road to Benissa, near the rather exotic Moorish-style building on the left of the road (Disco), is also very impressive, with many rugged pinnacles. Only the western cliffs are difficult to study at close quarters - the best views are from the *autopista*, but this is not a place to loiter and you have to be content with distant views from Pinos or Bernia. On all sides Olta is surrounded by steep cliffs – no trouble, I am sure, to rock climbers, but preventing the ordinary walker from reaching the top except by one straightforward route which climbs up Broad Gully on the eastern side.

During the summers of 1991 and 1992 there were extensive forest fires on Olta which burnt off all the vegetation, and this has made walking and route-finding much easier. The estate roads have been improved and extended and firebreaks constructed, so look out for roads not shown on the map. It is evident from the log book on the north summit that Olta is now a popular excursion for both Spaniards and visitors, which means that in places there is a semblance of a path.

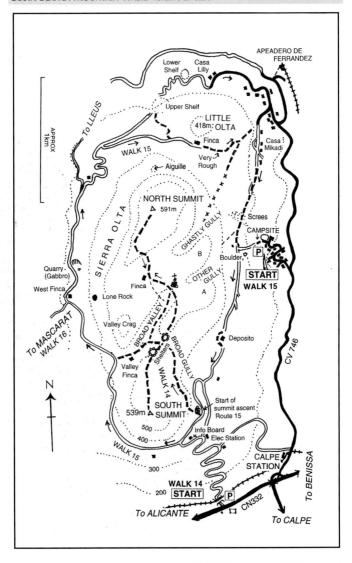

APEADERO DE
FERRANDEZ

Lower
Shelf

Casa
Lilly

Upper Shelf

LITTLE
418m OLTA

Finca

Casa
Mikadi

WALK 15

Very
Rough

TO LLEUS

APPROX
1km

Aiguille

NORTH SUMMIT
△ 591m

Screes

CAMPSITE

P

GHASTLY GULLY

B

Boulder

START
WALK 15

Quarry
(Gabbro)

West Finca

SIERRA OLTA

Finca

OTHER
GULLY

A

Lone Rock

Valley Crag

BROAD VALLEY

Deposito

CV 746

TO MASCARAT
WALK 16

Shelters

BROAD GULLY

WALK 14

Valley
Finca

SOUTH
539m △ SUMMIT

Start of
summit ascent
Route 15

N

500

Info Board

Elec Station

400

WALK 15

CALPE
STATION

300

To BENISSA

WALK 14
START

200

P

CN332

To ALICANTE

To CALPE

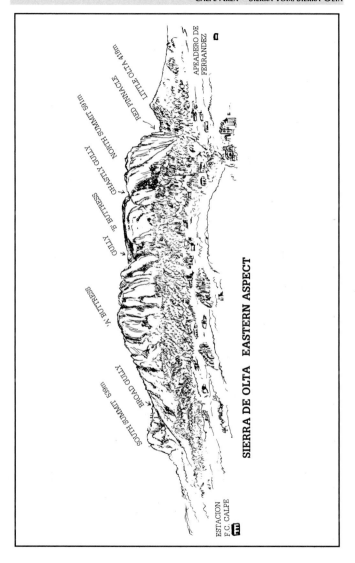

SIERRA DE OLTA   EASTERN ASPECT

APEADERO DE FERRANDEZ

LITTLE OLTA 418m

RED PINNACLE

NORTH SUMMIT 551m

CHASTLY GULLY

'B' BUTTRESS

GULLY

'A' BUTTRESS

BROAD GULLY

SOUTH SUMMIT 539m

ESTACION F.C. CALPE

This state of affairs cannot last for ever, and the spiky vegetation is growing well and in future years will return to harass walkers.

The Approaches

This is a stiff climb. Leave your car on the estate road (west side of the CN332), about 75m east of the KM 167.3 Disco. Before you set off get your bearings. The great rock buttress to the west guards the southern summit of the mountain, the rocks to the right of the summit form the eastern buttresses, and somewhere in between is the only reasonable pedestrian route to the summit, Broad Gully, which is your first objective. You should be able to follow the zig-zags of an estate road hewn out of the mountain many years ago, but happily never developed. Follow this rough but well-engineered route for the first 40 minutes of the walk. It is steep. Once beyond the electricity sub-station pick up the yellow and white markers that waymark Walk 15. At a junction, there is a route map with information.

In about 30 minutes there is a transformer station on the right of the track and then, at the next bend, an old *casita* on the right. From now on do not take any left turns and follow the road which skirts the crags, generally in a northern direction.   *45 mins*

The Gully

Soon you have a good view of the summit crags on your left, and ahead you can see Broad Gully and the narrow scree-filled path by which you can gain the top. Turn off at a cairn which indicates a short rocky scramble up the deepest part of the gully, and in 20 minutes you reach the summit plateau of Olta. The Broad Gully route comes out between two small shelters (see sketch), and from now on you have a choice of routes based on fitness or endurance, because most of the summit is limestone pavement, much eroded by water and overgrown with every spiky plant known to man!   *1hr*

Summit Routes

- South Summit route
- North Summit route

The summit of the plateau of Olta is geologically complicated. The waterworn limestone precludes the development of any reliable paths and the western side is sunken into a shallow valley which, at one time, was terraced and must have supported two small *fincas*, one at the head of Ghastly Gully (north) and one at the southern end. Care is needed walking in this area, but you can, in 20 minutes, reach the South Summit, and in 1 hour 15 minutes reach the North Summit, with dramatic views to the Bernias and into the many deep crevasses which scar this, the highest point of the mountain.

Calpe and the Peñon de Ifach seen from Sierra Olta

Southern Summit (539m)

On reaching the plateau top look for a small bothy (shelter) made of rocks, in a generally southern direction. Once past this there is a defined path, and in minutes you have a commanding view of the coast from Moraira to Albir and an intimate view of the Barranco de Mascarat, with its three tunnels carrying road, rail and *autopista*.　　　　*1hr 15min*s

Northern Summit (approx. 590m)

This walk is a little more demanding (remember that you have to come back the same way you went), but really this is the most exciting expedition on Olta.

Turn right (north) on reaching the plateau, look for the northern bothy and aim for the old *finca* just 10 degrees left of the North Summit (yellow arrows). Your first objective is a small cairn reached in 30 minutes when you can clearly see the old *finca* and its well to the north-west. Aim for these objectives by traversing the terraces and pass to the east of the *finca* to find a small track leading generally north across the eastern flank of the crags. In a short time cross a small col to a false summit and change sides of the summit ridge (west). In 10 minutes you are onto another limestone pavement with a clear view of the Northern Summit (90mins). Take care here, especially in windy conditions, but do try to take advantage of the close views of these dramatic gullies and the view to the north (Montgo – Benissa – The Balearics). To the west is Bernia in all its glory, and Puig Campaña, Benidorm and even Alicante to the south. At the time of writing a postbox and visitors' book exists on this summit provided by the Grupo Muntanya, Calpe.   *2hrs 45mins*

Descent

A descent by Broad Gully is recommended, but there is also an agreeable but more energetic alternative - Circuit Route by Broad Valley – **CARE NEEDED.** Broad Valley is the shallow valley running south–north on the summit, which at one time was obviously well cultivated. At its southern end, between imposing crags, is Valley Finca (ruins).

It is best to start the descent by following the good track along the western side of Broad Valley, which goes through some pines until it eventually descends to the bottom, where there are some terraces. Here cross over to the other side to pick up another track to the *finca* ruins.
3hrs 45mins

Below the *finca* ruins the path is subject to erosion each winter as rains funnel through Broad Valley and there will never be a really reliable path. There is a yellow marker on the south-west corner of the *finca,* and you should aim in this general direction for about 50m in the direction of a ridge with pine trees. Look for a path descending – but only for about 50–100m – and you should find a good unsurfaced road which is, in fact, part of Walk 15 heading first south then east which keeps to about the 350m contour and continues round the summit crags. You will descend to another *finca*, then in about 40 minutes you will regain the ascent road at the information board just above the *finca* previously mentioned in the ascent. Follow the waymarkings south-west for a few minutes to join a forestry road and turn left to join the ascent road.   *4hrs 45mins*

15: CIRCUIT OF SIERRA DE OLTA

Grade:	easy
Distance:	7.5km
Time:	3hrs 15mins
Ascent:	Negligible
Map:	Altea 848 (30–33)

When the circuit was first surveyed nearly 15 years ago it was a tenuous route connecting a number of badly overgrown and eroded mule tracks, which were marked with yellow circles, some of which still remain. Since then, the foresters have bull-dozed an almost complete road around the mountain, which has been waymarked in yellow and white by Calpe Mountaineering Club. As a result it is a much more enjoyable walk, with ever changing views and only on the descent from Little Olta is there any rough walking.

Getting There

Leave the CN332 at Km.168, where there is an underpass giving access to Calpe South, and follow signs to the Estacion Ferrocaril (railway station) by way of the CV746. After passing the railway station and crossing over the level crossing in 1.6km, turn off this road with a brown sign to Monte Olta and the camp site, which is reached in about another kilometre and where there is parking.

Making a Start, up to the Circuit

Above you, to the west, rise the Eastern Crags of Olta, and you leave the camp site by following a path, waymarked in yellow and white, up through the terraces marked out as tent sites to join a broad road, which climbs in ten minutes to a huge boulder on your left and the broad forestry road, which will take you around the mountain varying between the 300m and 400m contours.

Eastern Traverse 1

Turn to the left and continue south, climbing a little with views of the coast – Moraira Headland, the Calpe Salinas and Peñon d'Ifach are visible through the pines. Pass a large water tank on the right, an old ruin on the left and the road winds around Broad Gully to join the road coming up from the CN332 (see Walk 14), where there is an information board and map showing the routes on the mountain. On this section some of the old circle markers and even earlier red dots remain – now, of course, quite unnecessary.   *30mins   1.25km*

Round the Southern Summit

Turn right, with good views of the Southern Summit and its crags, until in a few minutes there is a finger post indicating your route on the left, and the road ahead leads to the main ascent route to the summits.

Pass a ruined *finca* on the left with good views of the coast, Calpe and its two harbours. Sierra Toix comes into view then the few remaining stones of Calpe's Moorish Castle, the Mascarat Gorge (with its three tunnels), Albir Headland with Sierra Helada and the eastern end of the Bernia Ridge with Puig Campaña in the far distance. When the road forks keep right. Below is the Estret Valley as you finally round the Southern Summit.

The Western Traverse

You start now to get views to the north, with the main summit of the Bernia and in the far distance the Ferrer Ridge. Above you on the right is Valley Crag and the cleft in the Western Crags which allows walkers to gain the summit plateau via Broad Valley (see Walk 14). Ahead in the middle distance is a prominent isolated crag and below it a ruined *finca* which is your next objective. On the way there, views to the north and north-west include Tossal de Navarro and the dramatic cleft of the Estret Gorge.

Leave the ruin on your left, and a road joins yours from the left from Mascarat (see Walk 16), Note that the terrace walls change colour to dark grey as you approach the abandoned gabbro quarry on the right with its spoil heaps. This small deposit of ornamental granite seems to have floated up through the granite as a Triassic diapar.
                                                                        1hr 30mins   3.5km

As you progress to the north the rough path up to Broad Valley is marked on the right, and your next objective, a large ruin under the pinnacles of the North Summit, comes into view and you reach a fork where you take the road to the right to climb uphill to the *finca*, while the road to the left leads to Lleus (see Walk 17). Do not wander off to the right as there are a number of dead end fire breaks.

Around the North Summit

Above you, on your right, are the pinnacles which guard the Northern Summit, appearing just as Montgo comes into view and as you reach a junction and can see to the right the modest crags of Little Olta. From here you have a choice of routes.

(a) The Civilised Route

Turn left (west) and after a few minutes the road returns to its eastern course under Little Olta to reach a level open space with pines, the shelf. Keep on along the road which still heads east and descends to join a surfaced road at a large villa, Casa Lily. Below you can be seen the start of the eastern traverse. On this section there are extensive views of the coast, with Monte Isadoro, Moriara Headland, Gata and finally Peñon d'Ifach.   *2hrs 15mins   5.5km*

(b) Little Olta Variation

Instead of following the above route, turn right to reach a small ruin in the col between Little Olta and North Summit, from where in a few minutes you can scramble up to this modest summit. Return the way you came, but look out for a small cairn and red markers on the right which indicate a narrow but distinct waymarked path to the shelf.

Direct Descent from Little Olta

This is a waymarked route through the rocks south from the col direct to the eastern traverse. Make sure that you descend down to the surfaced road and do not be diverted onto red-marked routes used by climbers to ascend Ghastly Gully (a dubious route up to the North Summit). This route has little to recommend it, is loose, very steep and dangerous in wet conditions.

The Eastern Traverse

Follow the surfaced road as it descends through villas until, in 1km, a surfaced road leads off to the right (waymark) near to Casa D'Agostina on left. Follow this road as it climbs gently towards the gash of Ghastly Gully seen above you and then south passing a marker indicating the route down from Little Olta. Pass two villas on the left, and at a third the surfaced road descends to the left as the route continue ahead on a path through pines and across a small scree shoot (from Other Gully) until you descend to a forestry road which leads to the Boulder and the route down to the campsite.   *3hrs 15mins   7.5km*

The nearest refreshments are at the petrol station at Km.169 on the CN332.   *3hrs 15mins   7.5km*

16: VAL DE ESTRET – A SECRET VALLEY

Grade:	**stroll**
Distance:	**14km**
Time:	**5hrs**
Ascent:	**Negligible**
Maps:	**Benisa 822 (30–32), Altea 484 (30–33)**

The Estret Valley was carved aeons ago by ice and rain, as the river first cut a deep notch in a side ridge of the Bernia mountain, then a broader valley and finally an equally dramatic gorge through the rocks, the Barranco Salido, between the Bernia and its neighbour Toix, under the ruins of Calpe's Moorish Castle, to reach the sea at Punto Mascarat.

This little valley has been ill-used by man in recent times: first came the modest road tunnel and bridge (now abandoned) to carry the main coach road north to Benissa, then ornamental granite (a rare find having floated up through the limestone as a Triassic diapar) was quarried on the western slope of Olta. Next, a Calpe family, the Crespos, established the first electric transformer station to take the electricity from the Hydro Electric Station at Chines, and the ruins can still be seen below the motorway. Then, being out of the way, it became useful for a number of essential but rather anti-social activities, such as a municipal tip, a dogs' home, a shooting range and even a proposed sewage treatment works. Finally came the rail and road tunnels and the motorway, which cut a swath right through its fruitful orchards and terraces.

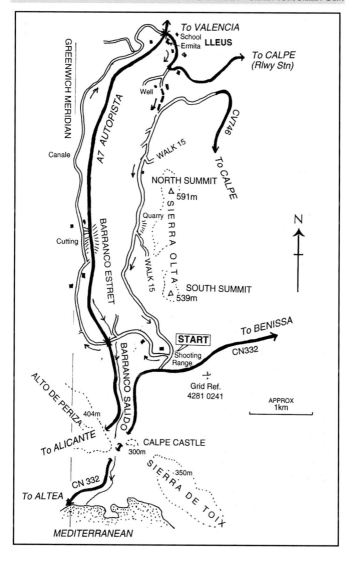

To VALENCIA
School
Ermita LLEUS
To CALPE
(Rlwy Stn)
GREENWICH MERIDIAN
Well
A7 AUTOPISTA
CV746
Canale
WALK 15
To CALPE
NORTH SUMMIT
△ 591m
SIERRA OLTA
Quarry
Cutting
BARRANCO ESTRET
WALK 15
SOUTH SUMMIT
△ 539m
N
START
To BENISSA
Shooting
Range
CN332
BARRANCO SALIDO
Grid Ref.
4281 0241
APPROX
1km
ALTO DE PERIZA
404m
To ALICANTE
CALPE CASTLE
300m
350m
SIERRA DE TOIX
CN 332
To ALTEA
MEDITERRANEAN

Happily, the tip is now extremely discreet and well managed, the sewage treatment plant has gone elsewhere and the valley is returning to its former tranquillity, so much so that a number of people are starting to restore some of the old fincas and local people are starting to cultivate crops. Despite the river running underground, there is plenty of water available.

Getting There

Leave the CN332 at the Calpe end of tunnels, at Km.165.5, and turn north onto a narrow surfaced road. At the first junction, fork right, with signs 'Campo de Tiro', to park at the Shooting Club. (At fiestas there might be a match in progress.)

Making a Start – North to Lleus

Return to the valley road, which is still surfaced for a while, and turn right, north along the valley bottom. For a while follow signs to the tip ('Vertedero Escombos') and admonishments to keep the valley tidy, under pain of penalties. Looking back and to the left you get good views of the one remaining wall of Calpe Castle, the crags of Toix and the various tunnels through the mountain. Above us on the right are the crags of Sierra Olta's South Summit and the great gully which divides the mountain on the western side. Finally across the valley is the col, Collado de Fachuch, which leads to the Eastern Ridge of the Bernia. The road, now unsurfaced, drops down a little; there is a quarry on the right-hand side and then a *finca* which is being restored. The road now starts to climb to the tip, but you fork off to the left to pass through a tunnel under the motorway and start your traverse along the western side by passing another *finca*, where a road forks off to the left to ascend to the Bernia Ridge. Keep straight on north, following the Greenwich meridian of longitude, and remain on the western side of the motorway (A7) until you get to the hamlet of Lleus.

Pass a number of small *fincas* and a newly constructed irrigation pipe and start to climb gently towards another attractive *finca* with a shady Umbrella Pine (*Pinus pinea*) and keep straight on, avoiding a road on the right which drops to a tunnel under the motorway.

The rather rough road now starts to climb, and if you look across the valley you might be able to spot your return route by the spoil heaps of the old gabbro quarry, which are a dark grey colour.

1hr   2km

There is another *finca* on the right and a road to another on the left as the deep gash of the Estret Gorge appears ahead, as you reach the brow of a hill with the motorway fence on your right. The motorway passes below you in a deep cutting, and at the top views open up to the north of the Loma Larga Ridge, with the two peaks, Tossal de Navarro and Silla de Cao, guarding the col over which the Greenwich meridian passes. To the east is the North Summit of Sierra Olta, with some attractive pinnacles. In the middle distance there is a large white *finca*, Casa de la Por, at Lleus, whilst in the far distance is the mountain Montgo, near Denia.

The road now starts to descend through a collection of ruined *fincas*, whilst ahead appears Benissa on its hill, with the Cathedral of the Marinas', its Gothic church, and the headland Cabo de Nao, near Javea. A little road now leads off to the left towards the Gorge of the Estret, which you ignore, as you get your first view of the Casas de Lleus, with the small white 'mission type' church on the eastern side of the motorway. Pass through *fincas* again to reach Casa de la Por, and another road joins from the left as you pass through the tunnel to emerge in the plaza of the village.   *2hrs 30mins   6km*

Lleus (pronounced Yows) is no more than a plaza, a stone cross, a tiny village school (rebuilt), the small *ermita* dedicated to St Abdon and St Senen, and a collection of farm houses on both sides of the motorway. It stands at the head of the Barranco del Conquet, through which a narrow country road leads north through unspoilt countryside (except, of course, for the motorway) to another tiny hamlet, Benimallunt, on the Pinos road. From the plaza there are excellent views of the surrounding mountains and of Peñon d'Ifach on the coast. When I first visited Lleus, the dusty windows of the tiny school house showed the room set out as it must have been when abandoned in the 1950s. The Caudillo and the Virgin Mary looked down on simple desks, a pile of slates and a heavily varnished map of the old provinces of Spain hung on the back wall. Since then the building has been completely rebuilt, sadly without its artefacts, which are no doubt in some folk museum. If you would like to see the rather spartan *ermita*, which is only used for mass on the saint's day in August, the lady at the farmhouse next door is the custodian.

Heading Back South to Calpe

Leave the plaza, pass the stone cross and follow the road as it drops down to cross the *barranco* between farmhouses. As you climb out on the other side, fork right onto another surfaced road and turn off left onto the first unsurfaced road, south-east, with the Northern Summit of Olta above you. Pass a *casita* on the left-hand side and a number of wells on the right as you climb up, passing another farmhouse, to gain a narrow and rather eroded path which climbs steeply out of the valley. The track has received some attention from trial motor cycles and the weather has done the rest. Above, to the right, you can pick out a large ruined *finca*, which is on the route. Now another track, which comes up from the Pou Roig Valley, joins yours from the left, and the track broadens as it climbs up the motor road, CV746 (believe it or not), which has come up from Calpe Railway Station.   *3hrs   8km*

To the Gabbro Quarry and Calpe Castle

Turn right, south-west, along the continuation of the surfaced road as it winds round a *barranco* and climbs to the extensive ruin of an old *finca* on the right-hand side. Look back for good views of Lleus and across the valley to the great cleft of the Estret Gorge, whilst above you are the cliffs and pinnacles of Olta's North Summit. The forestry road is now quite broad and your bearing always to the south. On this section there are a number of new forestry roads, constructed during the extensive fires some years ago, which can be a little confusing. At the first two junctions keep to the left, but at the next junction ignore a left-hander which goes uphill to E155, on the Olta Circuit (Walk 15) and waymarked with yellow circles. Keep going south on this route, however, for a short while, ignoring another forestry road on the left, as the dark grey spoil heaps of the old quarry appear ahead and then the small quarry itself on the left.   *4hrs   11km*

Calpe Castle and Sierra Toix appear ahead as you now leave the Olta Circuit to drop down, right, onto a road which contours for a while until you can see your transport ahead at the shooting club, and Sierra Helada, near Benidorm, comes into view.   *5hrs   14km*

17: LITTLE OLTA FROM POU ROIG VALLEY

Grade:	easy
Distance:	12km
Time:	5hrs 15mins
Ascent:	318m
Maps:	Benisa 822 (30–32), Altea 848 (30–33)

Little Olta is a small rocky crag, 110m below the North Summit of Olta, overlooking the Pou Roig Valley, an idyllic, unspoilt backwater, with the Barranco de Conquet running in the valley bottom from Calpe inland to Lleus.

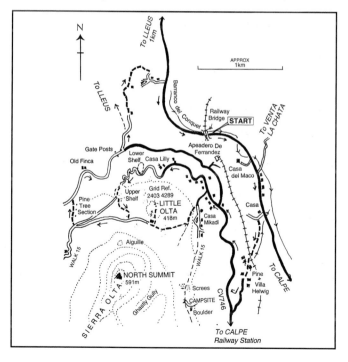

Getting There

This is easy for those approaching on the CN332 from Benissa. Just take the first right-hand road over the bridge at Km.170 and follow the narrow, unclassified road for about 4km until you reach the railway bridge over the valley. Those approaching from the direction of Calpe have a difficult choice to make – whether to obey the new road markings and drive a further 3km towards Benissa to turn round at the disco or to cross the white line and, if the Guardia should be watching, risk a fine!

Making a Start

Start by walking back, south, towards the main road, and after you have passed the road to the only restaurant, Casa del Maco, on the right and a few villas on the left turn right at a small *casita* (still a working farm). In a few metres leave the broad track, left, for a smaller one that climbs through pines and alongside a *barranca* containing a great many Strawberry Trees (*Arbutus unedo*) which in the autumn are ablaze with the reds and yellows of the ripening fruit (tasty but gritty). As you approach a culvert, the path leads to the railway line, so control dogs and infants.

With the greatest of care cross the railway line to find a narrow path, with steps, continuing upwards towards an old farmhouse. Take off left to follow a track through pines alongside and above the cutting through which the railway runs until you arrive at a surfaced road and villas, including Villa Helwig. Now follow the road as it climbs, through other villas, to gain the main access road to this part of Olta, the CV746, and turn right (north).   *1hr   2km*

Traverse Under Olta – to Casa Lily

Now follow the main, yet narrow, road through villas, but with good views to the east, until just as the road starts to descend a little you catch your first real view of your objective, Little Olta and the North Summit of Olta itself on the left (west) side of the road. Someone has tidied up the junction and landscaped it with shrubs, which means that you will be unable to find a sign to Casa Lily, which is the last of the villas at the very end of the road, another half a kilometre higher up the mountain. Pause for a moment to enjoy the views of Montgo, Cabo Nao and the town of Benissa to the north-east. Turn off here to the left and climb along the surfaced road until you find a road leading off to the left and some yellow circles as waymarkers of the Olta Circuit (Walk 15). Ignore this road and keep on climbing until the road loses its surface and you reach the large but never, it seems, occupied villa Casa Lily on the right.   1hr 50mins   3.5km

Upwards Towards the Shelf

There are, in fact, two shelves, probably old *eras* (threshing floors), and the unsurfaced and often badly eroded road zig-zags upwards to the first one, a popular picnic spot near an old ruined *finca*. Continue upwards until you reach the next flat area, a popular camping spot, under the impressive crags of the North Buttress of Olta. There are now good views of the Bernia Ridge and the great gash of the Estret Gorge, cut by ice and water aeons ago, with the tiny hamlets of Pinos and Bernia beyond, through the gap. To the east are the Cao Ridge, Montgo and Benissa, with its large Gothic church (Cathedral of the Marinas), and Moraira Castle and Peñon D'Ifach on the coast.
2hrs 40mins

To Little Olta

In the western corner of this upper shelf a broad track, which turns into a forestry road, leads off south-west. This is part of the Olta Circuit, and where this track begins I have built double cairns and red markers to show a narrow track which climbs south. In about 10 minutes, you join another broader track and turn left, east, until you arrive at a clearing and an old abandoned *finca* beneath the crags of Little Olta (418m). Climb the crags behind the *finca* to gain its modest summit, even more extensive views and the definite feeling of being on a mountain peak – until you turn around to see the intimate views of the pinnacles of big brother, the North Buttress of Olta.
3hrs 15mins   5.5km

Descent to the Pou Roig Valley

From the ruined *finca* retrace your steps, but ignore the ascent route and keep to the forestry road, west, with excellent views of the pinnacles of Olta above you until you meet up again with the yellow circles, waymarkings of the Olta Circuit. Your time on this route is very short and soon you come to a cairn which marks a short, rough section down to a large ruined *finca* below you.   3hrs 30mins   7km

The Three Pines Link

This path, which I have called after the three pines which at the moment act as your markers down to the road, is the only difficult section to follow, using an eroded water course then a reasonable track to a good forestry road which is, in fact, a continuation of the CV746. On reaching this road turn right, north-east, and in a few minutes reach what was once a large *finca*. Sadly, vandals have removed a great deal as souvenirs. The only thing that I took was a small piece of periwinkle from what remained of the old garden, which still flourishes in my own garden.   *4hrs   7.5km*

Leave the *finca* and follow the road to the east, around a *barranca*, whilst below can be seen the broad *autopista* snaking its way north to Valencia. Close to it is the tiny hamlet of Lleus, with its white mission-type church. As you pass through two gate posts, the road gains a surface and a number, but this luxury is not for you – turn off to the left down on a broad track. This track levels out near some walled terraces, and there is a marked path going down left which will lead in 20 minutes to Lleus. Keep going until you arrive at a ruined *finca*, beyond which a marked mule track descends to another ruined *casita*, which you pass on the left. Beyond this ruin I once built cairns, which seem to have been supplemented by red markers. Continue until finally you reach a concrete road, which in turn leads down to an unsurfaced road where you turn left, east still, passing small *casitas*, one named Riu-Rau, until you gain the surfaced road which follows the valley bottom and turn right, south, back to your starting point beneath the arches of the railway bridge.   *5hrs 15mins   12km*

Casa del Maco is a very select restaurant with a good reputation, but it may be able to provide light refreshments. The nearest bar is Ausinas, at the petrol station near Km.68 on the CN332.

Val de Jalón

18: CORDILLERAS DE ALMADICH FROM BENICHEMBLA

Grade:	moderate
Distance:	17km
Time:	5hrs 30mins
Ascent:	700m
Maps:	Benisa 822 (30–32)

This is a most scenic walk, and, for once, you do not climb to the summit of the mountain but start by walking up this attractive valley, then climb a ravine to a high plateau and, finally, enjoy a 5km traverse along a broad ledge 300m above the valley floor. The walk is all on good tracks and the high-level traverse is broad enough for the local farmer to graze his cows on in summer!

Getting There

Leave the lush lower Jalón Valley at Parcent and follow the CV720, signposted Castell de Castells, towards Benichembla. Just past Villa Menlu on the right and near Km.34 turn left (south) on a narrow surfaced road for about half a kilometre until another road joins from the left. This is, in fact, the return route. Leave the car here.

Up the Valley

This delightful, unfrequented valley makes a lovely walk in itself. First walk south on the road, climbing gently with plenty of time to admire the views. Behind you rises the Caballo Verde Ridge with Peña Roch at its western end. High above you on your left rise the cliffs of what the Mapas Militar call, rather unimaginatively, Cordilleras, which simply means a mountain range. The many bands of cliffs contain a number of summits, with the highest point Morro Enserra, 1000m. Across the valley, guarding the entrance, is El Mirabo, 695m, and to the left of

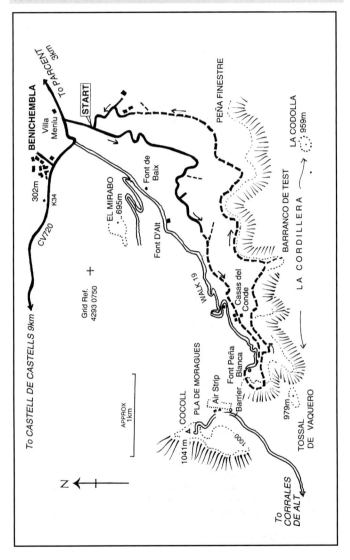

this peak (north-west) is the bulk of Cocoll, 1141m. To the left of Cocoll, right at the head of the valley, is the shapely cone of Tossal de Vaquero. The traverse is on the northern slopes of the Cordilleras.

To the Ancient Settlement

The road continues to rise, and ahead can be seen the great buttress of Peña Finestres, which you will pass close to later. In half a kilometre ignore a concrete road on the left-hand side – your road continues to zig-zag upwards. Look over your shoulder to see Orba Castle and Montgo on the coast. The road now loses its surface and you pass a *casita* in course of restoration and later a ruined one.   *1h*

You now pass very close to the base of the crags as the path narrows, and you pass a tiny *casita* with a fireplace and descend a little to negotiate the head of a small *barranca*. You should now start to find red markers to help you. Climb to a small col with a crag and a rock cairn.   *15mins*

Below can be seen the road which follows the valley bottom to the Fuente Peña Blanca at its head. Nearer, the ruins of an ancient settlement lie ahead, which you will pass through in 10 minutes' time.

To Fuente Peña Blanca

Now negotiate another narrow ravine and climb to another shoulder with an oak on it. Look back to see the village of Murla nestling under Peña Roch as you walk down to the troughs of the *fuente* (restored 1985), much used to water grazing animals including cattle, which, thankfully, are always in the charge of a *vaquero* (herdsman).   *2hrs*

The Ravine

The unsurfaced valley road ends here and at the head of the valley is a rocky stream bed in a narrow ravine (normally dry). To negotiate this obstacle follow a very indistinct path which climbs to the cliffs on the right-hand side, then under them to cross over the stream bed. Now follow a good path which heads generally east, gaining height. Over your shoulder lies the distinctive peak of Tossal de Vaquero (Hill of the Herdsman) and the higher one of Cocoll, with its new forestry road to the summit. First there is a shallow ravine to negotiate, then descend into a terraced *barranca* under Llometa d'Albordo, a good place for a break before starting the traverse.   *2hrs 30mins*

The High-Level Traverse

Start by climbing out of the *barranca* on a good path moving basically east. The traverse is 5km and will take about 2 hours, depending on how often you stop to relish your position some 300m above the valley floor, following approximately the 800m contour. Wherever the track forks, keep to the lower track; others lead up to the summits. There are, however, six major ravines to cross to prevent the route becoming boring. There is no need for waymarkings as the cattle keep the way clear (and well fertilized).The only reason for grazing this dangerous route is that, facing north, it probably retains grass during the summer when grazing in the valley is scarce. There are no walkers' routes off the traverse. There are a number of enticing gullies which, however, all seem to end in vertical drops, only suitable for those with plenty of abseil rope and a strong nerve. You will be walking under some very impressive cliffs, but only at the ravines is there any possibility of leaving the traverse to climb to the summit. The views are sensational and you can pick out your morning's route up the valley, including the dam constructed to hold back flood water, which you may have missed on the way up.

In some 2 hours, under Peña Finestre (Peak of the Windows), after the last ravine, leave the traverse along a good track which then joins a broad road. Turn left downhill and pass your first villa in 15 minutes. Descend through new villas until the road gains a surface and you reach your car after a dramatic and beautiful walk. There is plenty of hospitality in the bar at Benichembla and more sophisticated fare in Parcent. *5hrs 30mins*

19: TOSSAL DE VAQUERO

Grade:	moderate
Distance:	15.5km
Time:	7hrs 30mins
Ascent:	679m
Maps:	Benisa 822 (30–32)

This small, beautifully pointed peak rises to 979m (3000ft) and dominates the head of the quite unspoiled Almadich Valley, which leads south-west from the village of Benichembla at the start of the Upper Jalón Valley. The peak can also be admired, alongside its higher but less beautiful neighbour, Cocoll, from the high plateau of Val de Alt at the highest point on the Tarbena to Castell de Castells road (CV752). A direct ascent, for peak baggers, can be made from this point, but your route is more beautiful, but rather longer, along the Almadich Valley.

Getting There

Leave the road from Parcent to Castell de Castells CV720 at Km.34.7 near to a small bridge and take an unsurfaced road, south-west, to park in a clearing. A small party will be able to find parking in the village of Benichembla, refresh themselves at Bar Gat in the square opposite the church and maybe order a meal for afterwards. The patron, Francisco, does not run a restaurant, but will oblige a small party with a good, sustaining meal and a nice local wine. This will, of course, add to your overall time for the walk. The actual ascent of Tossal de Vaquero will only take just over an hour from the head of the valley, but those with limited time may wish to torture their cars by driving up to the Fuente Peña Blanca. For lovers of tarmacadam, the map will guide you along a surfaced road, which starts on the other side of the little bridge and will shorten the time spent on the rougher road.

The full walk will take 7 hours 30 minutes walking time and 15.5km, but is an interesting and not too strenuous expedition. Take a torch if you wish to explore the cave.

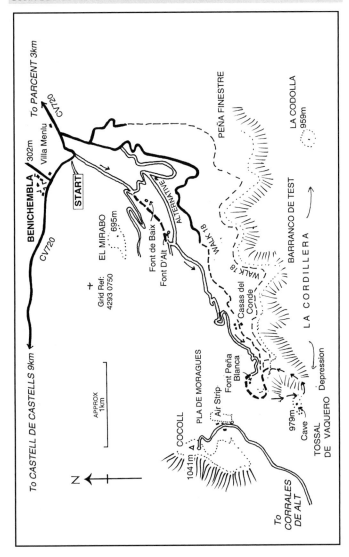

Looking through the Estret Gorge to Sierra Olta (Walks 14–17)

The cone of Tossalet de Vaquero (Walk 19) from near Serrella Castle

Orba Castle (Walk 26)

Making a Start – to the Fuente Peña Blanca

Continue along the unsurfaced road, which climbs gently along the western side of the Val de Almadich. There are good views behind you of the village of Benichembla, with the Caballo Verde Ridge and its two peaks of Peña Roc behind it. Mirabo is above you on the right, and across the valley is the long line of cliffs of the Cordillera, with Peña Finestre guarding the other side of the entrance to the valley. As you climb, Orba Castle is now visible, with the villages of the lower Jalón Valley. You keep on, as the road to Mirabo forks off to the right, and drop down to the dry bed of the *barranco* and the 'flash dam', constructed to hold back flood waters and so protect the motor road below.   30mins   2km

After crossing the bed of the *barranco*, where the road has been reinforced with concrete, the road starts to climb steadily in a south-easterly direction until you come to another concrete section, and it is here that you turn off sharply to the right onto a narrow track which starts to climb above the *barranco*. This section of the walk is a favourite of mine for its wild flowers. Facing north, the steep sides offer a habitat for many plants which cannot survive on the other sunny side of the *barranco*. Add to this the abundant supply of water running down the rocks, even in high summer, and it is no wonder that there is such a good display of beautiful flowers including the blue multi-headed Throatwort (*Trachelium caeruleum*), Pink Century (*Centaurium erythraea*) and Yellow Wort (*Blackstonia perfoliata*). Near the springs can also be found Hart's Tongue Ferns and even violets.

Across the *barranco* you can admire the cliffs of Mirabo and identify the route to the col by the small grove of pine trees below it. Behind you can be seen Orba Castle and the Caballo Verde Ridge, with its twin peaks of Peña Roc, and the Rocky Murla Arête leading down to the village from which it takes its name.

Watch out for a particularly lush vegetation on the left as you arrive at the lower spring, Font de Baix, with its six tiny troughs and reliable water supply. The bottom of the normally dry valley is now full of oleanders and a blanket of pink blooms as you climb in another 10 minutes to the upper spring, Font D'Alt, also with six small troughs. Below you the *barranco* cuts through a narrow gorge and you must move left in rough zig-zags to try to find a path in the overgrown vegetation. It really is my intention to make another visit to cut back the growth on this section, of only about 20m, but just in case you get there before me, put a pair of secateurs in your rucksack! Thankfully in a few minutes you find yourself on a good road, near a ruin (which leads to a *casita*). Turn left and you are on the main road up to the Fuente Peña Blanca.   1hr 15mins   3km

On to Fuente Peña Blanca

The road is broad and very pleasant as you head south-east along the northern side of the valley – the mighty cliffs of the Cordillera are above you on the left, and ahead now can be seen Cocoll. Eventually, the road twists and turns in order to gain height, and there are some steep sections, until you reach an old *finca* on the right and ahead you can see the dry waterfall at the head of the valley, which gives access to the route to Tossal de Vaquero and you reach the *fuente*.   2hrs 30mins   5.5km

Ascent of Tossal De Vaquero

Leave the *fuente*, where the broad road ends, and continue on a narrow path towards the dry waterfall (north-west). The path is, at times, badly eroded, as you cross under the waterfall and move right for a while on a reasonable track, through scrub, until it changes direction, left, to pass under some cliffs, once more headed for the dry river bed (south-west). There are good views as you climb out of the valley, with Mirabo guarding the entrance and Peña Roch with Orba Castle in the distance. As you start to climb the rocky watercourse, Montgo appears on the coast behind you. Continue this easy, if energetic, scrambling until you can see the craggy summit of Tossal de Vaquero to the south-east, and set a course, without the benefit of a path, towards it. You will have to negotiate some decayed walls and cross numerous well-worn cattle tracks. There is a large carob tree to aim for first, then make for the left (eastern) end of the crags, where the final ascent begins. As you gain height, your views of the summits of the Cordillera de Almadich expand to the east: there are 10 summits of over 3000ft. Sierra Aixorta now comes into view ahead and you can see a fertile *hoya* (depression) below you on your left, which will be visited during the descent.
                                                 3hrs 25mins   7km

Decision Time

There is now a sporting 15 minute easy scramble for the energetic along the rocky ridge to the summit, and for others a sedate ascent by means of a broad edge on the north side is available. As you climb,

you get good views of the neighbouring peak of Cocoll, with its fire lookout on the summit, and an improbable air strip, on Pla de Moragues, which rises to the north like an aircraft carrier in a heavy swell. The strip is a base for the fire-fighting aircraft which combat the forest fires. Step by step your views open up as you reach the summit.
3hrs 25mins   7.5km

Summit Views

The summit is perfect for photographers, with a handy rocky foreground, and due to its isolated position it has extensive views in every direction. To the north is the bulk of Alfaro, and beyond Caval the rocky Segaria Ridge and Montgo. Turning to the east you can look down the valley of the Amadich, with the whole of the Caballo Verde Ridge with Peña Roch at its eastern end and Orba Castle beyond. To the east, the Cordillera de Almadich can be admired. There are 12km of rough, high-level walking to join the Sierra Carrascal de Parcent at Tossal de Polupi, leading to Col de Rates (Walk 22). South-east are the jagged Bernia, Severino and Ferrer ridges with the coast beyond, with Sierra Helada and, in the middle distance, Bolulla Castle, Paso Tancat and Tarbena Castle. Aixorta and Moro Blau are in a southerly direction and on their right, south-west, Serrella Castle, Mala de Llop and Confrides Castle, in the Guadalest Valley. To the west and north-west, the mountains around Alcoy, including Monte Cabrer, 1389m, the third highest peak in the province, and Benicadell.

Descent – to the Cave

Leave the summit and descend through the rocks on the south side, keeping close to the base of the crags and a bit to the right, until in 10 minutes you find the entrance to a large cave in the limestone, which was inhabited in prehistoric times. There are stalactites and stalagmites, and on my visit a square hole had been excavated in the floor, with lots of animal bones and shards scattered around. It appears from the local newspapers that this excavation does not have the approval of Alicante University, so I suppose one day the cave will be fenced in. Use your torch to explore deeper if you wish.   *3hrs 50mins*

Descent – to the Hoya

Leave the cave and head, beneath the crags, in an easterly direction, with the Bernia main summit as your guide, and in 15 minutes you will be able to see the *hoya*, a small depression, below you, with its small buildings; head for it. The obviously fertile area is possibly a *polje*, where the limestone, eroded from beneath, has sunk, and the alluvial deposits have provided sufficient depth of soil for growing crops.

Head for the good path which passes through the depression, with recent signs of cultivation, passing the main *finca*, with a corral for the animals. Pass now an *era* (threshing floor) with two stone rollers intact, in a north-western direction in line with Peñon Roch, until you cross the cattle tracks again and eventually pick up red markers for the traverse (Walk 18). *4hrs 35mins 8km*

Follow these left (west) until you reach the dry river bed and reverse your ascent route. Do not forget to turn off left, above the waterfall, unless you are a very dedicated scrambler and reach Fuente Peña Blanca. *5hrs 9.5km*

Thoughts of refreshments or the meal which awaits you at the Bar Gat may encourage you to step out a little on the last 5km back to Benichembla. *7hrs 30mins 15.5km*

20: EL MIRABO

Grade:	moderate
Distance:	9km
Time:	4hrs
Ascent:	479m
Maps:	Benisa 822 (30–32)

The Barranco de Almadich is an unspoilt valley which leads south-west from the village of Benichembla at the start of the Upper Jalón Valley. There is an excellent stroll through the valley to its head at Fuente Peña Blanca, and an exciting high-level traverse of the cliffs on the southern side, Cordillera de Almadich (Walk 18), and from the valley you can ascend Cocoll (1041m) and Tossal de Vaquero (979m) (Walk 19). The modest mountain which guards the northern side of the entrance to the valley, El Mirabo, is the object of this walk. Mostly on good tracks, there is a very short section of rough walking to the summit, and the first section of the descent from the col takes a little finding. A torch and a small length of string could prove useful. The area is grazed by cattle, including bulls, under the eye of the vaquero and his collection of dogs. The animals tend to ignore walkers, but if you have a dog with you BEWARE, and keep it under strict control near to cattle.

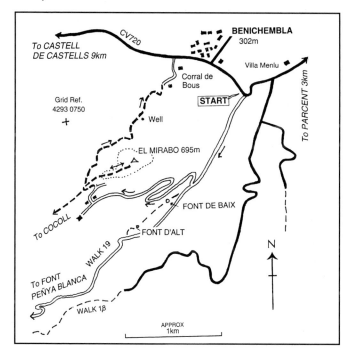

Getting There

Leave the road from Parcent to Castell de Castells CV720 at Km.34.7, just near a bridge, and take an unsurfaced road which leads south-west to a park in a clearing. If you are a small party, you could find parking in the main square of Benichembla, refresh yourselves at the Bar Gato and order lunch for later (there is no restaurant, but the patron will usually provide a good meal for a small party). This will put 30 minutes on my times.

Making a Start – Along the Valley Road

Continue along the unsurfaced road, which climbs gently along the western side of the Val de Almadich, with good views, beyond the village of Benichembla to the Caballo Verde Ridge, with the twin peaks of Peña Roc at the eastern end. Mirabo is above you, on the right, and across the valley is the long line of high cliffs of the Cordillera, with Peña Finestre guarding the other side of the entrance to the valley. Behind you can be seen Orba Castle and the lower Jalón Valley. The route to Mirabo now forks right and the road ahead drops down to the dry bed of the *barranco* and the Flash Dam, constructed to hold back flood water and so protect the village and road below.   *30mins   2km*

To the Col

You now reach a restored *casita*, Rosa Ferri, and the road climbs round it; views ahead now are of Cocoll and, to its left, the pointed little peak of Tossal de Vaquero (Walk 19). You are now well above the valley, with a small dam below in the normally dry river bed. You can also pick out the tracks which follow the valley bottom to Font d'Alt and Fuente Peña Blanca. The track now zig-zags to gain height and then levels out for a while. Ahead, in the distance is a white house, near which you will strike off up to the col. To the north-east you now have views of the coast and Montgo mountain near Javea. When you reach a ruined *casita*, turn right onto another track.   *45mins   4km*

Walk north-west, with a ruin on your left, and pass a restored *casita* on your right before reaching a prominent boulder, where you turn off, left, to follow an indistinct path, upwards, through pine trees to gain the col with some boulders with a brown deposit (probably iron). You are now at a modest cross roads: the path to the left is a fierce route to the summit of Cocoll; the path ahead is your descent route; and you take the right-hand one to climb north-east to the summit of Mirabo. There are new views now to the north of Carrasca and the western end of the Caballo Verde Ridge, at Puerta Garga.   *1hr 15mins   3km*

To the Summit

The path climbs towards some rocks and a unique sight in these hills – barbed wire! The badly constructed obstacle has been woven by the *vaquero* to persuade his herd not to descend to the south. With care, unweave it to pass through, and please close it as you leave. This is where you may need your two pieces of string. Continue north-east over another col to reach the rocky summit. *1hr 30mins   4.5km*

The views from the summit are extensive in all directions, and just below Cocoll can be seen the small airstrip that is so important in fighting forest fires. All the villages of the Lower Jalón Valley can be seen, including Murla, right under the eastern end of the Caballo Verde Ridge.

Descent Via Barranco De Bous

Retrace your steps to the col with the brown rocks and turn right, north-west, down the left-hand side of a little gully (there have been blue markers here as this is the only difficult part of the route to find). After a few minutes leave the gully to traverse left again along the terrace towards a ruined *casita,* which you pass above, in a westerly direction. Be careful here as this route will continue west to Cocoll. You need to look out for the start of a Mozarabic trail which turns off to the right and heads north-east, down the southern side of the Barranco de Bous. No more route-finding problems now: the Mozarabic trail will take you right down to the *finca,* Corral de Bous, from whence issues the herd of beasts mentioned earlier. Drop down in zig-zags to cross a little *barranca* where you can see your route ahead, and in about 15 minutes you reach the Moorish Well, evidenced by pipes and containers used to water the herd of cattle. It is interesting to speculate why this carefully domed well was constructed to take advantage of a reliable spring and then buried beneath the Mozarabic trail. A bit of bad planning, I suppose, by the Caliph's road engineers. This is where you reach for your torch to explore, beneath the trail, to examine and taste the cool, fresh water in the small trough, fed by a spring.

3hrs   6km

The trail now continues to drop gently, and in half an hour the village of Benichembla appears ahead. You drop now, passing an old *finca,* with the farm Corral de Bous, with its stock yards, below you. Pass by the farm, guarded by the dogs which the *vaquero* left behind. Reach the main road, turn right and the end of your route is only 2km away – unless, of course, as I usually am, you are forced to divert into the village by the attraction of Bar Gato, especially its sweet home-made wine and friendly patron. *4hrs   9km*

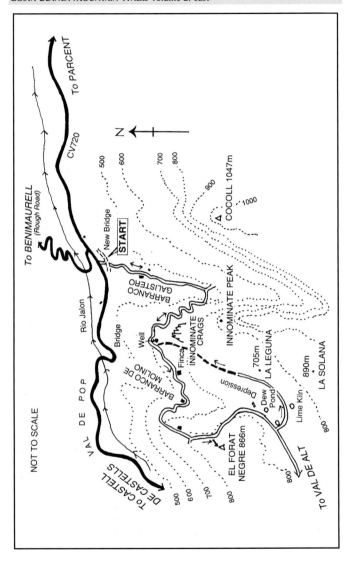

NOT TO SCALE

To BENIMAURELL
(Rough Road)

To PARCENT

CV720

New Bridge

START

Rio Jalon

Bridge

Well

Finca

BARRANCO GALISTERO

INNOMINATE CRAGS

BARRANCO DE MOLINO

INNOMINATE PEAK

COCOLL 1047m

500
600
700
800
900
1000

705m
LA LEGUNA

Depression

Dew Pond

Lime Kiln

LA SOLANA

890m

800

EL FORAT NEGRE 866m

V A L   D E   P O P

To CASTEL DE CASTELLS

500
600
700
800

To VAL DE ALT

21: FIG TREE WALK TO EL FORAT NEGRE

Grade:	easy
Distance:	15km
Time:	5hrs
Ascent:	486m
Map:	Benisa 822 (30–32)

To those who love the pastoral scenery of the lower Jalón Valley (Val de Pop), with its lush growth of vines and picturesque riu-raus, the upper valley beyond Benichembla provides a contrast, as the now dry river bed meanders between the crags of high mountain ridges. The ridge to the right (looking up the valley) is Caballo Verde, with its dramatic peak of Peñon Roch hanging over the tiny village of Murla. The Ermita San Sebastian, high on the mountain behind the village, seems to protect it from the threatening Peñon. To the left is another ridge, which is the objective for the day.

Making a Start

Leave Parcent by taking the CV720 towards Castell de Castells and past Benichembla. Stop at Km.29.8 (new road bridge). This upper valley has, over the years, suffered devastation in the winter storms, and as recently as 1988 the road to Castell de Castells was swept away in three places as flood water destroyed quite substantial culverts. It is at one of these newly constructed bridges, where the Barranco Galistero joins the Jalón river, that you start your walk. Here, a few years ago, stood a grove of old and fruitful fig trees. Sadly, the construction work has taken its toll, and only one wounded specimen survives. I still keep my original name for the walk as a tribute to the sympathetic engineer who converted the old mule track used on the walk into a forestry access road, and stabilised the edges with young fig trees. This is a gentle walk, and suitable even for prams (if fitted with four-wheel drive, good springs and a shock-resistant infant!). The objective of this walk is not an isolated mountain or a castle perched on a rock, but a lovely walk in majestic scenery: first above the upper Jalón Valley, then looking down into the Val de Alt. The forestry road makes the going comfortable, and there is little need for route-finding. With your back to the road, look up a broad valley (east of south). To the left is the bulk of Cocoll (1047m). Immediately ahead is a broad track and an unnamed peak (part of La Laguna); on the right the summit ridge ends in a rock gully, and between these points can be seen the new forestry track zig-zagging up over the ridge.

To the Barranco De Molinero

Follow the track up the Barranco de Galistero alongside the dry river bed, passing a *casita* on the right and a *fuente* on the left, and in 15 minutes reach a junction. Take the right-hand fork, which leaves the valley and starts to climb in well-engineered zig-zags to the right-hand flank of Innominate Peak. Gaining height, look back to see the Caballo Verde ridge appear to the north, and finally arrive at Innominate Crags, where you will find an old *finca*. Carry on round the edge of the ridge to a gully (which is the return route), where there is a *fuente*.   *45mins*

After a short climb, around another bend is an old, quite extensive *finca* with a well, oven and *era* (threshing floor), a wonderful spot to rest for a while with commanding views.   *50mins*

To the north-east is Peñon Roch, the end of the Caballo Verde Ridge, and Montgo is visible now. Leave the old *finca*, probably reluctantly, now moving south-west, and press on down into the Barranco de Molinero. Below, you can see the new substantial road bridge over the Jalón river. Seeing the river in its normally dry state, it seems hard to justify such a bridge, but when winter comes with its storms it will certainly prove to be of great benefit to the people of Castell de Castells and beyond. It seems a long way down to the head of this *barranco*, and a long climb (now north-west) up to regain the height lost, but you soon turn south-west again to reach another ruined *finca* and a deep roadside well on the left.   *1hr 30mins*

To El Forat Negre

This last stretch is very pleasant and more gentle. Go in a southerly direction up to an old *casita* on the left, then turn left (south-east). The track now levels out, with a small ruined house on the left. Follow the track for about 20 minutes, then strike upwards (no path) amongst the rocks to reach the highest point, where there is a rock cairn and a small shelter. You are now at El Forat Negre (866m), with extensive all-round views which include the Bernia, Aixorta, Serrella Castle, Mala del Llop and the highest of them all, Aitana. Only one village, Famorca, can be seen to the north-west. *2hrs 15mins*

Return Routes

Those who have become deeply attached to the forestry road can reverse the route; those seeking a little variation, and not afraid of a bit of rough walking, can rejoin the forestry road at the *fuente* by following the original direction (generally south-east and south-west), passing a ruined *casita* on the left; follow this route for 20 minutes before turning left at a junction near a dew-pond. After 5 minutes (generally north-east) pass an old lime-kiln on the right and the road then ends. *40mins*

Now the rough walking starts, as you turn off left into a *barranco* (north-east) to enter a gorge. Keep to the right-hand side (east), and descend carefully until a goat-track appears and leads down to the *fuente* on the forestry road, which you saw on the ascent. *1hr*

There is no handy bar for refreshments, but Benichembla is only 4km away.

22: CARRASCAL DE PARCENT

Grade:	moderate
Distance:	15km
Time:	6hrs
Ascent:	690m
Maps:	Benisa 822 (30–32)

As you pass through the Jalón Valley between Alcalali and Parcent you cannot fail to notice the Col de Rates, with the white-painted Merendero restaurant and the two sets of radio masts which dominate the skyline on the left-hand side and the twin peaks of the Caballo Verde Ridge on the right-hand side.

These notes describe a walk from Benichembla through the scenic valley of the Barranco de Almadich and the traverse across the ridge of the Sierra de Carrascal de Parcent, passing the radio masts to the Col de Rates. The walk is approximately 15km, with an ascent of 690m; it is moderately strenuous, with some rough walking, and necessitates the use of two cars or a support party.

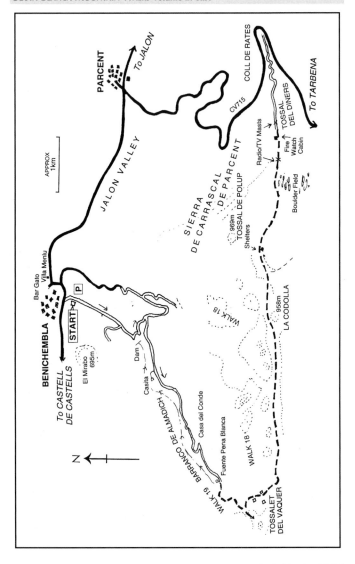

Getting There

From Parcent take the CV715 to the Col de Rates and park one car behind the restaurant Merendero. Return by the same route to Parcent and take the CV720, signposted Castell de Castells, towards Benichembla. Pass Villa Menlu, the bar Trompellot, go over the road bridge and turn sharp left up a track just before the 34km post. Park your car in a clear space 50m up on the right-hand side. This is the start point (see also Walk 18).

The Start

Turning right from the car park, walk up a track, leaving the village of Benichembla behind. The track, which ascends gently, becomes concreted after 50m, but soon changes back to a loose stone surface. Ignore all turnings to the left and the right, and soon you descend and see in front of you the concrete wall of a small dam. Here the track turns left and ascends again. Looking to the left you see the twin peaks of the Caballo Verde, humorously called the 'Marilyn Monroes' by some of my walking friends. Approximately 0.5km after leaving the dam there is a junction, but your wide path turns right and keeps ascending, passing through olive trees on the left and the right. The path now twists and turns, gradually gaining height, passing great crags and buttresses on the left, but the *barranco* previously on your left is now on the right.

In front of you, and slightly to the right of the centre of the *barranco*, the scene is dominated by the high peak of Cocoll, on which you can just see the airfield look-out tower. The head of the *barranco* is topped by the cone-shaped Tossal de Vaquero, towards which you are heading. The intention is to gain access to the ridge by traversing around the left-hand side of this peak.

Continuing along your track, you pass a *casita* on the right of an 'S' bend (Casa de Conde), and eventually come across the *fuente* Peña Blanca on the left of the track.   *1hr 30mins*

To Tossal de Vaquero and the Three Casitas

At a point 50m above the *fuente*, there is an indistinct path on the right, which you follow crossing the rocky dry river course of the *barranco*. The path twists and turns upwards towards the rock face on the right-hand side of the *barranco* and eventually turns left in a southerly direction, ascending and following close in, under the rock face.

Further up, the ravine or gully is full of rocks and the path crosses left over the ravine in an easterly direction. However, after 50m you turn right (look carefully and you may see a small cairn of stones at this point) and ascend towards the peak of Tossal de Vaquero across rough ground with no defined path. However, keeping the ravine on your right you may find a broken barbed-wire fence which you can follow upwards to its end. If you don't locate the fence continue upwards towards the peak of Tossal de Vaquero until you climb a few broken *bancales* and locate a plateau with a large oak tree to your right. Here you find a narrow track which you follow left, but after 200m it turns right around a rocky outcrop across old *bancales*, with Tossal de Vaquero on your right-hand side. Here you will find a small, sometimes cultivated, plateau with three *casitas*. *2hrs 25mins*

To the Ridge

Pass to the right of the left-hand *casita* and follow the path to the left of the cultivated area. Ascending slowly you arrive at the top of the ridge approximately 10 mins after passing the *casitas*. From here you can see the Serrella Castle to the far right and the Sierra de Aixorta and views down to the coast, looking back to see Tossalet and the airfield with its control tower.

The Traverse

Here you start to traverse the broad ridge following animal tracks in an easterly direction, towards the Col de Rates, leaving Tossal de Vaquero behind you. As you continue along the ridge, you will see in front and to the right the village of Tarbena, the Paso Tancat, the dominance of the Sierra Bernia and the high-rise buildings of Altea and Benidorm.

The earlier part of the path has some red markers, but the path is indistinct in places and the markers have faded. However, after the first rise, if you look carefully you may see the small broken walls of an old *casita* on the left of the path. In front, you will see a stone shelter on top of the hill which you can use as a guide, as the path passes approximately 7m to the left of this shelter. Be sure not to miss this shelter, as it is slightly hidden on the right when you get to the top of the rise. *3hrs 35mins*

Again follow the path to the two shelters on the top of the next hill. The shelter provides a nice place for a 5 minute break out of the wind. Four people in the shelter is very cosy, but five is definitely overcrowded.

The last 2 or 3km before the radio masts is rough underfoot. Continue in an easterly direction towards the sharp ridge which appears on the skyline in front of you. The radio and TV masts can just be seen to the left of the highest peak. It is easier to contour slightly left to gain the final ridge and avoid crossing the boulder field in front of you. After several ups and downs, the craggy ridge terminates in the final peak with the first set of radio and TV masts.   *5hr 20mins*

There are indistinct paths each side of this final craggy ridge, but I prefer to follow the rocky path on the right-hand side. From the radio and TV masts, follow the path to the new forestry lookout cabin (used for fire watching) and then down the wide track to the Col de Rates and back to your car.

If now your tongue is hanging out in anticipation of a beer, or if you would prefer to put your feet up with a coffee or something stronger, refreshments can be had at the Merendero, if open, or at one of the bars in Benichembla.   *6hrs*

23: PENYA TALAI (RATES)

Grade:	**moderate**
Distance:	**9.5km**
Time:	**4hrs**
Ascent:	**477m**
Maps:	**Benisa 822 (30–32)**

The Col de Rates, at 520m of elevation, is a wonderful mountain drive, as the main Pego to Benidorm road climbs 300m from the Jalón Valley to cross the mountains on its way to Tarbena. When you have shown your guests the beauties of Guadalest, there can be no finer introduction to the mountains of Las Marinas than to drive through the Algar Valley via Tarbena to reach this stunning viewpoint, where, suddenly, the whole of the Jalón Valley and the distant northern mountains come into view. The Merendero restaurant is the only hostelry in these mountains whose situation can be compared to those picturesque inns found at the top of alpine passes. The view from its terraces encourages the traveller to linger perhaps longer than he intended. As you look east into the Jalón Valley, the peak on your left, Tossal dels Diners (979m), is the terminal peak of the Carascal de Parcent, and there is a good road up to the radio transmitters which will take you about 30 minutes. The peak on your right (south-east), an impresive buttress of bare rock, has always been called Rates. The new edition of the MOPU maps, however, not only changes its name to Penya Talai, but reduces its height by 6m! The walk is mainly on good tracks, but there is rough walking in the Barranco de Pazules, and even the easiest way to the summit of Rates from the col is rough going.

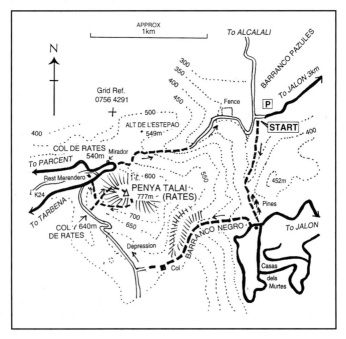

Getting There

The walk starts in the village of Jalón at the car park on the river-side, near to the bodega Pobre Virgen (Km.5.5 on CV750). The first 3km is on an unclassified surfaced road, which leads south-west from the restaurant El Teuler, opposite a bodega. Whilst this is a pleasant walk through vineyards and almond groves, it will put at least 2 hours on the total walking time, and you may wish to start the walk at the end of this road by taking your car to a parking point about 10m before the road ends at the bottom of Barranco Negro, which is a continuation of Barranco de Pazules.

Ascent of the Barranco Negro

Now walk south as the road loses its surface and reaches the head of Barranco de Pazules, where a track leads off right. This is your return route and leads toward Alcalali; your track continues along the east (left) side of the Barranco Negro. On your right are the slopes of Rates, and the end of the Ferrer Ridge is ahead of you. The track is easy to follow, and in 15 minutes the jagged ridge of the Bernia comes into view.

Now swing to the left through cultivated terraces and you see to the left Tosal d'Aspre, behind which, on the skyline, is the Loma Larga and Silla de Cau. Directly ahead is the north buttress of the Ferrer Ridge as you reach a steep surfaced road, which starts at Les Murtes (Km.2.5 on the Pinos road, CV749). *20mins*

Turn right up this steep road (generally west), passing a little *casita,* and in 5 minutes turn off right opposite a number of concrete culverts.

A Rather Difficult Section

You are still following the left-hand side of Barranco Negro and the section starts fairly well on a good clear path, but, sadly, this does not last very long. Whilst it remains, you have a marker to aim for – a tall pine stump on the skyline which you will reach in 10 minutes.

30mins 2.25km

Now you are assisted by a number of painted boundary markers, methodically numbered, on the left-hand side of what passes for a track. Be particularly careful near marker 38, where the easier track moves sharply left, uphill. Eventually these markers end and you aim for a small rocky pinnacle ahead. Some small cairns help. Pause a moment to admire the views back down into the Jalón Valley bounded by Sierra Solana. To your right a rocky arête comes down from the summit of Rates, and below you the dry rocky gully becomes narrower. In about another 5 minutes, you catch your first glimpse of the transmitters on Tossal de Diners, above the Col de Rates, and in a further 5 minutes the track levels out and you reach the top of the *barranco*, where there is a *finca* amongst small cultivated plots.

1hr   3.5km

From the *finca*, which is being restored, you can see a *hoya*, a depression between mountain ridges, where enough soil has collected to make cultivation possible. This one is quite extensive, and at its southern end there is a vineyard protected by two hedges of cypress trees to shelter the vines from the mountain winds, which blow cold at this altitude. Remarkably, this remote smallholding is still being cultivated. Views from the *finca* are, to the south, the whole of the north Ferrer Ridge, where the rock stratum has been twisted into an almost vertical position, and, to the north, the bulk of Rates peak, your next objective.

To Col De Rates

Leave the *finca* and walk and along a good unsurfaced road until it joins another road running north-west/south-east, then turn right. This road leads from the Col de Rates down into the Barranco del Llom and eventually to the banks of the Rio Algar. The road runs alongside cultivated plots, then zig-zags to gain height to a small rocky col which is the true Col de Rates (646m). From the col, the views open up to the north and you can look down on the Merendero restaurant and the motor road 100m below you, which most people think of as the Col de Rates because of the name plate you will see there (540m above sea level).

1.5hrs   4.5km

To the Summit

Just to the south side of this little col, turn uphill (north-east) along a narrow track which leads to a little shelf, with the last remaining stones of some former habitation and a few decayed terraces. From this shelf, you have a choice of routes to the summit. If you are attracted to a short but stimulating rock scramble, with fantastic photo opportunities down to the motor road beneath your feet, continue along a reasonable narrow path for a few minutes. Just before you reach a rib of rock with a pinnacle, strike upwards on steep ground, keeping to the right of the rib until you can leave it and climb up to the summit.

A less exciting alternative is to head almost east across the slope of the mountain, gaining height more gently and avoiding small bands of rock, if necessary. Both the ascent options use this route to return from the summit. Both routes take about 30 minutes.   *2hrs   5.5km*

The summit views include, to the south-east, Olta, near Calpe, and the ridges of the Ferrer and Bernia. To the south are the little Cortinas, near Benidorm, nestling under the towering Puig Campaña. Moving south-west you can see Ponoch, Sanchet and Peña Roc at the end of the Aitana Ridge, then Moro Blau and the Aixorta. Below you, in the Jalón Valley, you can identify all the little villages and the Caballo Verde Ridge, leading to the Val de Laguart. To the north-west are the col and, behind it, Tossal dels Diners at the end of the Carrascal de Parcent.

Down to the Merendero

If you are a rock-hopper (not the penguin variety), then by all means descend directly from the summit, but normally you move a little to the left (south-east) for a very short time, thus avoiding a band of mini crags. Start your traverse, losing height gradually, until you can see the shelf and the old terraces to aim for. From the shelf, a good path leads straight down to the road.   *2.5hrs   6km*

The Merendero

This restaurant has, as you may well expect, very variable opening hours, as no one lives here. Quite understandably, it opens when there is an opportunity of clients. Out of season do not travel without carrying refreshments, although, even out of season, we have been pleasantly surprised to find hospitality, a roaring fire and a good menu, which has considerably delayed your descent to the valley. From its terraces, even the car-bound motorist can enjoy magnificent views.

Peña Talai, or Rates

Return to the Jalón

Below the restaurant, by the side of the road to Parcent, can be seen a mirador (viewing point), with a diorama of the view. To visit the mirador, you don't even have to walk along the road, as there is a short cut which leads directly to it running from the junction of the access road to the restaurant. Your return route starts a few metres above the mirador, exactly on a bend in the road where an old trail leads north-east down a *barranco* to the valley.

Throughout most of this descent, the trail is easy to find, but the initial section has one or two traps for the unwary, where your route swings abruptly left, whilst another, equally inviting trail, continues to contour the mountain. The first of these sneaky zig-zags occurs about 20 minutes from the motor road, but if you have kept on course you will pass, on your right, a ruined *casita* in about 30 minutes. In a short time after this, you arrive at the head of the *barranco*, with some bare rocks and terraces.   *3.5hrs   7.5km*

This is the end of sneaky zig-zags, as the track settles down to a steady descent into the fruitful valley, with the villages of Jalón and Lliber in the distance. Ahead now, you will see a very unusual feature on these walks, a high wire-mesh fence which obviously stakes somebody's claim to a small plot of land. The fence is buried deep (rabbits?) and is 2m high (kangaroos, deer, or giant rabbits?). *3.5hrs 8.5km*

Follow along the upper fence, as the track turns into a broader unsurfaced road, and by now you should be able to spot your car parked below, amongst the almond groves. The village of Alcalali now comes into view, and in 10 minutes leave the road (which goes on to the village) and turn right between cultivated plots. This leads to another road which goes along the side of a *barranco*, with your morning's route on the opposite side. In another few minutes you will be back at the head of Barranco de Pazules and the end of the walk. *4hrs 9.5km*

24: ALT DE L'AMPLE

Grade:	moderate
Distance:	10.5km
Time:	5hrs
Ascent:	410m
Maps:	Benisa 822 (30–32)

This lovely walk to the Penon in the Jalón Valley is a circular route which includes the highest point, Alt De L'Ample (598m), overlooking the village of Jalón. As you sip your morning coffee in the Bar Juan in Jalón, you can glance up to the south to admire your objective, and at the end of a day filled with lovely views you can glance over your shoulder, as you re-enter the bar, for a last view of this beautiful little mountain.

From the road to Jalón from the Pla De Molinos, the rocky crest of this small ridge gives this mountain its distinctive appearance. The walk is all on good tracks and there is only one section where route-finding needs care, when you descend into the Jalón Valley via the Barranca Del Cau. During the walk you can visit lots of old fincas, where you can still find the remnants of eras, olive vats, corrals and wells, which will help you to imagine the rigours of rural life in these remote valleys. The wild flowers are also an attraction, and on the summit of the Peñon and Alt De L'Ample can be found orchids, Narcissus requienii (our own mountain daffodil) and that delightful little iris-like plant, the Barbary nut (Gynandrisis sisyrinchium). Spring is a good time to do this walk, as you often look down on a sea of almond blossom.

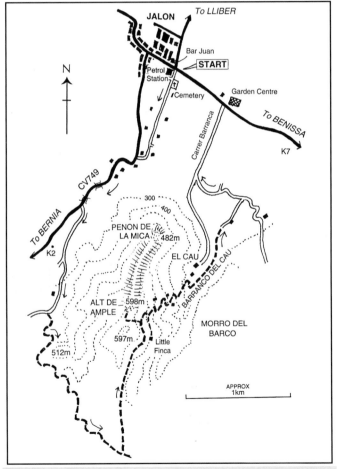

Getting There

Leave the CN332 road just outside Benissa (Km.175.8) and take the CV750 road to Jalón. As you enter the village, just after the Guardia Civil barracks on your right is the bar, on a corner opposite the petrol station. Meals can be ordered at the bar and there is plenty of parking on the broad side road.

Making a Start

Leave the Bar Juan, cross the road and walk south along an unsurfaced road (Carrer Cemeterio) which runs south by the side of the petrol station, passing the little cemetery on your left. After about 20 minutes, the road turns to the right and you join the motor road CV749 turning left towards Bernia. Cross and recross a *barranco*, Barranco de Maserof. At Km.1.5, turn off left, again south, along a good unsurfaced road which runs almost parallel to the motor road as it enters the Barranca De Maserof. You are heading towards a prominent but unnamed hill (point 512m on the map). On your right are excellent views of the rocky ridge of Sierra Ferrer and the prominent forestry road which runs to the central col. To the right of this ridge can be seen the eastern crags of Rates Peak above the col of the same name.   *45mins   2.5km*

As the road starts to drop, take to the *bancales* on your left and walk north-east on an old Mozarabic trail towards point 512. Cross the *barranca*, ignoring a little track which leads into it and starts to climb upwards towards point 512. In 5 minutes, pass a roofless *casita* on your right, and there are now views behind you of Sierra Solana. As you zig-zag upwards, you have views to the east of your objective, the Alt De L'Ample. Views now open up to the west of the extensive buildings of the Bodega Maserof; to the north-west Peña Roc, at the end of the Caballo Verde Ridge, comes into view, with Carrasca and Alfaro in the distance. Eventually, as you breast a rise, you get your first view of the jagged Bernia Ridge and the main (southern) summit of Sierra Ferrer, as the track swings to the left to go around point 512.
1hr 30mins   4km

A reasonable track now, it climbs to reach the ruins of an old *finca*, heading in a southerly direction. To the east can be seen the west summit of your mountain, with an old *finca* on its smooth slopes, and in 5 minutes you reach a turning and will wander off south through the Casas De Planisses and the Loma Larga.

Towards Alt De L'Ample

Follow the track north-east towards the summit and reach the ruins of a group of small *fincas*, with water still in the wells. To the south-east is the long ridge of Loma Larga, and in the dip between Silla De Cao and Tosal De Navarro runs the line of longitude of the Greenwich meridian. Follow the track as it heads north-east, keeping the ruined *finca* on the slopes of the southern summit to your left, and you will reach a large, unusually mature pine tree. Beneath this tree is a convenient stone wall, which provides an inviting and shady resting place. To the north-west, you can identify the Val Laguart by the long wall of Fontilles sanatorium and you are high enough now to see, behind Col De Rates, Carrascal De Parcent, with the transmitting antenna overlooking the col. To the north-east, Montgo comes into view on the coast. As you follow the track, note a deep ravine on your right-hand side; this is the Barranco Del Cau and it has a vertiginous Mozarabic trail climbing its far side. Below you, on a little shelf, can be seen a tiny *finca*, with its circular *era* (threshing floor), which you will visit later on your way back to Jalón. On reaching a ruined *casita*, your track continues above it, and within a few minutes you have a view ahead of the two peaks of L'Ample with a small col in between them. In contrast to the rounded southern summit, the northern one is crowned by modest, but impressive crags; these are the coxcomb you can see from the valley at the start of the walk. On the way to the col, note a very small *nevera* (ice-pit), and once there views open up to the south and south-west, including Puig Campaña. On the col, there are cross-tracks; you go ahead to the summit, and the track to the right is your descent route to Jalón. *2hrs 25mins   5.5km*

To the Summit Rocks

To gain the summit it is necessary to do a short rock scramble, which needs care, but it is well worthwhile for the views which await you on the summit. Views to the south are restricted slightly by the bulk of the Loma Larga Ridge, but there are enough views to satisfy everyone – from the Caballo Verde Ridge, with Orba Castle on its right, across the vast *huerto* of the Rio Girona to the jagged ridge of the Segaria and to the lighthouse on Cabo St Antonio, nestling beneath mighty Montgo. To the north, the Jalón Valley, you can actually see and identify the Bar Juan, your starting point. The rocky ridge drops invitingly down to the Peñon de la Mica, 100m below, but do not be tempted, as from the

Peñon there is no track and the descent is extremely tedious, even though it does lead directly to the front door of the Bar Juan.

2hrs 30mins   5.7km

Descent to Jalón by Barranco Del Cau

Leave the summit and reverse the rock scramble down to the col and turn left (north-east) on a reasonable Mozarabic trail which zig-zags downwards, passing two *fincas* and a water-hut (used for collecting water to pipe down to the valley). In 10 minutes reach the small farmhouse perched on its little shelf, which earlier you looked down on from the route to the summit. The situation is, without doubt, a dramatic one, looking down into the deep gorge of the Barranco Del Cau and up to the distant mountains. Here, I often speculate on how the old farmer and his family must have felt, wresting a meagre living from such harsh terrain, so far from the civilized life of Jalón. I doubt very much whether they had the time or the inclination to admire the view. His descendants probably are now plumbers or restaurateurs in more civilized spots on the Costa.

Apart from this tiny farmhouse, where numerous families must have been reared, there is a tiny sheepfold built under an overhanging crag, complete with small water bowls, laboriously carved out of the rock. In front of the farm building is an *era*, with its heavy stone roller still in place, where it came to rest after the very last harvest, and there are two wells still containing water.

Return to the junction and follow the now eroded Mozarabic trail, which traverses under the summit crags. Pass another old *finca* as you zig-zag downwards, and you can now see the bottom of the Barranco Del Cau ahead.   *3hrs 30mins   6km*

From this point you can see, in the bottom of the *barranco*, a substantial *finca*, with its roofs intact; this, in case you get lost, is your next objective and the key to finding your way back to Jalón. Between you and this old *finca* are some smaller ruins which you will visit on the way.

The Mozarabic trail is now very eroded, but you can keep to it if you remember that the objective of the Moorish builders, when making a trail, was to gain or lose height by constructing zig-zags or hair-pin bends. It is on these bends, where the trail changes direction abruptly, that the walker is most apt to lose his way. You now reach a collection of tiny *fincas*, the first of which is worth exploring. In addition to a stone olive vat, used for curing olives for eating, there is an *era* with its stone and, very unusually, inside the house a heavy wooden *era* roller, the first I have ever seen. There is no well at this *finca*, but there is evidence of a system of drains to collect rainwater. You will see the well which served this small community built into the wall before you.

4hrs   7km

After these *fincas* comes the only section of the walk which presents any difficulty in finding your way down, due to the eroded nature of the track. If in doubt, traverse right for a couple of minutes and you will see the valley bottom below you through the trees.

4hrs 15 mins   7.5km

Surprisingly, the track now climbs a little, and you get views of the *finca* mentioned earlier above you on your left. You are now walking between broad terraces of carob trees, but carry on, just above the *barranco*, until the track reappears, improves and passes through groves of almonds and carobs to join an excellent unsurfaced road, passing a restored *finca* on the way.

The road now crosses, for the last time, the Barranco del Cau and wanders generally north and west through almond groves and vineyards until it settles on a north-westerly route through villas and *fincas*. Now the traffic on the motor road can be seen ahead. You join the motor road near Km.6.5, and find that the road you have just travelled has the distinctive name of Carrer Del Barranca.

4hrs 45 mins   9.5km

Turn left along the main road, remembering to face the traffic, which can be busy at times, and enter the Bar Juan. I feel that I must declare that I have no financial interest in this establishment, except for having lavishly invested my money in the hospitality it provides. It could well be that the patron of the bar is a descendant of one of the old farmers who used to live on the mountain.

5hrs   10.5km

25: LLOMA LARGA

Grade:	moderate
Distance:	9km
Time:	4hrs 20mins
Ascent:	586m
Maps:	Benisa 822 (30–32)

When I first looked upon these mountains of the Costa Blanca I was excited by the rugged ridges of the Bernia and the exquisite shape of Puig Campaña, but realistic enough to accept that such bare rock might well be outside the capabilities of a retired mountaineer. But one mountain, which stirred memories of British hills, gave hope of rather less exacting exercise and, in fact, has proved to be a great joy to me. That mountain is Cao, which is the next best thing to a British fell walk in Spain (without, of course, the bogs and the driving rain).

The Mountain

The ridge runs north-east to south-west from the Jalón Valley to Pinos, and is 3km west of Benissa. You can see the two main peaks at the end of Benissa's main street and from most parts of Calpe, but the best view of all is from the CN332 as you climb out of Calpe towards Benissa, from which the whole ridge can be clearly seen. Cao has no great crags, but it does have impressive bands of rock and deep gullies. Some of these small cliffs have been identified as old sea-cliffs. The mountain has a distinct advantage over other peaks: it has excellent Spanish restaurants at each end! Some experience is required in finding the best route to follow on the ridge, and boots are essential as much of the walking is on bare rock. The ideal way to do this walk is north-west to south-east, and obviously needs two cars.

The Start

Originally the route started near Venta Roja Restaurant, just inside the Jalón Valley at the northern end of the Paso de Molinos, but the area has now been developed for housing. It is now preferable to tackle the

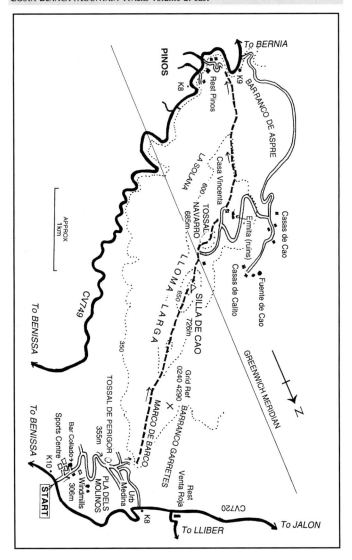

ridge from the southern side at the col (Collado), near Km.10 on the CV720 from Benissa to Jalón (signpost to the Sports Centre for Benissa (Polydeportivos)).

Follow the surfaced road, passing the Bar Collado, where refreshments are available, as it climbs and swings left at the water tanks. Pass one villa and bear right at a junction, and you are on one of the developer's access roads which contours, twists and climbs, eventually, right up to the ridge at Tosal de Perigor.   *45mins*

The Ridge

At times there are good paths, at times there are only bare rocks, and in some places there are even red markers, but treat these with caution, because *some* are only boundary markers. Best to keep as near to the crest as possible, and do not be deceived by false summits: there are between seven and nine intermediate summits on this ridge. Remember that Cao is 1 hour 20 minutes away, so settle down to enjoy the magnificent views in all directions. Note the Jalón Valley to your right and the distinctive limestone flora.   *2hrs*

Silla De Cao (726m)

There is no mistaking this summit, with its lofty triangulation station of the Institutio Geografico. It is a true mountain summit, all rock, with extensive views in all directions. Note especially the vines of Maserof in the valley to the west. The views of the Pou Roig Valley and its railway bridge and the distant Peñon d'Ifach, and to the north-east a far away vista towards Pego, can all be enjoyed from this point. Due south-west, but out of sight below, lies the col with its *casitas*, behind which is the Tosal de Navarro, and it is not a bad idea to plan your route up to this from the summit of Cao. To descend to the col keep as near to the right of the ridge as is prudent, as the nearer the edge the easier the going. Continue until you can see the col and its *casitas*.   *2hrs 30mins*

At the Col

This is a lovely place for a meal break, right on the Greenwich meridian of longitude. The peak Silla de Cao, to the north-east, is in the eastern hemisphere, whilst Tosal de Navarro, on the other side of the col, is in the western one. There is a modern structure, right in the col, but to the north of this is an old *finca* with an *era*, and in season there is watercress in a small stream. A road which has come up from Pinos via Casas de Cao can be followed to Casa Vincent by the faint-hearted who do not wish to ascend the Tosal.

Tosal De Navarro (683m)

Do not attempt a direct ascent from the *casita*, as the lower slopes are full of dead trees and debris. Better to traverse left until clear ground is encountered, and then traverse right to find the weakest point in the rock bands and continue to reach a rock summit with a cairn (3hrs). From here keep as near to the crest as possible, and eventually you will descend to another col with a *casita* and join the road previously mentioned.

From the col you can descend on the northern side to the bridge at Km.18 just north of Pinos, via Casas de Cao and Barranco de Aspre. There is also a very rough path to the east down the Barranco Garretes to Venta Rotja. Your descent follows the ridge to the west.

Turn left, south, along the road until you come to a *finca*, still occupied, Casa Vincent. Keep going south-west, dropping down to a ruin on the right and a path which crosses the ridge at right angle to your route. Ignore this and keep on the same bearing to the north of a small hill, with the Barranco de l'Aspre and Casas de Cao below on the right (north-west). The ridge has been ripped up for planting pine trees, but you will still be able to find a path heading down to the surfaced road to Bernia (CV749), which soon comes into view, at the bridge over Barranco de l'Aspre, near Km.18. If in doubt bear left, a little away from the bridge, and find a good track which becomes a road, passing a *finca* and reaching the surfaced road a few metres to the east of the Pinos Restaurant, where refreshments are available.

4hrs 20mins

26: ORBA CASTLE

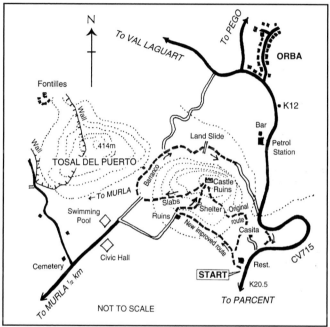

Grade:	moderate
Distance:	6km
Time:	3hrs
Ascent:	100m

As you drive on the CV750 from Parent towards Orba and Pego, you will be treated to a good view of the ruins of this ancient castle on the left as you approach the pass. Returning by the same route, the eastern aspect is even more impressive. This is a lovely walk with rewarding views, first of the Jalón Valley with its vines and almonds to the south, then the contrasting vista of the Girona huerto to the north, lush with citrus groves. This is a circular route with few good paths, and is well within the capabilities of most walkers. If you only wish to ascend to the castle then start from Murla (an unsurfaced road leads north-east from a stone cross at the eastern end of the village), as this is a much easier route.

Making a Start

The restaurant on the col is just to the south of the watershed between the Girona and Jalón valleys. It is the start and finish of this walk, at Km.12.5 on the CV715 at Murla. First walk along the car park on the south side of the restaurant for a few metres. Look for markers on the cairns which have been erected to stop camper-vans entering the almond orchard. The route to the foot of the castle is waymarked in yellow. Here, turn right through the orchard and a path will appear. It will lead in 25 minutes to a broad road coming up from Murla. Go along this road until it turns into a track near an old ruin.

To the Castle

From here, it is 15 minutes to the castle, which is directly above. Whichever route you choose, you will not have a continuous path. Avoid the vegetation by keeping to the rocky slabs as much as possible. If you keep to the left (west) you will find more bare rock and eventually pick up the marked track to the col. If at the ruins you traverse right (east) for some time, you will come to a cairn under a carob tree, which marks a good path to the shelter and then on to the summit. There is little to choose between these routes in getting to the top. The western view is of the

Orba Castle

Benimaurell and Barranco del Infierno (Walk 42)

Terracing on the way to Collado del Pas de Benimeli (Walk 32)

The Caballo Verde Ridge, with Penon Roc at the end (Walk 27)

Val Laguart from Caballo Verde Ridge (Walk 27)

continuing ridge of Tosal del Puerto and the impressive boundary wall of Fontilles Sanatorium. To the left of the ridge can be seen the Caballo Verde Ridge and Peñon Roch, with the Ermita of San Sebastiano perched high above the tiny village of Murla. Note Benimaurell high in the Val de Laguart with the village of Campell below it.

Walking through the ruins to the eastern side you look down into Orba and the lush *huerto* of the Girona, backed by the Sierra Segaria, with the sea in the distance.   *1hr*

Descent and Circuit

At the south-western end of the summit a track leads onto bare sloping slabs and some more red markers. Care is needed at one or two points to negotiate the rocks. Move slightly right (following the direction of the ridge) for a short time, passing a water deposit, to arrive at a small *casita* with a corral. Here an unsurfaced road joins from Murla, and you can break off the circuit to visit the village, which is half an hour away. Turn right along a reasonable track and enter the small col on the ridge along almond terraces. Watch out for a red marker which indicates the need to drop down one *bancale* to join the rough track which descends the stony *barranca* between cliffs. Below can be seen a large water reservoir. The tracks swings north-east through a grove of pines and drops down to a badly eroded area. A broad track to Orba should be ignored. Look for a red marker on the right.   *2hrs*

After a rough start a passable track appears through the pines, moving east, with the crags of the castle above on the right. After 20 minutes there is much evidence of erosion, and the going is again rough; but take heart, the best track of the walk now appears and leads gently down to the main road just above the petrol station.

2hrs 40mins

Turn right towards the pass, and at the first bend look for a red marker on the wall indicating a path which zig-zags upwards avoiding the hair-pin bends of the road and the traffic. Rejoin the road again near the pass, always being careful to walk on the left-hand side of the road, facing the oncoming traffic. Happily, it is then only a few metres back to the restaurant and welcome refreshments.   *3hrs*

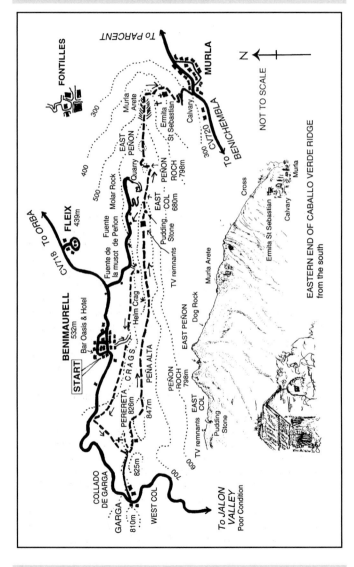

EASTERN END OF CABALLO VERDE RIDGE
from the south

Val de Laguart

27: CABALLO VERDE RIDGE
FROM BENIMAURELL

Grade:	strenuous
Distance:	14km
Time:	5hrs
Ascent:	450m
Map:	Benisa 822 (30–32)

In 1609 a great battle occurred on this ridge, as the troops of the Spanish king subdued the last remnants of the Moorish occupation, destroyed their castle of Peñon Roch, and deported every man, woman and child to Africa via the port of Denia. The last refuge of these Moriscos had been this long, high rocky ridge, which divides the Jalón and Laguart valleys, running due west to east, with the rocky mountain El Peñon Roch overlooking the little village of Murla at the eastern end. The Moors had defied the expulsion orders of the Spaniards and continued to lead a peaceful co-existence with their Spanish neighbours, but by 1609 they had been joined by other refugees, and totalled over 20,000, which eventually caused alarm amongst the Spaniards. The name El Caballo Verde is based on a mystical Moorish knight who was said to ride from the mountain on a green charger to drive out the Christians.

This walk offers a complete traverse of the ridge from the western end to the col under Peñon Roch. The rest of the ridge to Murla needs some rock climbing, and cannot be considered a walk. The approach and the first and last sections of the walk are on surfaced roads or Mozarabic trails. The ridge itself is rough walking, mainly on rock with hardly any paths. The ridge rocks are very dangerous in wet conditions, and in poor visibility route-finding is difficult, especially at the broad western end. So far, no safe way has been found off the ridge on its flanks.

Making a Start

Leave the CV715 at Orba, with signs to Fontilles and Val de Laguart, and continue along CV718 to reach Benimaurell.

From the Placa de Sacrement, with its church, walk west in the direction of the *fuenta* to turn left into Calle de Principe, south, to the edge of the village, where you join a concrete road which climbs towards the ridge. At a signpost turn off to the right along a Mozarabic trail which is waymarked as PRV181 to Col de Garga. There are magnificent views east down the valley, with the sea and Montgo in the distance. You can now nearly touch the crags as the cross of Perereta appears on the ridge ahead. In 30 minutes you rejoin the road, but only for a few metres, when you leave it again at another signpost to rejoin the footpath and gain a col on the ridge itself. The waymarked track on the right leads to Col de Garga.

Onto the Ridge

Your route is left on the south side, along the ridge to the east as views down into the Jalón Valley appear, with distant Aitana and Cocoll across the valley. At times there is no path, and at other times it seems that there are two or three. Try not to lose height, and reach a small ruined *casita* with point 847 ahead (the highest point on the ridge). Overhead on a crag (Perereta 826m) on the north side of the ridge is a stone cross from which views of the valley are obtained. At this point the ridge is very broad.   *1h 20min*

Keep going towards the col, then move right to aim for the summit rocks, in which you will find a rock gateway leading to the south side of the ridge with views of the Jalón Valley and the eastern part of your ridge, terminating in Peñon Roch.   *1hr 40mins*

From here to the Peñon there is seldom a continuous path, and it is often better to keep to the ridge rocks. First pass a small cairn, then reach a small col with *bancales* coming up from the northern side. For another half-hour keep on the ridge, until you reach a small depression with crags on the far side.   *2hrs*

Keep left going down and avoid the crags, bypassing them on the south side. Use a narrow terrace, and pass a circular shelter with views of the narrowest part of the ridge and some prominent pinnacles of rock (Helm Crag).   *2hrs 50mins*

On the north side of the largest pinnacle is a large cave, well worth exploring. This is a wonderful place to stop for lunch.

Descend from the pinnacles on flat slabs to a craggy ridge, which is a very sporting scramble for those with good balance and nerve. Ahead on the right is the Cao Ridge near Pinos. Slowly the ridge broadens again, and you can see first the Peñon and its quarry on the northern flank, then the walls of the sanatorium at Fontilles, and finally, at a small shelter, the blue TV cabin and Pudding Stone.

3hrs 20mins

Pass the scant remains of the TV transmitter.

3hrs 50mins

Then pass the Pudding Stone, which you pass on the left (north) to reach the col under Peñon Roch. *4hrs*

Peñon Roch on the Caballo Verde ridge

Return to Benimaurell

Linger awhile, because this is where you will leave the ridge to return to Benimaurell. The next section is very overgrown and is notorious for its briars (shorts *not* recommended). Go down on the south (right) side on a new waymarked path past a quarry to a surfaced road.

Now follow the surfaced road west, until about 800m beyond the Font de Penyo a concrete road leads off left to a *casita*, where you join a Mozarabic trail, waymarked in red, which leads to the start of the walk and Calle Principe.

On the way, it is fun to pick out the pinnacles and other points on the ridge, and to bask in the satisfaction of a hard walk well done.

5hrs

There are three bars, three restaurants and even a hotel in the village of Benimaurell. Bar Oasis has the most reliable opening hours.

Ascent of the Peñon (Diversion)

This ascent is suitable only for those experienced in rock-climbing.

To reach the summit of the Peñon is a rock scramble, and to cross the two summits follow a rocky arête and ridge down to the Ermita San Sebastian, and then go via a calvary to the village of Murla. It is a very rough expedition, with no paths, but is very rewarding. Allow 2 hours 30 minutes to Murla. There are orange markers on the ascent and descent of the summits. Start on the south side of the summit crags by crossing a maze of large boulders well vegetated with spiky plants. If this does not put you off, perhaps the 4m wall will. This obstacle, however, has its weakness, and is the last difficulty before traversing carefully upwards towards a small belvedere. From here, strike straight up to the summit on broken ground. The small holes made by treasure seekers, and a few broken pots and tiles, indicate that you are nearing the summit. To descend, go down a short rock pitch (easy) on the north side, which is a little exposed, and traverse up to the eastern summit. From here, keep to the ridge as far as possible, passing Dog Rock on the left whilst descending slabs to gain the short but delightful Murla Arête. Then make for the metal cross above the village, descending through old terraces to the *ermita*, then down to Murla on a good track.

28: DAY OF 10,000 STEPS

Grade:	strenuous
Distance:	18km
Time:	6hrs 30mins
Descent/Ascent:	950m/950m
Maps:	Benisa 822 (30–32)

I do not pretend to be able to date or explain the ancient stepped mule tracks which can be found all over these mountains and are commonly known as Mozarabic trails. The word Mozarabic is usually reserved to those Christians who accepted Moorish rule. They are well-constructed tracks showing considerable engineering skills, as they take in their stride precipitous ascents and descents across the gorges and valleys of the rugged mountains. During this walk the route descends three times into the depths of gorges and climbs out of them again. In one or two places even the solid Mozarabic construction has succumbed to the forces of nature and the track becomes difficult to follow, but generally the whole long day is spent on good trails with magnificent views. You will not pass a single inhabited dwelling during the whole walk, but there are good water supplies at three wells on the route.

Making a Start

Benimaurell is the last and highest village in the beautiful Val de Laguart. Seen from Montgo, you can really appreciate its elevation of 532m at the head of the valley. To reach the village, leave the CV715 at Orba, follow the CV718 (signposted Val Laguart) and start the walk at the Bar Oasis at the western end of the village.

Go down through the village in an easterly direction until you reach the Cooperativa Agricola San Roch, and turn left down to the village well and wash-house. From here, a lovely lane descends gently through orchards of cherry, almond and apple, until in 20 minutes you see the wash-house of the neighbouring village, Fleix, ahead. Just before reaching the wash-house and its *fuente*, turn left to join your first Mozarabic trail, which leads to the very bottom of the gorge. *20mins*

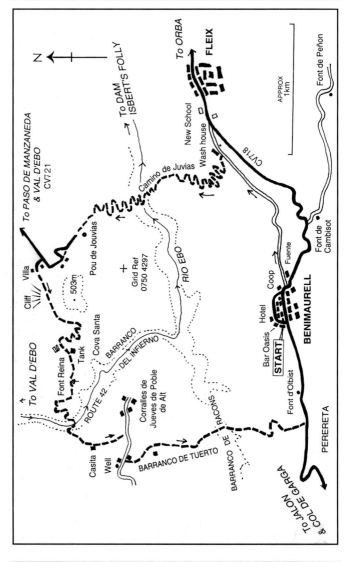

N ←

To ORBA

FLEIX

To PASO DE MANZANEDA
& VAL D'EBO
CV721

To DAM
ISBERT'S FOLLY

Font de Peñon

APPROX
1km

Camino de Juvias

New School

Wash house

CV718

Villa

Cliff

Pou de Jouvias

· 503m

Grid Ref
0750 4297

RIO EBO

Font de
Cambisot

Fuente

To VAL D'EBO

Font Reina

Tank

Cova Santa

BARRANCO
DEL INFIERNO

Coop

Hotel

BENIMAURELL

Bar Oasis

START

ROUTE 42

Corralles de
Jueves de Poble
de Alt

BARRANCO DE RACONS

Font d'Olbist

PERERETA

Casita

Well

BARRANCO DE TUERTO

BARRANCO DE RACONS

To JALON DE GARGA
& COL DE GARGA

168

Down to the Rio Ebo

Across the valley as you descend you can see a complementary trail zig-zagging upwards on the other side of the gorge. This is on your route. In another 15 minutes cross a small stream and go down through a cave in the cliff. Descend now by zig-zags and get your first view of the beautiful waterfall, which drops some 70m from near the cave to the base of the cliff. Sadly, the stream dries up in the summer, but in winter or after rain it is worth doing this part of the walk to appreciate the beautiful cascade. After another 30 minutes, recross the stream to reach the east side of the valley. *50mins*

Keep to the trail as it passes under some cliffs and zig-zags down to the rocky bed of the Rio Ebo. For most of the year there is no water in the river, but after stormy weather not only does the river flow, but the dam downstream (Isbert's Folly) holds water for a few weeks and a lake is formed. Diversions upstream to the Val de Infierno and downstream to the dam are possible.

Camino De Juvias

Cross the dry river bed to find the Mozarabic trail, which keeps to the left-hand side of a deep ravine for about 30 minutes. After passing a squarish boulder, the track climbs left away from the ravine. On this section, you get good views up into the Val de Infierno and back to the Fontilles Sanatorium, with its great boundary wall, the Caballo Verde Ridge, and in the distance Montgo on the coast. Eventually, a stream invades the trail, which becomes very eroded and overgrown. Thankfully, this section is very short, so push through to reach a level area with almond groves and a well. This is Pou de Juvias. *2hrs 25mins*

Leave the well, and go uphill on a broad surfaced road in a west-north-westerly direction, passing some small *casitas*, until in about 5 minutes the track levels out and comes to an extensive ruined *finca*. To continue on this road would lead over the Paso de Manzaneda to Pla de la Molino, above the village of Val d'Ebo. Turn left, once more down into the gorge in a generally south-west direction, with a signpost indicating PRV147 to Val de Infierno and Font Reinas, which is waymarked in yellow and white. The track at times is badly eroded, but there are dramatic views down into the gorge as you pass under some cliffs to arrive at a flat area with a spring, Font de Tres Abeuradors. *3hrs 15mins*

CostaBlanca Mountain Walks volume 2: east

Down Again to the Rio Ebo

There was once a good trail leading to the river bed just above Cova Santa, but sadly it has nearly all disappeared. As there are cliffs immediately below the Font, it is necessary to move left (south) downstream for a while to avoid them and reach the stony bed of the river. Turn right upstream, and in a few minutes you should find a crag with two cairns on top, on the left-hand side, which indicates the start of the ascent. Avoid the gully immediately above by keeping to the left (south side of it) and head for a small *casita*, seen high up amongst the terraces. *4hrs*

To Corrales De Jueves Del Poble De Alt

From the old *casita*, a reasonable Mozarabic trail leads upwards towards a well seen on the skyline, which is reached in 20 minutes. Once there, you will find the Corrales, a collection of restored *casitas*. Turn west on a good road (which would eventually lead in 5km to Collado de Garga) until you reach a level area with a well and some ruined *fincas*. *4hrs 20mins*

Down into the Barranco Del Tuerto

On the opposite side of the road from the well, close to one of the farm buildings, find yet another Mozarabic trail, which in 2 hours will take you down into the Barranco de Racons (a tributary of the Ebo) and up again to join the road near Collado de Garga. First follow the trail down the east side of the Barranco del Tuerto, passing an extensive *finca* on the other side. In 30 minutes the track levels a little, is invaded by a stream and crosses the larger Barranco de Racons. *4hrs 40mins*

Ascent to Benimaurell

Your final objective can be seen above, a large buttress to which the trail leads via many twists and turns. It offers beautiful views down into the Val de Laguart. *5hrs 20mins*

Pass to the right of the buttress, and in a few metres you reach the top of the slope and the track becomes a wide lane, which leads you in a few minutes to the road. *6hrs*

Turn downhill to pass the picnic site at Font de Olbist to return in 15 minutes to the fleshpots of Benimaurell, after a very full and happy day following in the steps of the Moorish muleteers. *6hrs 30mins*

170

29: ISBERT'S DAM FROM TORMOS

Grade:	easy
Distance:	9km
Time:	3hrs 30mins
Ascent:	Negligible
Maps:	Benisa 822 (30–32)

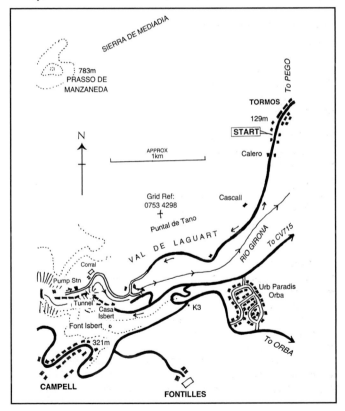

Some 30km west from Javea, as the eagle flies, are the two vast remote mountain valleys of Val d'Ebo and Val d'Alcala, where time has really stood still, with the inhabitants concentrating on agriculture, especially fruit and vegetables. Most of the rain which falls has only one outlet, to the Laguart Valley in the east, and over the centuries the Rio Ebo has carved and polished the rocks and boulders which make up the deep narrow defile of the Barranco del Infierno, through which all of the winter torrents must pass to gain the sea. The barranco is dry for most of the year and provides a magnificent challenge for the experienced and well-equipped rock climber (Walk 42).

Below the gorge the dry, boulder-filled bed of the Ebo can be walked (the river has gone underground), passing beneath the cliffs on the right where the villages of the Val de Laguart are to be found. Beneath Fleix is found the stepped Mozarabic trail Camino de Juvias, which crosses the gorge and then climbs up towards Ebo in many thousands of steps (see Walk 28).

Further downstream, east, you find that the river, now the Girona, has one more obstacle in its track, a high band of rock, through which it has been able to exploit a weakness to cut out a gorge of no more than 5m width to enable its waters to reach the vast heurto of citrus trees on the plain of Denia, on its way to the sea near Setla, just west of Denia.

At the beginning of this century, a dam was constructed in this most inviting spot, with a view to solving all future water problems not only for the farmers but for the towns of Orba and Denia. Access tunnels had to be cut through the rock to get materials to the top of the dam, but it would seem that the little building work needed to plug this natural gap did not cause much trouble. The winter rains came and the dam filled with precious water, just as it still does today, but, sadly, after only a few days the level dropped as the water found its way down into an ancient underground watercourse, with its many underground chambers and lakes. Isbert's Dam, named after the nearby finca and spring, is called by some Isbert's Folly. Your route is a delightful stroll to this piece of industrial archaeology from Tormos, through citrus groves all the way.

Getting There

The lovely little village of Tormos lies to the north of the vast *huerto* of citrus groves, under the crags of Sierra de Mediadia. Take the main road, CV715, which runs from Benidorm to Pego, and Tormos is the next village, north after Orba at Km.17.5. There is an excellent restaurant right beside the road near to a new *glorieta* (and bus shelter) across from the almond crushing plant and warehouses of the Cooperativa.

Making a Start – Through the Huerto

If you have time, please explore this lovely little place, with its unpretentious charm and courteous inhabitants, then make your way from the Plaza Major, via Calle Martin, and then turn right, south-west, along Calle Cacall, straight out into the country. The road is narrow but has a good surface as you continue down into a *barranco* then climb up again to views ahead of the great wall of Fontilles Sanatorium. The best opinion is that the wall only indicates the boundaries of the Leper Colony, perhaps to allay the fears of local inhabitants in less informed times. The Sanatorium has played a vital part in research and in the eradication of the disease from Spain. Whilst its laboratories will remain active, its future seems to be as a retreat for elderly folk.

Close to the walls of Fontilles, the main valley road climbs upwards with the small urbanisation of Paradiso Orba beneath it. This is also a lovely position from which to admire the impressive Caballo Verde Ridge, which towers above us. To the left are the twin peaks of Peña Roc and then the long ridge which leads in 8km to Puerto Gaga, just above the upper village of Benichembla.

30mins   1.5km

Your road is now unsurfaced as you keep to the same bearing, between oranges, lemons and almonds, passing a small *casita* on the left. You drop a little then climb again, then on the right is a small *finca* with a barbecue.

40mins   2km

You are now following the valley of the Barranco del Infierno and get your first views of the cleft in the rocks which is your objective. On the skyline to the left can be seen the first houses of the village of Campell, built high up on the cliff top. At a fork you bear right, and to the right ahead can be identified the mountains of Mediadia, with the highest peak, Prasso de Manzaneda (783m), to the north.

To Casa Isbert

The large white house ahead at the top of the valley is your objective, Casa Isbert, whilst towering above it are the houses of Campell. From Campell you can see a rocky ridge which descends to the valley bottom. It was this ridge which the constructors of the dam had to tunnel through to get to the site of the dam, and through this very tunnel you too shall soon travel.

You now reach a small *casita* on the right-hand side with roses round its door, and here you turn off to the left on a rough road (chained) which leads down to the valley bottom. *1hr   3km*

Reach the river bed with its thick growth of bamboo and reverse your course for a little while to follow the north bank, east, until at a concrete wall you can cross the river bed and start to ascend again, passing a small *casita* to join a surfaced road near another *casita*. This road seems to be heading in your direction towards Casa Isbert, but be warned: do not follow it (it soon disappears). Turn left and climb to another road where you do turn right, along a level section, with the substantial house Casa Isbert ahead as you pass a stream issuing from Font Isbert, a little higher up the slope. The house commands a lovely view down the valley, with the majestic heights of Sierra Mediadia above to the north.

To the Dam

Pass to the left of the house's boundary wall on a narrow, descending brambly path to gain a better track across a *revêtement* into a small tunnel, with a small stone hut at its entrance. Use a torch here as there is debris on the tunnel floor. Emerge from the darkness after 150m to get your first clear view of the defile which tempted the engineers to construct the dam. Ahead is a narrow gallery, cut into the rock to get materials to the dam site. The way ahead is barred by a protective steel fence to prevent access. If you are minded to trespass, the catwalk will take you to the very parapet of the dam.

Otherwise, you must break off to the right on a good track which leads down into the river bed, which has been colonised by oleanders and wild figs, to walk to the base of the dam. You can reach the wall, with the great iron valves which were to regulate the flow of water rusting above you. It is obvious that adventurous folk enjoy scaling these walls, making use of some pretty unstable metal ladders left by the builders, and have even placed graffiti high on the dam itself.

2hrs   5km

Back to Tormos

Follow the dry river bed, ignoring your approach route, and make for a pumping station on the left-hand side of the valley where you will find a good, unsurfaced road which will take you back to Tormos. First you reach another pumping station, cross over a ford and pass a wooden corral for the cattle which graze in the valley. After passing a rather long ruin on your left you are back at the rose-covered cottage where you turned off on the route up the valley.   *3hrs 30mins   9km*

The restaurant, The Tormos, is highly recommended.

30: CRUZ DE CAVAL

Grade:	moderate
Distance:	9km
Time:	5hrs 30mins
Ascent:	468m
Map:	Benisa 822 (30–32)

This may be the lowest summit of Mediadia, at the very eastern end of the range, but the ascent of nearly 500m makes it the hardest day. Whilst the walk up to the col at Pla de les Poets is delightful, the actual ascent to the cross is rather a 'bone shaker'.

Getting There

The walk starts from the village of Tormos, at Km.17.5 on the CV715 road from Orba to Pego. It is, as you may have gathered, one of my favourite starting points, not just because the people are so friendly but because of its bars and, particularly, the Tormos Restaurant, where simple traditional fare is dispensed in generous helpings and at a very modest price. But beware, you may have to fight for a table if it is harvesting time.

Start from the main road and the Tormos Restaurant, and walk along heading south-west until, at the church, go north along to the cemetery, with its lovely gardens, and seek out your first yellow and white waymark, near to the Stations of the Cross. (Cars can be taken this far.)

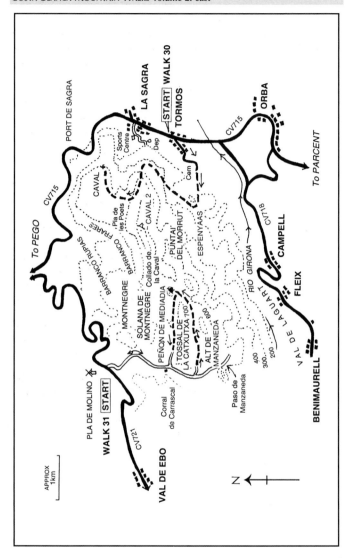

Making a Start to the Summit of Espenyaas

Above you is a rock buttress, Espenyaas (344m), which the ancient Mozarabic Trail negotiates by winding around its base and ascending its south-western end to reach a col behind the summit. I have often thought that, in ancient times, it must have been a likely spot for a look-out, and it is possible that the stone ramp, by which you may climb to the summit, bears out this theory. Having negotiated Espenyaas, your track now starts to climb more gently in a north-easterly direction below a spur of Caval 2, which is above you to the left.

To the First Rock Gateway

Settle down now on the old Moorish trail until, just before you round the eastern end of the rock ridge, red markers appear, indicating that the trail from Sagra, a little steeper but shorter than yours, is joining the trail. You can trace the route from the village, below to east, and perhaps pick out the water tank which is on the route.

Now you head north-west, under the crags of Caval 2 and above a deep but broad valley which separates you from your rather undistinguished objective, Cruz de Caval, over to the north; however, without the benefit of an identifiable summit, or even a cross, it is difficult to locate.

To the east, on the skyline is Montgo and the Mediterranean, with the jagged ridge of the Sagaria rising out of the green *huerto* of citrus groves. Over to the south is the Caballo Verde Ridge and the Val de Laguart.

Pass a convenient flat boulder under the crags and ahead can be seen some trees which are your next objective. A rocky ridge now divides your route from the rest of the *barranco*. There are still some yellow and white waymarks to help as you reach the first rock gateway and descend, passing a number of ruined *casitas*.   1hr   2.5km

Sierra de Mediadia from Benimeli, with the village of Tormos on the far left

To the Pla De Les Poets

Keep on the same north-westerly bearing, descending for a while until you reach some terraces where a red marker invites you to turn off to the right. If you follow this route, you will have to climb the terraces when you reach crags of a second rib of rock descending from Pla de les Poets. Keep climbing, close to the crags on your left-hand side, until you reach the last broad terrace, which you walk along, west, to find a well with troughs. As you again start to climb on waymarks you reach an old ruin and emerge onto the Pla de les Poets. *1hr 30mins*

Over to your left can be seen the summit of Caval 2. There is a route from here to the summit by making for the weakness in the crags between the main mountain and the ridge which you have followed up from Tormos. It is a rough climb of over 270m, first to the old *finca*, then on to the 'Lomo' and finally across the limestone to the summit.

As you walk north along a good path, still on waymarks, you will note that this area must have been well cultivated in ancient times, as there are a number of ruined farms, and at the last one you can rest, with views now to the north. *2hrs   4km*

To the Summit

I cannot think that I have ever, in all my years of mountain walking, decided that any mountain was not worth the effort of climbing it. I came pretty close on Kinder Scout on a bad day, and Cruz de Caval was another candidate, but then you may disagree.

The waymarks will lead you to the edge of the level area, with excellent views along the Cavals to the Carrascal de Ebo and, to the north, the town of Pego, Almisira and the coast near Gandia. You can also see the 'alpine' road which wends up to the Pla de Molino on its way to Val de Ebo.

A yellow sign points confidently to the north-east and the Pic (the summit). Someone has liberally anointed the 'route' with waymarkings, which I suspect were painted from a helicopter by using a very long brush! It would be an understatement to say that I did not enjoy the next three-quarters of an hour very much, and only those who enjoy karst limestone could possibly do so. There isn't really anything to aim for until you catch sight of the twisted remains of the metal cross and are rewarded by the new views to the east and down to the Port de Sagra. Even these were tainted by the thoughts of an even longer time spent carefully negotiating the grykes and clints back to the Pla.

3hrs   4.5km

Return by the same route, which, after the summit traverse, is even more enjoyable, to the hospitality of Tormos.

31: PEÑON DE MEDIADIA

Grade:	moderate
Distance:	9km
Time:	5hrs
Ascent:	286m
Map:	Benisa 822 (30–32)

This, the highest point on the Sierra del Mediadia, is not even named on the Mapas Militar, and the most recent 1:25,000 series show the height as 786m, some 31m higher than the old maps – so it still seems to be growing! Naturally, the views from its summit can be considered to be the best on the Sierra and can be achieved with only modest effort.

Unlike the hard climb from Tormos in the south, this route approaches the peak from the north, thus allowing cars to climb the first 500m.

Getting There

Leave the CV715 road from Parcent, near Km.19.5 just outside Pego, and head south-east on the CV721 signposted to Val de Ebo. This is, without doubt, the most dramatic of all the region's mountain roads: in alpine fashion it twists and turns, snaking along the contours, as the road-makers used all their skill to reach 500m above the coastal plain. The views from the car are fantastic, but make sure that the driver keeps his eyes on the road. At Pla de Molino, with its mill converted into a house, stop and park near to Km.8, as the road starts to drop down to Val De Ebo. Across the road, a road leads to a *refugio* for climbers opened by Pego Council. The first section of this route is suitable for vehicles.

To Paso de Manzanera

From the main road, a good forestry road heads south-east along the 500m contour and is a delight to walk, with hardly any gradient and extensive views. To the right, ahead, can be seen the Cavallo Verde Ridge in the Laguart Valley, then, further to the right, the Carrascal de Ebo. In the far distance, to the north-west, is the elegant mountain of Benicadell, near Beniarres. Above you, on your left, appear the crags of Montnegre (649m), and to the right you can see the defile of the Barranco del Infierno. After dropping down to negotiate a *barranco*, the road resumes its course, and you get good views of the northern end of the Sierra del Mediadia and Cruz de Caval (597m), overlooking the pass, and Port de Sagra. Pass a ruined *finca* on the right, Corral de Carrascal, and you now have a view of your return route along the northern flank of Tossal de la Catxutxa (688m).   *30mins   1.5km*

   Now pass a *finca* on the right as you cross the modest pass, and in another 0.5km look out for a good track which leads off left, into the valley between Tossal de la Catxutxa on the left and Alt de Manzaneda (702m), the southern end of the Sierra del Mediadia, on the right.
                                                    1hr   2.5km

Ascent of Peñon de Mediadia

The good track heads east along the northern side of the valley, level for a while, until it reaches a *finca* with a well and a corral for cattle, where you cross over to the other side of the valley and start to climb a rough track which improves as it heads for a col, where the farmer has built a wire netting corral. The col is the starting point for the ascents of Alt de Manzaneda and Tossal de la Catxutxa.   *1hr 30mins   3.5km*

The farmer has thoughtfully provided a number of building blocks so that walkers can continue their way without serious injury, and you continue your way up the valley. Go ahead, east, heading for a ruined *casita*. Once there, you see that the valley is split by a rib of bare rock, and you keep to the right of it as the path continues and drops a little. Now on your right is the deep gully of Barranco dels Oms, between the peaks of Alt de Manzaneda and El Parat dels Oms. As you continue eastwards there are good views down this gully to the south-east into the Val de Laguart, with the mountains of Sahili and Carrasca de Parcent beyond. Then the first village of the Laguart appears, Campell, with the wall of Fontilles on Tossal del Port.

Pass a ruined *casita* on the right and continue through terraces of long-abandoned almond trees as Helm Crags, on the Cavallo Verde Ridge, appear. Drop down now to negotiate the bed of a ravine, and climb out to pass another ruin.

This section is grazed by the cattle which use the corrals, and they have made their own paths to compete with yours; thankfully you are all, it seems, going the same way. Eventually some trees appear ahead and you head for them. The trees are on the Pla, a small level area beneath Peño de Mediadia, and you now have to climb up the rocks to gain the small shelter on the summit.   *2hrs 30mins   5km*

View over Paradis Orba to Sierra de Mediadia (from Walk 26)

Summit Views

As you climbed up from the Pla, the views to the south increased to include the Bernia Ridge, Aixorta, Cocoll, Tossal del Vaquero and Aitana, but now there are extensive views in all directions. The new views are to the north and east, with the ridge of the Mediadia in the foreground, extending to the two summits of Caval 2, with an old *finca* nestling under the crags, on the south side, at the head of Collado de la Malladoro Rasa and the Barranco de la Palla, which drops down to the valley of the Laguart. Below you, to the east, is a remarkable pinnacle of rock by the side of the gully, Puntal del Morrut. Beyond Caval 2 is Cruz de Caval and the Segaria Ridge. To the east is the Mediterranean, the coastal plain, Denia, Montgo, Cabo Nao and, on the horizon, the island of Ibiza. To the west are Monte Cabrer, the Forada Ridge, Benicadell and Azafor, while further to the north is Almisira. Is there no end the peaks that can be identified? Looking back on your ascent route you can pick out the line for the ascent of Alto de Manzaneda from the col. You can also plot your course east over very rough ground to the twin summits of Caval 2 (about 1 hour).

An Alternative Descent along the Flank of Tossal De La Catxuxta

Leave the summit and retrace your steps until you reach easier ground and can traverse east, under the summit rocks, to the col, where you make for some trees which mark the beginning of a good trail, heading north-west. The trail will descend steadily along the northern flank of the Tossal, and heads directly for the old *finca* Corral de Carrascal on the forestry road to the pass. It has to negotiate four modest gullies on the way and at times suffers from the extra trails made by the grazing cattle, which you now should be good at coping with. On this section, as the distant views disappear you can still admire the peaks of Montnegre and Benicadell as well as the 'alpine' road up to the Pla de Molino from Pego. Eventually the forestry road and Corral de Carrascal come into view ahead, and you reach a double-trunked pine tree near the ruins of an old shelter to pick up a broad road which leads down, left, to the forestry road.

Turn right, north-west, back to the Pla de Molino, where, sadly, there are no refreshments. Drive 8km into Val de Ebo, where there are a number of bars and restaurants, and ask for the folk museum if you are interested in finding out how these country folk once lived. The interesting caves, Cova de Rul, are a little way along the road to Alcala de Jovada and are worth a visit. *5hrs* *9km*

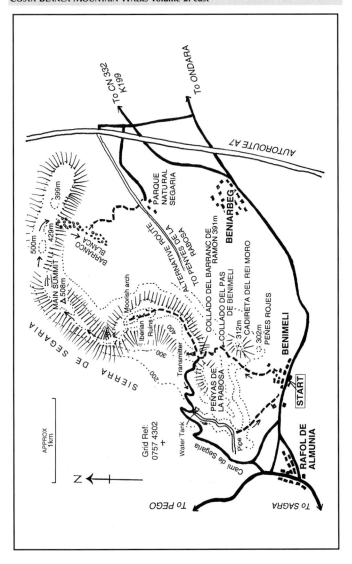

32: SIERRA DE SEGARIA
– FROM BENIMELI TO THE IBERIAN RUINS

Grade:	moderate
Distance:	9km
Time:	2hrs 45mins
Ascent:	207m
Maps:	Gandia 796 (30–31), Benisa 822 (30–32)

VARIATION: SUMMIT AND CIRCUIT

Grade:	strenuous/scramble
Distance:	13km
Time:	6hrs
Ascent:	500m

On the northern boundary of the Province of Alicante are two very different areas of intensive cultivation. The northern one, east of Pego, has not only extensive citrus groves but also the Marjal swamps, once cultivated as rice fields. The southern one is the vast huerto of the Girona, well irrigated to provide a superabundance of citrus fruit. The jagged ridge of bare rock which separates the two is the Segaria Ridge, which runs from near to the village of Rafol de Alumnia, on the northern edge of the Girona huerto, for just over 2km north-east to end as Peña Roja, above Vergel. Although of modest height, like all mountains which rise from near sea level it presents a noble sight, especially from the main coastal road, and is easily identified by the transmitters on the western col to the west of the main summit. The main walk will take you to the col and to explore the Iberian ruins which crown the summit. The alternative route from the ruins to the summit is a rock scramble, and there is also a direct descent over steep rocky ground down to the picnic site on the south side of the mountain near Vergel. To make use of this extension you will need to arrange transport back to Benimeli.

Getting There

From the coastal road, CN332, take the road north of Ondara signposted Benimeli at Km.25 to pass through the pleasant little villages under your mountain until you reach Benimeli. From the inland road, CV715, turn off north-east at Sagra to join the CV729 to Benimeli. Note that Benimeli does not appear on some road maps, but is between Rafol de Almunia and Sanet y Negrals.

Alternatively, to reach the eastern end of the walk ,a few metres north after leaving Ondara on CN332 turn left near Km.199, with signs for Sagra and Beniarbeig, and immediately follow signs to the car park for Segaria Natural Park (2km).

To Collado Del Pas De Benimeli

If you have patronised the bar on the main road for your coffee, you will have to walk up into the village square, where there is another bar, Bar Hogar. Now walk east into Plaza Danach, then continue by way of Calle Calvaria to follow the lovely Stations of the Cross upwards until you pass between two water tanks to find some old calvaries alongside a rough mule track. This will take you up the eastern side of a broad gully which leads to the col. Already you have lovely and extensive views to the south, across the *huerto* to the distant mountains, with the village in the foreground. You get particularly good views up the Val de Laguart, with its villages, reaching up to the Col de Garga, under the crags of the Caballo Verde Ridge. The track is at times rather eroded, but there are one or two red markers to help, and after passing a small ruin on the left, you arrive at a more extensive ruined *finca* on the Col del Pas de Benimeli.   *30mins   2km*

To the Ridge – Collado De Barranc De Ramon

Above can be seen the transmitters on the ridge, and you aim for them, sometimes finding a track going in that direction. At other times there are only the rocks to negotiate until you join the surfaced motor road which has taken a more circuitous route on the northern side of the ridge. Walk along the road and reach the transmitters.

Your views are now extended to the north, including the coast as far as Gandia, with Sierra Falconera behind the town, and across the wetlands of the Marjal Mayor. Denia and its castle are also visible to the east.   *50mins   3km*

Sierra de Segaria from the grassy belvedere

To the Iberian Ruins

Pass to the left, north, of the wire fence surrounding the transmitters and continue along a good path on the southern side. There are, in fact, a number of paths all leading in the same direction until you find the remarkable ruins of an extensive Iberian settlement which date back to 3rd century BC. The ruins are impressive, with lots of dressed stone, and the winter rains wash out a lot of shards, which can easily be identified as Iberian by the double glazing over a grey basic pot, leaving a sandwich of brown, grey and brown. You can compare these ruins with the cruder remains of a Moorish fort at the col. Continue along the path, east, to arrive at the col, with a lovely grassy belvedere which invites you to linger a while.   *1hr 15mins   3.5km*

Across the other side of the col, at the base of the crags of the Segaria summits, there are the remains of a Moorish gateway and defensive wall. And you can enjoy intimate views of the dramatic northern crags of the Segaria's summits. This ends the main walk, but those who are competent and fit enough for a rock scramble can go on to the ridge and gain the main summit (508m) in about an hour. (See 'Variation: Summit and Circuit' below.)

Descent to Benimeli

If you enjoyed the ascent then by all means reverse it down to Benimeli. An alternative is to follow the motor road on the northern side of the ridge, which gains the main road about 1km west of Benimeli. A variation of this route is now described.

Follow the surfaced service road for about 1km, until you pass a house on the right-hand side and can see a large water tank on the left. Just below the tank, at a large rock, leave the road to head south-east along a broad, level unsurfaced road. Keep left at a fork and pass a well on the left. You now have good views of the eastern end of the Sierra Mediadia, with Cruz de Caval overlooking the Puerto de Sagra. Above you is the true, western end of the Segaria Ridge, the rocks of Penyas de la Rabosa, and ahead is a large concrete pipe which will be your guide down to the valley, which you reach in about 30 minutes.

2hrs 15mins

Down to Benimeli

Follow the pipe, but only for a few minutes until you turn off to the left to follow red markers along a Mozarabic trail, south-east, down to Benimeli. You will cross the water pipe, and views will open up over the vast *huerto* of the Girona, with the Bernia, Rates, Caballo Verde Ridge and the high valley of the Laguart, with Orba Castle and Fontilles. Pass a *finca* on the right to join a broad road which leads directly to the Plaza Major. *2hrs 45mins* 9km

Variation: Summit and Circuit

The ridge should not be attempted in high winds or in wet weather. The route is not marked and goes upwards from the Moorish ruins to gain a cleft in the ridge. A tooth of rock is passed on the north side. Once on the ridge there is another cleft, which can be avoided by descending on the south side and climbing up again through a green groove. Once back on the ridge the summit, with its trig point, is only a further 200m to the east.

Descent of South Flank from the Summit

For those who have gained the summit there is a rough descent to the picnic area at Vergel. This descent is fairly straightforward in good visibility; there are intermittent waymarks, in white, but with some paths to help you.

From the summit with its trig point continue east along the ridge towards a prominent clump of holly oaks, which you pass, then keep to the top of the ridge, avoiding some crags by moving a little to the northern side until a saddle is reached.

You are now at the head of Barranco Blanca, with its white rocks leading down the steep southern slopes of the mountain. At the bottom of the gully, in line with distant Isadoro with its antennae, is a small collection of buildings, a children's playground and the car park for the Segaria Natural Park. This is your next objective. Follow the white markers to descend the rocks on the right of the gully, then after 15 minutes start to cross the gully, aiming for an ochre deposit on the crags. White markers now lead you down a reasonable path which zig-zags down towards the car park, with a quarry on your left. But beware, the waymarkings give out as the path improves and navigation is easier, until you cross an irrigation channel (dry) and admire the beautiful ceramic panorama (the mirador). *45mins*

There is a perfect path now with railings down to the warden's office and the car park. *50mins*

For those who forgot to arrange transport, the conduit can be followed west for 2km, where it ends. Drop down to a river bed and past a large tree to join a track which soon turns upwards towards Penetes Roches. Turn right now and follow it nearly all the way to the saddle, then climb *bancales* up to Collado del Pas de Benimeli and rejoin the main route down to the village. *6hrs*

Limestone clints lead from Collado del Pas de Benimeli

Val de Llosa

33: CASTELLET DE L'OCAIVE
FROM LLOSA DE CAMACHO

Grade:	moderate
Distance:	10km
Time:	4hrs
Ascent:	250m
Maps:	Benisa 822 (30–32)

I first discovered the charming little village of La Llosa de Comacho, the only village in the Llosa Valley, quite by chance on holiday. I was starting to explore inland from the coast and stopped for coffee at Alcalali, where I saw a poster which declared that La Llosa was celebrating its main fiesta. We spent the rest of the morning sitting under the palms in the tiny plaza in front of the church, as the Clavelles Band cavorted in and out of the streets, putting everyone in a festive mood. Eventually a modest procession, led by the priest, with children in national costume carrying bread, flowers and gifts, led us into the old church for mass. In fourteen years the village has changed little: they still cultivate only lemons (no oranges here), there is no public telephone and only one tiny shop. True, they now have their own Ajuntiamento and a popular Alcalde, and since gaining their independence from Alcalali in 1996 the very basic bar has improved. It is decorated with paintings by a village artist and a display of local pottery, and now offers a good selection of meals and tapas. There is also rather a posh restaurant as you leave the village and a lovely ceramic near to the pottery which records that the village lies on the Greenwich meridian of longitude, dividing the hemispheres. The walk starts in the western hemisphere, but spends most of its time in the eastern one!

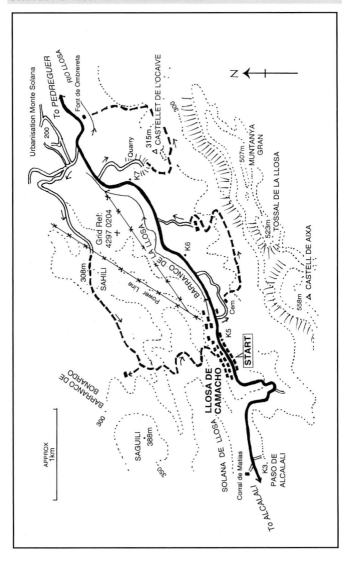

Getting There

The valley runs slightly north of east from the pass, Puerta de Alcalali, to Pedreguer. The CV720, which runs from Alcalali in the Jalón Valley to Pedreguer, is the only road in the Val de Llosa. The village where the walk starts is at Km.5.

La Umbria de Beniguasi

Leaving the village, head east on the road to Pedreguer, passing the restaurant and the pottery on the left-hand side, and cross the bridge over the normally dry river and take the first road on the right after the village sign, with the crags of the summit of La Umbria above you. Walk at first between villas, passing the village cemetery on your right, to fork left at a junction and start to climb as the road loses its surface. On this section there are lots of inviting tracks leading off left; ignore them as they only lead to terraces and keep on upwards towards the crags of Castell de Aixa, 300m above you. Some red markers have been placed, and after about 10 minutes a good road leads off to the left and levels out to contour through orchards and lemon groves. There are excellent views of the ruins of Casellet de L'Ocaive ahead, with the whole valley of Llosa below and the Solana ridge, along which you will travel on your return route, across the valley. Behind you can still pick out Peña Roc, on the Caballo Verde, on the western horizon. Below is a small *finca* hugging the side of the mountain, which you will pass later. Now you can see a noble crag ahead, with a boulder perched precariously on a ledge above you, as the track gives out and the almond groves show neglect. Now wild flowers take over, and in December there is a good display of Alpine Aster (*Aster Alpinus*). There is now a broad almond grove with a tall wall on the right, and you cross it to seek out markers which will lead to the edge of the terrace, where a narrow Mozarabic trail leads off the terrace to zig-zag in a south-westerly direction downwards. Pass a small ruined *casita*, then walk in front of an occupied *finca*, between two water tanks, to seek out a rough, rocky road leading down to the valley bottom and the road, near Km.6.5, where you turn right for a short while, until at Km.7.6 you start your return journey. On a pointed crag on the right-hand side of the road, you can admire the ruins of the tiny castle on its summit, against the skyline of La Solana (494m) (Walk 34).

1hr 15mins   4.5km

Ascent to Castellet De L'Ocaive (Optional – add 4km/2hrs)

A few metres on the village side of Km.7, a steep road (sign Campo de Tiro), surfaced for a short while, leads upwards towards the impressive crag which supports the castle ruins. It ends in a small quarry, the Campo de Tiro, and you wade through used cartridge cases to continue upwards to the castle ruins, passing a water tank on the way.

To the west the twin peaks of the Caballo Verde can be seen, with the village of Benimaurell, and, on the horizon, the Serrella peeping over Alfaro. To the north is the Solana, and you can pick out the track which you will follow from the new urbanisation which is being built as its eastern end.

Down to the Valley Again

Return to the col and now move east, towards a ruined *finca* and a corral, to drop down towards another *barranca* and an ancient path, a little overgrown at times, heading towards a lone pine tree. After you have passed an old ruined *finca* a better path zig-zags down and crosses another *barranca* to climb up to another ridge, where the left (western) side of the *barranca* eventually becomes a good track, leading through almond groves to the main road at a bridge over the Rio Llosa (Km.7.5). There is a picnic ground under the trees. (Add 4km/2hrs/140m ascent.)

Traverse of La Solana De Llosa

Walk up through the imposing archway and landscaped approach to this new urbanisation, Monte Solana. Future walkers will find that they have to pass through villas for a few minutes until the surfaced road ends and you can join the ancient track which heads west towards the skyline. As you climb, the rugged ridge of the Segaria appears to the north-west, rising from the plain of Denia, and in the distance Montgo, with Denia Castle, appears beyond the two small hills at Sella, Picaxos and Peña Roja. Throughout the traverse you will be able to admire the 5km ridge of the Sierra de Castell de la Solana, running from Pedreguer to the highest point at Castell de Aixa (606m) (Walk 34).

When the surface ends, the rough road continues for a short while on the same bearing until it ends and you take off to the right, with a red marker on a rock, to follow a narrow but reasonable path upwards with the help of cairns and markers. There is quite a lot of broken limestone, so take care. Views open up to the south-west of the Forada

Ridge and to the north-west Cruz de Caval, the terminal peak of Sierra de Mediadia, as the gradient eases a little and the track changes direction for a while to north-west. Ahead, in the distance, the villages of Tormos and Sagra appear, whilst below are the villas of the urbanisation at Benidoleig.

The track moves back to south-west as you approach power pylons and set a course in line with Castell de Aixa, on the skyline across the valley. Ahead to the right is a continuation of your ridge, Seguili, above Alcalali, guarding the pass to the Jalón Valley. Also ahead are the peaks of Cocoll and the pointed Tossal de Vaquero, in the Val de Almadich, and to their left the high ground is the Carrascal de Parcent (Walk 22). When this ends in the transmitters on Tossal de Diners, you can just see Puig Campaña, then the Bernia.

Now pass under the electric cables (for the first time), following the track as it weaves from side to side until Sierra Falconera appears to the north-east, near Gandia. There are a number of tracks across this section, but keep heading south-west until you see an old ruin with a lone pine tree to aim for and pass to the right of it as your traverse nears its end. At a cairn you join the trail up from the valley (your return route). It is worth going on a little to find, to the north-east, another old *finca* with a natural rock pool and, finally, another old ruin with lots of Prickly Pear (*Opuntia*), from which you get good views down into the Barranco de Benardo, with its track leading to Orba. Views up the Val de Laguart to the Barranco del Infierno are particularly good from here.

3hrs 30mins   8.5km

Back Down to Llosa De Camacho

Return to the cairn and seek out the start of the old Mozarabic trail which will lead you down to the village again, but it is not easy to find. Make a line for Castell de Aixa, across the valley, and you will find the well-constructed ancient trail, which zig-zags downwards until you reach the first of the village houses, including one under construction, with a tall crane. Time really does stand still in this lovely backwater: the crane has been there since my first visit, over a decade go. A concrete road now leads into the village. There is plenty of hospitality in the Bar Emilio and at the restaurant, Le Perroquet, on the main road by the bridge.

4hrs   10km

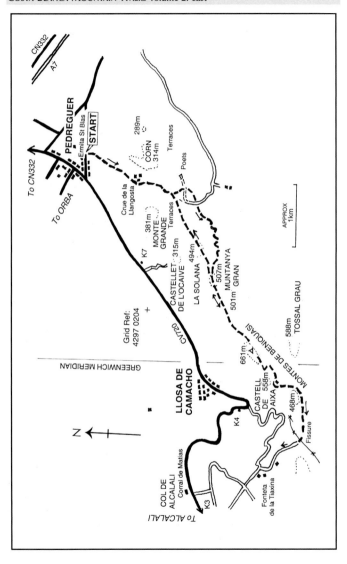

34: CASTELL DE AIXA FROM PEDREGUER

Grade:	moderate
Distance:	15km
Time:	6hrs
Ascent:	500m
Maps:	Benisa 822 (30–32)

The Sierra de Castell de la Solana is an 8km ridge of high ground which extends from Alcalali to Pedreguer, separating the Jalón from the Llosa valley. The new maps not only change the spot heights, but call the mountain Montes de Beniquasi; the highest point, the Castell de Aixa, retains its name however. The route is now being waymarked, and there is a guide sheet issued by the local council, available from the town hall in Pedreguer.

Getting There

Pedreguer lies 1km south of the CN332, 5km north of Gata de Gorgos. Head for the main square, with its interesting ceramics, pass the town hall and keep going up the narrow streets until you reach the ancient Ermita St Blas. There is parking beneath its walls at the end of Carrer El Cid, where there is also an information board and maps of walking routes.

To Barranco De Poets Via Crue De La Llangosta

From the information board head south-west, across the gully of Barranco de Poets and an old Mozarabic trail which is waymarked in yellow and white. On the left of the valley is the hill Corn and on the right is Monte Grande, part of the Solana Ridge. Cross over the *barranco* and note, on your left, the well-constructed ancient Moorish terraces, designed to make every bit of this inhospitable terrain productive. Behind you there are views over Pedreguer, with the *ermita* at the bottom of the *barranco*. The track widens and starts to zig-zag under the high terrace walls of an extensive farmhouse, whilst across the valley there is another old *casita* and a well on the skyline. This old *finca* is Crue de la Llangosta, which, when I first saw it from the ridge,

I mistook for a castle. Pass between its ruins to emerge from the gully, with views now of Montgo to the east, with Cabo Antonio beneath its summit. To the south-east is the Serrella and Tosal de Moro, and you pass a *casita* on the left as you head for the small hamlet of Poets. One of the old *fincas*, on your right, has a collection of wind generators, and on the left notice a well with troughs as your track becomes an unsurfaced road. *1hr   3.5km*

To the west the jagged ridge of the Solana rises above as you walk south-west along the road, with a clear view of the *finca* with the wind generators on the right, and the ruin with a well and troughs on the left. As you gain height, Peñon d'Ifach, Toix and Olta appear to the south, with Caballo Verde, the Bernia and Ferrer Ridges. All too soon you must leave this good road and the waymarkers, as it drops a little into the Barranco de les Fonts and heads for Pedreguer. You leave it to head west up a small rocky barranca (La Ponderosa, marked in the concrete of the road).

To the Col and Muntanya Gran

The track becomes wider as it moves away from the *barranca* to head for two *casitas* on the skyline. Still climbing west with the rocky ridge of La Solana above you, the track levels for a short while then climbs again to gain a broader road, passing a *casita* with a well, and finally zig-zags up to gain the col between La Solana and Muntaña Gran (507m). There are new views now to the north, with the Llosa Valley and the village below, with Sierra Seguili behind it and the vast *huerto* of the Plain of Denia. To the north-west the Segaria, Mediadia and Almasira with the Forada are visible. *1hr 45mins   4.5km*

Along the Ridge to Castell De Aixa

To the south-west, on the northern slope of Muntaña Gran, are three very wide terraces, which when I last did the walk were bright green with a crop of oats. Walk along the track above the upper terrace, with the summit ruins of Aixa in the distance and the intervening ridge of Tossal de Llosa. Follow a good track now to the south-west traversing the northern side of Muntaña Gran, not forgetting to look over your right shoulder to get your first view of the lovely little castle, Castellet de Ocaive, on its improbable crag, below. Reach a ruined *finca*, then the track takes to the south side of Tossal Llosa and climbs towards the summit, with a couple of lonely trees. *2hrs 45mins   7km*

Castell De Aixa

The castle, named after Mohammed's last wife, 'the mother of the faithful', was known to exist in the 12th century as part of the domain of Huydahl al Sahuir, the father of the last Moorish king, Al Azraq, who died at the Battle of Alcoy in 1276. There is little of the castle remaining – probably due to the earthquakes of 1644 rather than to military action. There is a trig point on the summit, with all-round views of most of the mountains of the Costa Blanca.

Along the ridge, to the south-east, you can see all of your ascent route, with Montgo and Denia Castle to the east, and Ibiza far away across the sea. To the left of the remaining summits of the Beniquasi Ridge is the Barranco de la Fontdaxia, leading down to the Font of the same name, whilst in the distance, to the south, there is Peñon d'Ifach, at Calpe, Olta and Toix. To the south-west are the Jalón Valley, with the mountains of Loma Larga, the Bernia and the Ferrer Ridges, whilst in the distance are Puig Campaña, Ponoch and Sanchet. What views, indeed!

Return Down the Ridge to La Solana

Return along the same track to the col, unless you fancy a rocky ridge walk instead, with good views of the whole ridge and with Pedreguer at its north-eastern end. At the col keep to the rocky crest, north-east, to gain the summit of La Solana (494m), either on the crest, or by a track on the right, southern side, but do not descend too much, with the *finca* with the wind generators below you.

4hrs 30mins   11.5km

To Crue de la Llangosta

Leave the ridge by following a good track off the south side, under some crags, and head for an old ruined *finca* with an *era* (threshing floor), with what looks like another castle, Crue de la Llangosta, in the distance, which you will pass by. It is in fact a very large *finca*, but its position on a large spur of rock gives it a distinctive appearance. There are distant views of the coast and Montgo. Pass an old *casita* ruin and gain another trail beyond it on the left and descend into a *barranca*; cross it and climb up the other side for a short distance to reach Crue de la Llangosta. Unless you wish to explore the *finca*, avoid it and descend a good track along the right-hand side of the ravine below it.

5hrs 30mins   14km

Back Down to Pedreguer

Across the other side of the ravine, the ancient terraces are still cultivated with olives and almonds, and you have to admire the determination of those who constructed them to take advantage of every inch of this inhospitable place. Cross over to the other side of the ravine and reach the first house as the Ermita of St Blas comes into view, with a penitent's cross, then continue to your car and the hospitality of Pedreguer.   *6hrs   15km*

Descent from Castell de Aixa to Fonteta De La Tiaxina

If you have left a car at the Fonteta (by leaving the main road at the col, near Km.3, and following a road to the south for 800m), leave the summit and retrace your steps to the south-east until you find a track which descends south-west, under the summit, to gain a col on the ridge between the other peaks of the Beniquasi.   *3hrs 15mins   8km*

From the col, seek out a track heading west of south-west, which leads to the Fonteta de la Tiaxina. First head for some pines and pick up waymarkings, which will lead you down to the Fuente, following a valley on the south side of the Beniquasi Ridge. Pass a well and reach the extensive ruin of an old *finca*, and you can now see the village of Lliber, in the Jalón Valley, and the little hill Montaneta behind it. Walk around the ruins and drop down one terrace to pick up a cairn and the waymarked path, which now heads for the line of pines on the skyline and changes direction a little to the north to reach a col on the edge of the escarpment. Now follow the escarpment west and climb a little to see below you a last col with power lines. Beware of a deep fissure just to the east of the pylon on the col. Now reach a number of cairns which mark the junction with the path down to the Fuente. Follow the track down to the north, pass an old ruin on the left and reach the surfaced road; a few metres to the west (left) is the Fonteta de la Tiaxina.   *4hrs   10km*

Montgo Area

35: MONTGO TRAVERSE FROM JAVEA

Grade:	moderate
Distance:	12km
Time:	6hrs
Ascent:	571m
Maps:	Benisa 822 (30–32)

Montgo certainly stands out from the region's other mountains, being an isolated rocky ridge on the coast between Denia and Javea with, some say, a close resemblance to a sleeping elephant. Certainly from the east, you could imagine the summit as its great head; the trunk sloping down to Cabo St Antonio; the eye, the great cave, inhabited by early man; and the red cliffs as its ears. The back, of course, continues west for some 8km, and the tail is in La Jara. This was my very first ascent in Spain, and a recent traverse of the ridge has shown that not only have vandals demolished the 3m high plinth and the large wooden cross on the main summit, but the mountain's popularity, since my first walk over a decade ago, has resulted in the erosion of the footpaths, which are now much rougher than they were.

This is a lovely traverse, with a steep climb up from the Pla de Just, then a long walk along the elephant's back down to Jesus Pobre. You will, of course, have to organise transport back from Jesus Pobre.

Getting There

From the Javea to Denia road, CV736, turn off west towards the mountain, at Km.2.5, to follow an unsurfaced road for 1km, ignoring a right-hand fork (to the shooting club), until you come to a noticeboard for the Natural Park and find parking for your vehicle.

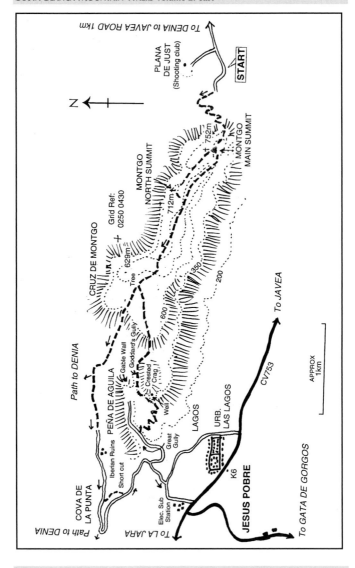

To DENIA to JAVEA ROAD 1km

PLANA DE JUST (Shooting club)

START

N

Grid Ref: 0250 0430

MONTGO NORTH SUMMIT

752m

712m

MONTGO MAIN SUMMIT

CRUZ DE MONTGO

629m

Tree

350

200

600

Path to DENIA

PEÑA DE AGUILA

Gable Wall

Goddard's Gully

Crested Crag

Well

LAGOS

To JAVEA

CV753

APPROX 1km

URB. LAS LAGOS

Iberian Ruins

Short cut

Great Gully

Elec. Sub Station

K6

JESUS POBRE

COVA DE LA PUNTA

Path to DENIA

To LA JARA

To GATA DE GORGOS

Ascent to the Summit

A broad track heads north-west, through scrub and pines, towards the mountain until the track ends and you join a distinct, but rather eroded, Mozarabic trail which will take you right to the summit via the north-east face of the mountain. First the direction is more to the north, below some honey-coloured cliffs, which you will pass on the route. Already you have good views to the south-east of Cabo San Antonio, the watch tower on the cliffs at Rotes, Cabos Martin and Nao and, below, the pilgrims' route, Camino de Colonia, which girdles the lower slopes from Denia. Eventually, the northern track is halted above the deep Barranca Raco Del Buc and swings south, as a marked path joins yours at a cairn. Already, you are high enough to pick out the nearest Balearic island of Ibiza to the east-north-east.   *30mins*

The path levels a little to pass under the cliffs, then steepens in shorter zig-zags to gain height until you leave the track to take to the rock for the final scramble up the arête.   *1hr 30mins   2.5km*

There is no path, but there are one or two red markers to keep you on course; if in doubt, just keep on upwards. Now you get views to the south and south-west including Isodoro, Peñon d'Ifach, Toix, Puig Campaña and many other mountains of Las Marinas. Follow a small ledge on the southern side of the rocks which goes directly to the main summit. An impressive plinth and a lofty wooden cross survived until 1999.   *2hrs   4.5km*

As might be expected, being so isolated, the summit gives excellent all-round views, not only of the coast but of most of the inland peaks, including the northern ones of Almisira, Monte Cabrer and Benicadell. To the north-west are Gandia and Sierra Falconera. To the west, on the northern summit, can be seen a cross commemorating an aircraft disaster in 1938. The decayed original was replaced in 1999 by a cross donated by a local craftsman.

The Long Traverse

Leave the summit and head north-west on a reasonable track across the broad summit plateau until, at some boulders, the path descends on the southern side. A marker on the rock indicates one route to the northern summit, going off to the right. The path, now much eroded, descends to a lone pine tree and a cave. And here again, a better track leads off to the right, north, to the other summit.

Diversion to the Northern Summit

Those who wish to visit the northern summit should now leave the main path and fork right along a narrow track which leads to a rocky arête and, with a bit of scrambling, to Montgo's second summit with its cross in about an hour. You now get a better view of the coast and Denia. Strike down, without a path, and over broken limestone, south, to rejoin the traverse route, just before it starts to climb. Progress will be slow, so add at least one and a half hours to the time.

To Great Gully

You continue to descend on a very eroded path, with the exposed limestone rocks giving the impression that you are walking down the spine of the elephant's skeleton: take care! You will also have to be a supreme optimist to be able to pick out the route – across a shallow valley to climb again to a shoulder. As you start to ascend, just below the cross, those who have been to the northern summit rejoin your route. *3hrs   6km*

As you gain height, you get your first sight of the Great Gully, which divides the southern cliffs and views towards Gandia. Soon you can pick out the honey-coloured cliffs of Gable Crag, on the route from Jesus Pobre (Walk 36). There is a handy tree at the head of the gully, just a little on from where the route across the limestone to Jesus Pobre heads off to the left (south-west). In the middle distance are the two small hills Picaxos and Peña Roja, near the Sella Urbanization. Beyond the jagged ridges of Sierra Mediadia and the Segaria and in the far distance are the towns of Pego and Almisira. *4hrs   7km*

Cross Over to the Northern Side

The well-worn path is now fairly level as you head north for a while, and in season is clothed in a carpet of small iris, 'Barbary Nut'. Now the northern cliffs come into view and as you gain the top of the northern escarpment, Denia and its castle. On the left above you the ridge continues to the Penya de L'Aguila, the site of an early Iberian fortified settlement, and you can pick out the remains of the outer wall as you reach a cairn which marks a dramatic route down a gully to La Pedrera, near Denia. The old Mozarabic trail is much eroded and very steep, but is a good way off the mountain. *4hrs 30mins   9km*

To the Punta De L'Aguila

In 0.5km you pass close to another Iberian wall, and the track now broadens and levels out a little to reach the rocks which mark the end of the main ridge, with a lot of small rock crystals in the strata. Just before you start to descend, note on the left the start of another, more ancient Mozarabic trail, the original route onto the ridge before the bulldozer carved the broad route up to the pass – no doubt paid for by a prospective property developer. (Everyone wants to build on the Montgo – even after it became a Natural Park.) To follow this old trail, leave the main route and turn off left to traverse under crags on an impressive rake until you find cairns which will lead you down, keeping to the left of a large boulder to descend through terraces to the main route.   *5hrs   10km*

Down to Jesus Pobre

As you pass between a rock gateway to change direction to the east, you are still at over 1000ft, with views now over the extensive *huertos* of Denia and Gandia, and to the west the 'tail' of your mountain descending gently down to La Jara, passing another Iberian settlement, at Benimaguia, on the way. As the broad but, at times, rough road descends, passing a cave on the left, Cova de Punta, note a marked trail leading off to the right, which again leads to La Pedrera, via the Urbanizaton La Marguesa, in about an hour. There are views now of Great Gully as you pass through pines to a cairn, where the old Mozarabic trail takes off on the left-hand side towards a large crag and traverses left on a rake to the Punta de L'Aguila. Finally you reach an electricity substation (a good place to find your transport waiting for you) as the now surfaced road leads through a small urbanisation to the main road and the hospitality of Jesus Pobre.   *6hrs   12km*

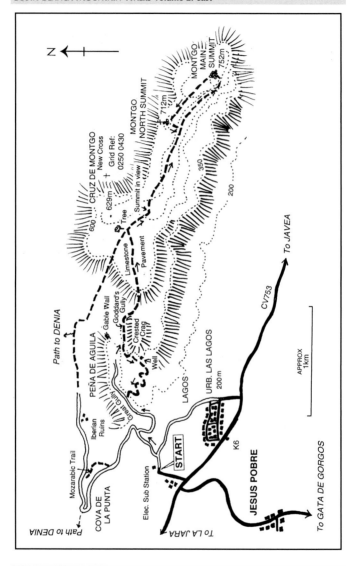

36: MONTGO FROM JESUS POBRE

Grade:	strenuous
Distance:	12km
Time:	7hrs 30mins
Ascent:	593m
Maps:	Benisa 822 (30–32)

Montgo is probably the most identifiable of mountains, a great elephant of a thing (yes, it does look like one when seen from the south). It is isolated from the other Sierras by the flat huerta, and is in close proximity to the coast. Both Denia and Javea shelter under its protection. With the exception of Peñon d'Ifach, it is probably the most popular mountain on the Costa Blanca. The large cross which once graced the main southern summit was once the object of an annual pilgrimage, with the penitents ascending the mountain from Plana de Just at night, carrying torches. There are four normal routes of ascent. This one breaks fresh ground.

Getting There

Jesus Pobre (Poor Jesus) is an unspoilt village 3km north of Gata de Gorgos which sustains a thriving brush-making industry. There are bars, shops and a restaurant. Leave the village and go north to join the La Jara to Javea road (CV753). Turn right in the direction of Javea, and within a few metres turn left (north) through a small collection of villas until the surfaced road ends at an electrical substation. The road, which continues upwards and to the north-west, leads to the Cova de la Punta, which is, in fact, the tail of the elephant, and continues south the entire length of the mountain to the summit. You, however, turn right on a track which at first goes south for a few metres, but settles down to a generally north-easterly direction, heading for the Great Gully, which splits the south-western flank of the mountain.

Making a Start

This walk is mainly on reasonable tracks, but there are some short scrambles, and the middle section, over a featureless area of limestone pavement, is difficult to navigate in poor visibility. Follow the track north-east, and note high above you to the right a handsome crag, Crested Crag, which you will pass on the way down. You cross a clearing and then pass a cairn, which marks the junction with your return route.   *30mins*

Ahead can be seen the rust-coloured Gable Wall, which divides Great Gully from your route (Goddard's Gully). In another few minutes the track narrows and eventually deteriorates into a jumble of boulders, which lead to the base of the wall. Now traverse right and enter Goddard's Gully, which is a rock scramble, passing a sheep-fold built into the crag as the gully narrows and is finally blocked by a wall of rock. Now take to the steep right-hand slope, without the benefit of a path, for 15 minutes until you reach the rim of the gully and can see the vast expanse of the flat limestone pavement to the north-east.
1hr 45mins

Across the Limestone to the Main Summit

You now have about 30 minutes of very rough walking with, at first, no apparent objective to aim for. A bearing of approximately north-east (30°) is the best advice. At present there are some dead trees roughly on the line of your route, which are helpful as markers. Eventually, and thankfully, Denia appears to the north, and the cross on the northern summit of the mountain to the east becomes visible. Finally, you reach a cairn on the ridge track and turn right for the main summit. It is prudent to look around and fix the position of the cairn in your mind, as well as taking a bearing to help you traverse the limestone on your return route.   *2hrs 15mins*

To the Main Summit

There is little need for route-finding now, as you move east on a good track and views open up to the south of Jesus Pobre and Gata de Gorgos, whilst to the south-east Peñon d'Ifach and Olta appear near Calpe. In a very few minutes, you breast a small rocky ridge to see the southern summit ahead. From here, you can also identify the ascent by picking out a large pine tree near a cave, which you will reach in an hour. Beyond the cave, the track leads upwards over some slabs to the broad summit plateau, which once had a massive cross. The plinth of the cross, once 3m high, contained a penitents' offertory box, but has now been demolished by vandals. However, beautiful views open up in every direction. Below you is Cabo St Antonio, with its lighthouse, with the south-east arête in the foreground. This is the route up the mountain from Plana de Just. Note the Val de Laguart, with its high villages to the west, and see if you can pick out the island of Ibiza to the north-east, visible on a clear day.   *3hrs 30mins*

Montgo (Walks 35 and 36) from Segaria, with the low, light-coloured hills of Picaxos and Peñya Roja (Walk 37)

To the Northern Summit

Those with experience of rock scrambling may enjoy a diversion to visit Montgo's other peak, with its metal cross, which commemorates an aircraft disaster. There is a path up onto the rocky ridge just as you leave the summit plateau, but for most of the way you will be on a delightful rocky arête. It will take about an hour to reach the cross, from which you can enjoy some different views down towards Denia. Your penance is, however, to descend to the main track by way of steep broken limestone. Allow an extra hour and a half for this diversion.

The Descent

Retrace your route along the ridge track as far as the cairn.   *5hrs*

Now continue your route across the limestone pavement to the south-west. It is useful to aim for a small urbanisation on the hillside behind Jesus Pobre, with two prominent hills on its right-hand side. In poor visibility, it may be more prudent to continue along the ridge track to the Peña del Aguila on a clear route, which takes you back to the starting place in about 3 hours. Eventually, the red cliffs of Montgo's south flank appear, and when you can identify Gable Wall, reverse the route down once more into the rocky gully and regain the marked path. Watch out for the marked boulder, at which you turn left to head for the base of some cliffs through pines and flat slabs.   *5hrs40mins*

At the base of the cliffs, move right under Crested Crag, where you gain a rough shelf with a water *deposito* dated precisely 11th July 1969.
6hrs

Down to Jesus Pobre

A well-engineered Mozarabic trail now zig-zags down through the pines, and in 1 hour you regain the main track. At present, a number of fallen trees obstruct the path. Continue now to reverse the ascent route back to Jesus Pobre and some well-earned refreshment.
7hrs 30mins

37: PICAXOS AND PEÑYA ROJA

Grade:	moderate
Distance:	8km
Time:	2hrs 30mins
Ascent:	70m
Maps:	Benisa 822 (30–32)

*This modest ridge, rising from the **huerto** of the Rio Girona beside the main Valencia to Alicante road, near to Pedreguer, is crowned by three modest but rocky summits. The two western peaks of Picaxos (244m) have been called the 'Camel's humps', but a more accurate description must be 'Bactrian'. The equally rocky eastern summit is Peñya Roja (242m). Your route is mostly on unsurfaced roads along the 150m contour, and only the short* *ascent and descent are rough walking. Those with the energy to do so can scramble up to the summits, where the views are more extensive.*

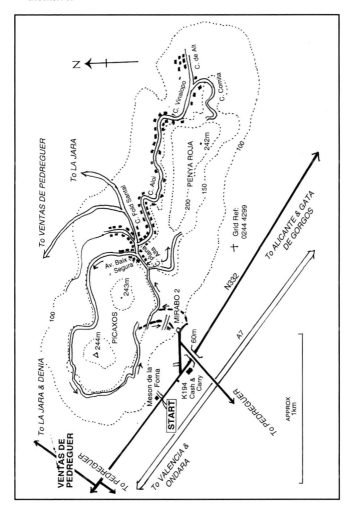

Getting There

Those starting from La Sella or La Jara can reach this walk without any need for climbing by using the estate roads on the northern side of the ridge. For the rest of us the start is at Meson de la Forna, an excellent traditional restaurant at Km.194.5 on the CN332, 0.5km south-east of Ventas de Pedreguer.

The Ascent

Walk south-east along the very busy road, thankfully only for a few minutes, passing the depot of a drilling company on the left and a supermarket across the road, and fork left onto the slip road which leads to the flyover to Pedreguer. Ignore a narrow road on the left, but take the next one and continue on it until you come to a villa, Mirabo 2. On this section you have good views to the south-west of the Segaria Ridge, on the edge of the *huerta*, and the town of Pedreguer with the Ermita San Blas above it, below the mountain of Monte Grande. Above you on the right are the twin summits of your objective, Picaxos.

Ahead, south-east, across the motorway, is the little hill with two windmills on the summit El Molino (180m).

Turn off at the villa onto a good track at a red marker between citrus groves, and in 10 minutes leave it to join a narrow path which climbs through decayed terraces to reach the unsurfaced estate road.

20mins   1km

The Traverse

At the moment only the northern side of the mountain has been developed for housing, so for a little while at least it is possible to enjoy a gentle stroll, with excellent views, on a decent road by courtesy of the builders. In years to come, all that you will be able to admire is the opulence of the villas – so make the best of it.

Turn to the right, south-east. Your gain in height has now given you views to the south-west of Sierra Media Dia and Caballo Verde Ridge, with the town of Gata de Gorgos ahead, with the transmitters on Isadoro, overlooking Benitachell in the distance, on the coast. There are signs of 'civilisation' now – a new rubbish tip on the col between your mountains and the roofs of the first villas.   *7mins   3km*

The map shows a projected road continuing to girdle Peñya Roja, but the developers were a little ambitious, and if you follow it you will reach the point where the bulldozer driver lost interest in the project at some crags. It is, however, a worthwhile diversion, for 10 minutes, with views of Jesus Pobre (more windmills), the Garganta Gorge, Caballo Verde Ridge and Fontdacha.

Northern Traverse

Cross the col to the north side and follow the estate road, through villas with views now, to the north of Benimaquia and Montgo. Turn off left, north-west, onto Carrer de Plana Alta, enjoying civilised walking for a while, whilst ahead can be seen the road continuing to contour under Picaxos. Now climb a short hill back up to the 150m contour, Avinguda de Baix Segura, until it becomes a rough, level track again. Views to the north are of Denia and the coast towards Gandia, as you round the western end of the ridge, and the eastern buttress of Segaria appears above Oliva and the other towns on the plain of Denia. On a clear day, there is a bonus, as the island of Ibiza can be seen across the sea.

1hr 30mins   4km

Back on the South Side Again

The road continues in a south-easterly direction for a short while, with the highest summit of Picaxos above you, until you can see the Meson (and your cars) below you. Again the crags have prevented the constructors from continuing a level road, and it ends. Take off to the right on a narrow and at times rather overgrown mule track to reach another contour road.

2hrs   6km

Bee Warned

This is the road which was used on the southern traverse, but at the time of writing it is as well to heed the apiarist's warning and avoid hives of man-eating bees.

Descent

There is a marked path, which descends through almonds and olives, crosses a water conduit and passes a *deposito* to reach Villa Mirabo 2 to use the outward route back to the start and the hospitality of Meson de la Forna.

2hrs 30mins   8km

38: BENIMAQUIA AND THE IBERIAN RUINS

Grade:	moderate
Distance:	2.75km
Time:	1hr 45mins
Ascent:	160m
Maps:	Benisa 822 (30–32)

Montgo is said to resemble an elephant, with the head over-looking Javea and the trunk reaching down to Cabo St Antonio. This walk on the very western end of the Montgo massif explores the tail of the animal, and for a modest amount of effort you can enjoy extensive views of sea and mountain scenery, whilst pondering on the pre-Christian ruins of another civilisation. There is a little rough walking on the summit. This is one of the few walks which can be reached by using the railway, but remember to remind the guard when you leave Gata (or Denia) that you wish to alight at La Jara, which is only a request stop (apeadero).

There are a lot of interesting features to be seen on this modest walk, evidence of man's impact on the landscape over 4000 years. The earliest are the vineyards, which can be claimed by the Bronze Age about 2000 BC, then the Iberian ruins from the seventh century BC. The orchards of oranges, lemons and many other fruits, along with the irrigation systems still in use today, were innovations of the Clif Abel el Rahuran III in 929 AD, during the Moorish occupation, whilst the 20th century is repre-sented by the railway, the golf course and the beautiful villas just below the summit, which will, no doubt, continue to be built into the 21st century.

Getting There

The walk starts from the Restaurant Punta de Benimaquia, which is near Km.1.5 on the CV735 Denia to Jesus Pobre road. If you use the train, alight at La Jara and walk 0.5km south.

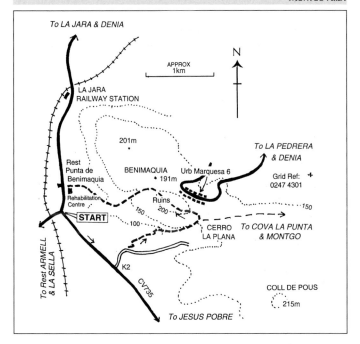

Making a Start

Follow the motor road to the south-east towards Jesus Pobre for 1km, and opposite the hotel near Km.2.7 turn off left along the second track, which has a green barrier and a Montgo National Park sign, just before the Narriot development. There are, at present, no waymarkings on the walk.

To Cerro La Plana

Follow this broad track, which leads east, for only a few minutes before taking off left on a narrow path which climbs steeply in zig-zags. Across the golf course to the south are the small hills of Picaxos and Peña Roja (Walk 37). Pass an old well on the right and a *casita* on the left, and admire the views of the western peaks of the Montgo, Peña de L'Aguila and Cova la Punta on the right. A track joins yours from the left, and then you reach a junction with another track which leads to

Montgo, and you turn off left, west. This is Cerro la Plana; you are on the ridge and views open up to the north with the coast and Denia.

20mins   0.75km

To the Iberian Ruins

For a while the track runs north-west between stone walls. As the exotic roofs of the Moorish-style villas appear (Marquesa 6) you pass a small *casita* which is being restored. Descend on the northern side of the ridge to the road (Calle Medussa) and follow it left (west) until it starts to drop, then take off left to follow a very rough path upwards towards the ruins of Benimaquia. The ruins date from the seventh century BC and are the oldest in the province. Approach and follow the remains of the six defensive towers and wall, and the shape of a number of dwellings can be seen. The southern side was deemed not to need any protection due to the steep crags.   *45mins   1.7km*

Summit Views

To the east Montgo dominates the view and this is one of its best aspects, with Peña de L'Aiguila (where there are the ruins of another Iberian settlement) leading on to the summits. The newly restored memorial cross on the northern summit can clearly be seen.

To the north-east the island of Ibiza is visible on a clear day, and there is the vast *huerto* of the Girona, with the attractive ridge of Segaria and the coast towards Gandia beyond to the north-west. More to the north is Mediadia, and to the west Carrascal de Parcent; the Sierra Bernia blocks further views to the south.

Descent to La Jara

Leave the ruins at the western end through what seems like a gateway and start your descent, without the benefit of a path, towards a pair of trees below and reach some narrow terraces. Follow the fourth one south for a while along a poorly defined path until you reach a decayed Mozarabic trail, which zig-zags down in a westerly direction until it reaches the top of a broad buttress. Follow a track to the west across it and then descend a gully to get your bearings now of La Jara and the motor road below you. Your track ends at the north-east corner of the fence surrounding a rehabilitation centre, near to the restaurant from which you started your walk.   *1hr 45mins   2.75km*

Outlying Areas

39: CRUZ DE BODOIX FROM PEGO

Grade:	moderate
Distance:	11.25km
Time:	5hrs
Ascent;	455m
Maps:	Gandia 796 (30–31), Benisa 822 (30–32)

Bodoix (556m) is a prominent hill to the south of Pego and south-west of another summit which is crowned with the remaining walls of Castillo d'Ambra. Both of these dramatic viewpoints are visited during this circuit, with ever changing views of distant mountains. Being a circuit there are a number of other starting places, but I have chosen the interesting old town of Pego, 20km inland from the coast at Denia. The walk is all on good tracks except for the short, rocky ascent of Cruz de Bodoix, which is optional.

Getting There

From the main coastal road, CN332, turn off west onto the CV3311, immediately to the north of Vergel, with signs for Pego. Leave the CV3311 at the first roundabout and turn left onto Carretera del Mar, and at the second junction bear right along Calle San Rafael to cross the market square. Your objective is the Paseo Cervantes in the south-west corner of the town, but you will have to negotiate a one-way system, made necessary by the old, narrow streets. There is plenty of parking and varied refreshments are available in the Paseo.

Making a Start

Leave the Paseo by the road from the south-west corner and follow the dual carriageway of the Cami del Calvare, with its Stations of the Cross, until you turn off left with a signpost to the Escuela de Escalada (climbing school). Follow the surfaced road for another few metres until the road to the left leads to the school and its practice crags; your

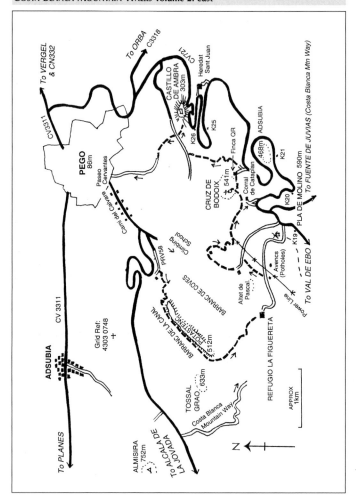

road, to the right, is waymarked and signposted as PRV58 to Refugio La Figuereta and Val de Ebo. After only a few metres bear left at the first junction and right at the second to follow a rather steep, unsurfaced road, which is chained and marked 'privade', preventing vehicles from going any further.

Right from the start of this lovely walk you have good views, which of course improve as you gain height. To the north is the town of Pego, with its two prominent churches and its little *ermita*, in a pleasant setting of orange groves and Lombardy poplars. In the distance to the south-east, across the Barranco de Coves, are two of your objectives – the castle and Cruz de Bodoix.

Refugio La Figuereta

This first part of the route climbs between two valleys, Barranco de Coves on the left and the more dramatic Barranco de Canal on the right, whilst ahead are Crinkle Crags, the end of a rocky ridge, Potastenc (512m). Behind you to the north-east is the jagged ridge of Segaria with Almisera, with its summit transmitters ahead looking quite impressive. The road ahead leads on to an old *finca* which is being restored, but you take off, left, onto an old decayed Mozarabic trail which climbs up, with crags on the left, towards some trees. On the right, Montduva and Azafor come into view to the north as you climb through more pines to reach an old abandoned almond grove with ruined farm buildings. *50mins   1.75km*

The waymarked route is below the wall on your left but it is badly obstructed by rampant fan palms! The view is now to the south-south-east of Sierra de Mediadia, while below to the right are the impressive depths of Barranco de Canal and ahead is a large cave in the eastern buttress of the Potastenc Ridge. Behind are Crinkle Crags, as you cross a small col to follow waymarks along the northern flank of the ridge below the crags, with the *barranco* on your right.

When you reach the end of this traverse, climb a little to round the western end of the ridge and, still following marker posts, climb south-east towards a grove of trees on the horizon which mark the *refugio*, with Cruz de Bodoix to the left. As you reach the top of your ascent take an unsurfaced road with the Refugio La Figuereta on the right. This is a mountain hut run by Pego Council and has very basic accommodation for 40 climbers. *2hrs   3.25km*

To Pla De Molino

The road from the *refugio* leads south-east and climbs a little until ahead, to the east, is Monte Negra, overlooking the Molino Pass and then Mediadia, whilst to the south, in the far distance, are the Caballo Verde Ridge, Serrella Castle and the Forada. On the right is the peak of Tossal Grau (633m), whilst on the skyline, in the far distance, is Benicadell. Between this point and the motor road at Km.19.2, there are three *avencs* (potholes) which have been well explored and documented by local enthusiasts (marked on the map), and as you reach the end of the road there are excellent views of the dramatic depths of the Barranco de Infierno Gorge, with the Carrascal de Ebo beyond. Shortly before you reach the road a waymarked path leads off right down to Val de Ebo and the nearest refreshments.

To Finca De Quatre Robles
Alternative

You can avoid this section by following the unsurfaced road then turning left to descend by the motor road to rejoin the route at the *finca* for the descent back to Pego.   *1hr 30mins*

Main Route

Just after a marker on the right of the road indicating the route to a pot hole, on a bend under an electric power line, leave the road and climb, without the benefit of a regular path, to the north, heading for a col on Altet de Pascal. At the top you can see your route, a broad unsurfaced road below you to which you descend and turn left. The road has come in from the Paso de Molino. In 10 minutes leave this road and follow a narrow track north along a broad ridge. Below the ridge to the right (east) is an old *finca* which is on your route, whilst above is the highest part of the walk, the peak of Bodoix with its cross.

Follow the intermittent path for about 10 minutes until, at a cairn, descent to the right down through the terraces to the ruins of the old *finca* with its *era*.   *2hrs 40mins   4.5km*

You now find a good, clear path heading north-east towards your goal, Cruz de Bodoix and a lone pine tree on a col to its right which is your next objective. The path negotiates the head of two *barrancos* and then climbs to the col, where you get views down to the winding, tortuous motor road leading up from Pego towards Val de Ebo, the most demanding road on the Costa.   *3hrs 10mins*

Note now a track leading down on the right to the road, which is an escape route for those who wish to avoid the arduous ascent to the summit of Cruz Bodoix. The path descends through terraces, which at the time of writing are cultivated with cereals to tempt game birds to tarry, then joins a rough road from an extensive *finca*, Corral de Cataplan, and reaches the motor road near Km.21. It is only a short walk down the road to the next *finca*, Casa de Quatre Robles.

Ascent of Cruz De Bodoix

This is not recommended in wet conditions, when, in any case, it is unlikely that there will be a rewarding view from the summit.

Follow the ridge from the lone pine. There is a good path on the northern side, past a small well, and when the path runs out address yourself with determination to a short but vigorous ascent of about 100m over broken limestone and boulders heading, as best you may, for the summit cross, avoiding the main rock pitches.

There is a rusty metal cross installed on the summit with a cut-out of a chalice and the host. The old decayed wooden cross lies abandoned below you.

As might be expected from such an isolated, even though modest, peak, the vistas in every direction are excellent as you renew acquaintance with the mountains identified earlier. To the north, of course, Pego, at the end of the walk, dominates the view, but beyond you can see the coast as far as Gandia. Your next objective, the castle, looks well from this vantage point, and note below you, to the east, the large *finca* with its four mature oaks, which is your key to the descent.

Descent to Casa De Quatre Robles

I have never fully appreciated the joy of descents over broken ground, and this one is far from pleasant. Pick your route carefully between the boulders and try to keep heading to the right, remembering that the *finca* is to the east. I have heard that some valiant souls prefer to descend the sharp rocky ridge direct to the *finca*, and I wish them well.

Eventually you descend through old abandoned almond terraces to easier slabs and can explore this long neglected farm, with its well, corral for the animals, oven and old *era*. How long it has been since wheat was threshed here can be guessed by the age of the four magnificent oak trees which now claim the site.

Follow a broad road in the direction of the motor road, but in 5 minutes turn off to the left with a waymarking to join a good path down to Pego.   *3hrs 30mins   7.75km*

Down to Pego

Now follow a good track, north, descending with waymarkings and zig-zagging to lose height, passing an old ruin on the left, to pass under power cables before gaining a broad unsurfaced road.

4hrs   9.25km

Turn right and follow this road to the north-east, and in a very short while a signpost indicates the path up to the castle.

Diversion to the Castel – Castillo De Ambra

This well-worn path climbs up to join the main unsurfaced road which comes up from the motor road. Turn off to gain the remains of the castle. Return the same way.

The castle, which is of Arabic origin (although artefacts would seem to indicate a Roman and Iberian site), guarded the entrance to the Val de Ebo and was in the possession of Al Azarac until 1258. The thickest walls are on the vulnerable south side, while cliffs protect the north. Sadly this commanding site has been obliged to accommodate modern antennae. *Allow 1 hr*

The Final Section

Continue along the good road (it will eventually join the motor road to Val de Ebo near Km.1) and watch out for a yellow and white marker on a wall which indicates a change in direction to the left. Unfortunately waymarkers on this section are sparse, but near a large boulder on your left descend one terrace and persevere until you find a good track; this passes a water tank with vine trellis installed on its top, where you join a broad road and walk through orange groves, passing the municipal football field, to join Calle San Pedro and return to the Paseo. *5hrs   11.25km*

40: TOSSAL DEL MORO

Grade:	moderate
Distance:	8.5km
Time:	3hrs 30mins
Ascent:	293m
Maps:	Benisa 822 (30–32)

40a: SERRILLAS

Grade:	moderate
Distance:	14.5km
Time:	6hrs
Ascent:	423m
Maps:	Benisa 822 (30–32)

This delightful walk through the valley of the Rio Gorgos to ascend a modest peak lends itself to a number of variations. The route described here starts and finishes at Gata de Gorgos, but, firstly, the ascent of Tossal del Moro (in less than 1 hour) can be added to the walk. The walk can also be extended by ascending to the summit of Serrillas and continuing along the ridge to descend to Gata via a barranco. For those who are desperately short of time and for 'peak baggers', cars can safely be taken along the first hour of the route.

There is a handy, if rather anonymous, bar in the square.

To Fuente De Mata

Head south, crossing the bridge over the dramatic gorge of the Rio Gorgos (the Rio Jalón until it gets here). It is well worth a visit after winter rains have brought the river to the surface. Continue on, with the school at the end of the road, and take the last street on the right, Carre San Jose, at the end of which turn left again onto the Cami De Fuente Mata and a lonely waymarking in yellow and white. In 0.5km,

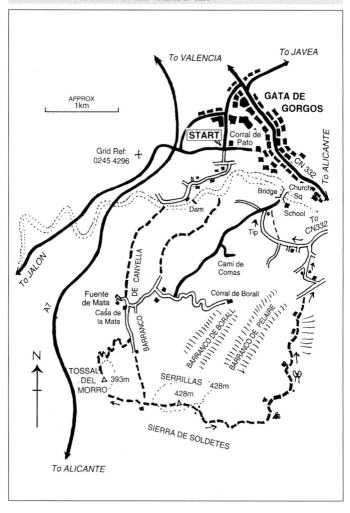

fork right at a junction with another road (your return route if you extend the walk to Serrillas).

Ahead, as you head mainly south-west, are the rocky arêtes on the western flanks of Fontdacha, in the Jalón Valley and beyond the Carrascal de Parcent. This is a delightful road: no traffic, good surface and no real gradient as it rises and falls on its gradual climb of about 100m to the Fuente. Above you, on the left, is the highest point of the Sierra de Soldetes, Serrillas (428m). The sierra is better known for its eastern crags, which overlook the defile of La Garganta (famous for its quarries) on the road between Gata and Benissa. Over your shoulder you can look back on the bulk of Montgo. Ignore a road on the left, and then across the valley can be seen the route up from Corral de Pato, passing between small *casitas*. Now, ahead above you can be seen the ruins of the Masa de Mata as you descend into the Barranco de Canyella and climb up to the ruins, passing signs on the left which indicate your descent route.

This was a very extensive *finca*, with its *era* and a very unusual building, half buried, but with a beautifully constructed stone 'barrel roof' and no apparent entrance except for two small square holes in the roof. (Any ideas?) Beyond the ruins, the track drops down a little to the *fuente* (passing a narrow waymarked path on the right, which has come up from Corral de Pato).

The *fuente*, a spring issuing from a grotto, festooned with shade and moisture-loving plants (which have a hard time here on the Costa), is an idyllic place to rest and even have a meal on the seats and table thoughtfully provided by the authorities. *1hr   3.25km*

To the Col

In front of the *finca* ruins is a broad unsurfaced road which heads south, and you follow it in the direction of the col between your peak, Tossal del Moro, and its neighbour Serrillas. There are now yellow and white waymarkings for a short while, thoughtfully providing a *paseao* for those taking lunch at the *fuente*. These markings are lost as your road crosses another marked track. The track on the left you shall use on your descent. Turn left and continue along the broad road up the right (western) side of the Barranca de Canyella; the concrete road on the right is the direct route up to the summit for 'peak baggers'. Now pass through what once must have been a prosperous farm, with broad terraces and orchards, to reach the ruins of a *finca* on the left. As the terraces come to an end, cross over to a narrower and rather overgrown path on the eastern side, which starts to climb towards the col. Pass a small ruin on the opposite side of the *barranca* as the more extensive ruin on the col comes into view ahead. Take to some broad terrace walls as the path becomes overgrown, and as you do so note the track heading for the summit of Serrilla on the left. At the col views now open up to the south of the coast, with Peñon d'Ifach, Toix, Olta, the town of Benissa, with its distinctive church, and eventually the Bernia.

1hr 30mins   5km

To the Summit

Pass the old *finca* and its well on the left to follow a path for a few metres, until another path to the summit forks off right, directly in line with the summit above you. Your bearing is north-west, and the path, which is sometimes difficult to find, will with care lead right to the summit. For the first section, a line of metal notices (hunting rights) is a rough guide. On the upper sections there are a number of cairns (help them grow please). After crossing a collapsed terrace wall reach the ruins of a shelter right on the highest point.   *2hrs   5.5km*

Views

To the south-east, with its transmitter masts, is Isadoro, near Benitachell, with Montgo to the north-east. To the south is the Bernia Ridge, and south-west, behind it, is Puig Campaña. To the north are Aixorta, Rates, Carrascal de Parcent, Cocoll, Orba Castle and the Caballo Verde. To the north-west lies Gandia with Segaria and Mediadia, whilst across the sea is Ibiza, the nearest Balearic island.

Descent to Fuente De Mata

Reverse your ascent route, and when you have passed the *finca* take off on a right-hand track which is marked in yellow and white for a short cut that will lead through a sylvan glade back to the road, just below the *finca* De Mata. All that is now required is to enjoy your stroll back to Gata de Gorgos for refreshments.

Variation – Ascent of the Serrillas

From the old *finca* in the col, leave the track down the *barranca* and join a narrow track which climbs steeply to the east, direct for the summit of the highest point on Sierra Soldetes, the Serrillas (428m), where there is a trig point and better views to the east.   *30mins*

Return, if you wish, to the col and rejoin the normal descent route to Fuente de Mata.

Traverse East and Descent Direct to Gata

Leave the summit and keep going east along the ridge, but leave it when it starts to descend steeply over rocks into the Barranco de Pelaire (there is a route, but it is rough and unmarked). A much more civilised route is to make for the two ruins of old *fincas* below on the southern side of the ridge, by way of another, easier ridge; this has some cairns, and on the lower slopes a line of metal hunting markers are of some assistance.   *1hr 10mins   2km*

From the second *finca*, keep on east along a good track which seems to have been used by tractors to supply water to animals during the summer. The high ground is on your right and would eventually lead you to the great gorge, La Garganta, where the main road and the railway cut through the Soldetes. You keep below the ridge as the track leads south, but only for a short while, before heading east again along some broad terraces to a trough and water drums. Montgo is ahead as you pass through some pines now and head east again for another set of terraces.   *1hr 40mins*

The second set of broad terraces also has a water trough and a supply for animals, as you cross the broad terrace to reach a large cairn which marks your track down to the valley of the Gorgos again.

Head first for the summit of Montgo as you drop down a little to the north to reach a deep, domed well.   *2hrs   4km*

From the well set a course to the north, heading first for the middle of the Montgo ridge, along a very rough track, with the help of some cairns (please help them grow). On the coast, to the east of Montgo, can be seen the capes of Nao and San Antonio, as the town of Gata now appears below you. Head for and cross a patch of bare limestone as the railway bridge across the gorge of the Rio Gorgos comes into view. Below, you should also be able to pick out a grassy lane running through orchards, which is your next objective as you descend between two ravines, Pelaire on the left and an innominate one on the right.

On the left ahead is a small pointed rock which you will pass on your left, with some rough sections before you gain the cart track.
                    2hrs 30mins   5.5km

Back Down to Gata

Turn off at a junction, down to the left, and continue until the road gains a surface, passing a *casita* and in 0.5km a clearing where the track down the *barranca* from the summit of Serrillas joins from the left. Continue as the road now leads north for a while, until at a junction you turn left, west, for a while (the road on the right will lead back to the CN322). The road climbs a little, passing a riding school on the left, with good views of Fontdacha ahead. Keep right at another road junction to pass an abandoned sports field on the right and the town tip on the left-hand side, until the road swings north again to join the main valley road back to Gata (there is a footpath shown on the map which will provide a short cut). *3hrs 30mins*   *8.5km*

41: ALCALA DE LA JOVADA CIRCUIT

Grade:	moderate
Distance:	13km
Time:	5hrs 30mins
Ascent:	200m
Map:	Alcoy 821 (29–32)

The valleys of the Ebo and Alcala are as isolated and remote as they have always been, although in recent times adventurous coach drivers have ventured over the slightly improved roads bringing determined tourists from Benidorm. In the past, these valleys were part of an ancient Moorish kingdom, so it is not surprising to find so many 13th-century relics.

The walk takes you past the ruins of Al Azrac's former capital. Al Azrac was a Moorish wazit, who was born in the village of Alcala de la Jovada about 1213 and died in battle against the Christians in Alcoy in 1276. Despite having been treated generously after an earlier defeat, he was leading the Moors in revolt against the King of Aragon, James I. His castle (Benisili) can be seen to the north at the western end of the Forada Ridge.

The walk is all on forestry roads which are normally in good condition.

Getting There

From Pego follow the CV712 through Val de Ebo to Alcala de la Jovada.

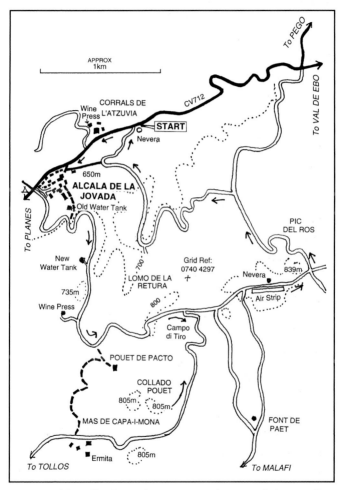

From Jalón Valley leave the CV720 road to Castell de Castells at Km.28.5, with a signpost for Val de Ebo and the Pinturas Rupestres (prehistoric cave paintings), passing on the way the ruins of an ancient *ermita* (Pixacos) on the right-hand side. At Val de Ebo turn left with signs for Alcala de la Jovada and pass the interesting caves, La Cueva Del Rull, discovered in 1919 and now open to the public (11am–5pm).

From Planes head along the CV700 east towards Pego, turning off at Km.21 towards Margarida then on to Alcala de la Jovada.

There is parking at the picnic place near Km.6.5.

To the Ancient Remains of Adsubia

Walk (west) towards the first houses, but just past Km.6 turn off to the right to explore the ruins of Al Azrac's original capital, Adsubia, with an old *finca*, Corrals de Llatzuvia. The village was abandoned in 1610 when the last remaining Moors were deported to Africa, being considered unreliable whilst Spain was at war with the Ottomans. You can find other Moorish ruins on the left-hand side of the road back to Val de Ebo. These were the original Moorish village of Cariola.

The valley was repopulated in the 17th century with settlers from Majorca and other parts of Spain.

In Adsubia, just off the road on the right-hand side, are the remains of a 19th-century wine/olive press carved out of the rock. The wine presses are redundant now due to the spread of phylloxera some 60 years ago, which destroyed the vines. Whilst other villages imported foreign vines, Alcala was either too poor or too abstemious to do so.

35mins

Into the Village

Retrace your steps to the main road and follow it right, turning off along a narrow road on the left to enter the village, which during weekdays is a haven of peace and quiet. In the little square is the house, where it is believed Al Azrac lived (No. 6). Reminders of what he is supposed to have looked like appear on the water fountain and on a memorial to him. There is an information office open at weekends.

Pass an old wash-house on the right (still used), between soaring stone houses which seem to sprout from the rocks, as does the ancient church on your left. Dedicated to La Virgen de los Desamparados (the virgin of the helpless), it was converted from a mosque when the Christians came back in the 17th century. There is a fountain and a bust of Al Azrac against the church wall, and you take the next turn to the left to enter the square, Placa del Bisbe Vilaplana, and see another monument to him built into a *fuente*. Pass the Casa Consistorial and head for the top left-hand corner of the square, where there are the remains of a Moorish tower, used now as an information office.

Ascent to Mas De Capa I Mona

On the left of the tower is Carrer la Torre, and you follow this street until the road ends in a path, which follows the right-hand side of a valley towards a new white water tank. Pass an old water cistern on the right and then cross an old aqueduct which carried the village's water supply in days gone by and follow the faint track amongst rocks to gain a broad forestry road. Turn left, south-east, passing a modern water tank (a present from the EEC) on the right, and in about 1km, on a very sharp bend, with a *casita* on the left of the road, follow another track off to the right for about 150m to admire another 19th-century wine press, again carved out of the rock, about 30m on the right-hand side. The discoverer has carved his name and the date on a nearby rock.   *1hr 30mins*

Return to the road at the *casita* and continue on your way, but stop on an acute bend to note below you on the right a small Moorish tower which marks the spring which was the site, in 1244, of Al Azrac's surrender to James I. A reasonable path can be followed into the *barranca* to visit the tower. Those who have made this diversion can, if they wish, continue south-west to arrive at the next destination, Mas De Capa I Mona. There is one snag, however: there isn't a reliable path to follow, only sheep tracks.

Continuing along the original route, a little further on take the road which forks to the right and then pass through the remains of an ancient holly oak forest, passing a *campo de tiro* (shooting range), and in 2km arrive at Mas De Capa I Mona, a 17th-century fortified farm house which was worked as a farm until 1950, but has since suffered from decay and vandalism.   *2hrs 30mins*

The need to fortify such a remote settlement against raids by Berber pirates is explained by the presence amongst the raiders of former inhabitants of the valley, who had sufficient local knowledge to advise the raiders.

You are now at over 700m, with a panoramic view of the surrounding mountains. Starting from north there is the Forada, with Benisili Castle, then, moving anti-clockwise, Azafor, Benicadell, the Mariola, Serrella, Pla de la Casa, Alfaro, Aixorta, Cocoll, Sierra Carrasca, Almisira and finally the Mediterranean.

To Pic Del Ros and Nevea Altas

Return the way you came to the fork, past the *campo de tiro*, and turn right, east. Note two roads leading off to the right which join at a lovely picnic spot, Font de Paet (4km diversion). Now arrive at a fire brigade tower and an air strip, onto which you turn right (south-east). Walk along the airstrip, with a water tank on the right and the Nevera Alta on your left. At a crossroads turn left and start your descent back to the village.   *4hrs*

Back to Alcala De Jovada

After about 1km, turn off to the left on a rougher but still reasonable road, which negotiates the Barranco Hondo and climbs out (keeping right at the top) to meet a track coming up from the village. Turn right at this junction and continue north to pass the Nevera Baixa on the right and reach the end of the walk. The *nevera*, which was used to store ice on its journey to the coast, is 18th century and has a capacity of 700 square metres. It has a lower access to remove the ice.

Refreshments will be found in the lower village at the sports centre.

5hrs 30mins

42: BARRANCO DEL INFIERNO

(route by Roger Massingham. See also *Costa Blanca Mountain Walks*, volume 1, 'Costa Blanca Way, Stage 2: Val d'Ebo to Fleix')

Grade:	**British VDiff, continental Grade 3 (climbing grade)**
Distance:	**1.5km**
Time:	**4–5hrs**
Map:	**Benisa 822 (30–32)**
	(See also map to Walk 28)

The Barranco del Infierno is a cave without a roof. Traversing it is one of the most exhilarating mountaineering experiences on the Costa Blanca. Those who have skills in caving or climbing should have no difficulty at all in getting through the gorge. It is a fairly easy climb even for the very inexperienced, providing there is a competent and experienced climber/leader.

A word of warning. *There have been numerous rescues in this gorge and a few fatal accidents. The majority of these incidents were caused through inexperience and being ill-equipped.*

In all there are some five rope pitches or drops to descend and at least four considerable wells or swirl holes to traverse, with the odd little rock obstacle in between. None is of great difficulty to experienced rope handlers, although extreme caution must be taken due to very precarious rescue conditions. It is not wise to try this in wet weather as the gorge is prone to flash flooding. Local knowledge or advice is essential if attempting this route after storms as the state of some pitches are then in constant flux. Sometimes swirl holes are full of debris, other times they are full of water, too deep to wade through. After such conditions any pegs and ropes remaining need to be treated with extreme caution.

The climb through is approximately 1.5km long, this being the throat of the gorge. In parts it is so narrow it is possible to reach out and touch both sides, and in other places so high and narrow you can't see the sky. It is as formidable as it is beautiful.

Equipment

The gorge is regularly traversed and is fully equipped with bolts. You will need climbing rope (at least 30m), safety line/rope (30m), harness if possible, safety helmet, gloves (not Nylon), six or more karabiners, etriers, descenders or other rappelling device, caving ladder (10m) – not necessary but useful, variety of slings, good climbing tape for tying off and abandoning, and lots of drinking water. It goes without saying that personal safety equipment, stout boots, first aid equipment, torch, clothes, etc., should be present in your day sack.

Time

The approach to the descent is from Val d'Ebo. Follow the track along the river bed for about 5km. You will arrive at the neck in about an hour or so. A much more sensible approach is to leave the CV721 from Pego to Val de Ebo at Pla de Molinos Km.19 and drive south along the new surfaced road for 3km to Font de Juvias, where the car may be parked. Using the map for Walk 28 (10,000 Steps) retrace your steps to follow the route down to the river bed (waymarked PRVI 47), where the first pitch is 15 minutes on the left, downstream.

After emerging from the gorge follow the river bed downstream until you can ascend the Camino de Juvias (see same route) back up to your car.

There is also a signposted route (PRVI 47) from Col de Garga, above Benimaurell (see Walk 27). Cars can be taken 4km along an unsurfaced road. The start of the climb is fairly obvious. Give a comfortable 4–5 hours to complete the climbing part and, if you go out through Fleix, another 2 hours or so to climb out. These times are only approximate; depending on the size and ability of the party these could be considerably altered. The above estimate is based on a first trip through for a party of four adults, in fairly good shape, and with one experienced climber leading. The grade of climbing skill required is about a good V.Diff (Grade 3).

Pitch 1   A short 4m drop. *Belay:* bolt(s) on the face.

Pitch 2   A short 4m drop slightly more exposed and overhanging than the first. *Belay:* bolt(s) on the face.

Pitch 3   A shallow well with an 8m wall with five bolt holes on the right wall. Here, especially in wet conditions, you must do an aid traverse using etriers, etc. Once round and on the lip of the well you will find a bolt to secure a caving ladder for the rest of the party to ascend (could be very time consuming for all the party to traverse). A short rope from the same bolt is needed to drop down off the lip onto the other side.

Pitch 4   A 10m overhanging drop into a well. Because of a difficult edge, start-off is easier done with a caving ladder. *Belay:* Bolts on the face. **Once down this pitch you are committed to complete the climb as return is only possible by very experienced rock climbers, and at great risk, or by prudent climbers who have left a fixed rope in place.**

Pitch 5   A bit of a tricky traverse along the right side of a stagnant pool (4m) finishing on a precarious narrow ledge (room for two only) which gives onto pitch 6. *Protection:* bolts on the face.

Pitch 6   A 6m ladder or rappel drop. *Belay:* bolt(s) on the face.

Pitch 7 A 4m traverse on the left wall of a stagnant well. The wall initially had bore holes with pegs in to walk across; use these as best you can as hand holes. Quite intricate moves involved here: rock dancers will enjoy the moves; the not so agile will get a wet boot. *Protection:* bolts on face.

Pitch 8 A short drop of 2m off which you lower yourself or jump down.

Pitch 9 The final and longest traverse, being some 30m, and the most exposed. Below is a deep well; a shepherd who ventured alone here fell in and, unable to climb the smooth sides, drowned. A slightly difficult start to the climb on the left wall leads onto a series of iron pegs and a fixed rope (not to be counted on) on which to swing along. This ends on another small ledge, enough for two people, where a bolt belay should be used to rope the rest of the party round the well and down the next and last pitch.

Pitch 10 As you bring someone round the wall to your stance it is advisable to keep them roped up to manoeuvre the very intricate move onto the last wall. This is a 10m drop furnished with iron rungs to climb down. The difficulty here is that the rungs are not entirely visible from the top. To help gain the first rung you have to lower yourself down a smooth wall. A bolt is placed above where you can fix a sling to hang on to. The last climber must take great care here. Indeed the last one down or across each pitch should be top roped. This is where the climbing tape is necessary in order to tie a piece off to come down on, and so abandon.

Pitch 11 A free ground-level traverse on the right round a boulder; no danger here, it just saves getting your boots wet. And you're out!

Appendixes

1. Costa Blanca Mountain Walkers

'An informal group of those happy people who enjoy taking strenuous exercise in the magnificent Sierras of the Levant, formed to provide companionship on the mountains, sharing enjoyment and knowledge of the high places of the Costa Blanca.'

What was true in May 1987, when the group was formed on the summit of the Peñon d'Ifach, is still true today. We have always resisted the temptation to form a 'club', and remain still extremely informal. There is no membership, therefore no membership fee. The modest expenses of organising the group are provided for by members donating 200 pesetas (twice per year), for which they receive a full programme of walks and a comprehensive newsletter, which keeps them in touch with group activities. All other publications, badges, etc., are the responsibility of individual members who voluntarily accept this work, subject only to two criteria: (a) that the items be supplied at cost to members, and (b) that no charge falls on the group.

The group comprises about 50 regular residents of the Costa Blanca, supplemented by an increasing number of 'Winterers' and, of course, holiday-makers.

Every season, from the beginning of October to the end of May, the 20 Leaders of the Group (Cuerpo del Guias) take over 2000 walkers into the mountains and, what is more important, bring them back again, tired but elated. We basically still remain an English-speaking group but, at the last count, 21 nationalities were identified. In 1993, we welcomed our first Spanish leader, with the distinguished name of Cristobal Colon (Christopher Columbus).

We maintain friendly relations with all other walking groups on the Costa Blanca, especially the Spanish Mountaineering Clubs at Alcoy, Altea and Calpe.

In 1992, the group celebrated its fifth anniversary in grand style, again on the summit of the Peñon d'Ifach. Founder members were invested with special souvenir medals, and the chairman was pleased to present certificates to those who had completed the Costa Blanca Mountain Way. This 100–150km long-distance walk, right across our walking area, Las Marinas, was instituted especially to celebrate our fifth anniversary.

In our fifth anniversary year, we were flattered and gratified to find that Lookout Magazine (the premier English-language magazine in Spain) had chosen our Group out of 80 others to feature on the cover and in the main article as 'an example of a new type of Club and a new type of resident, a Group of active people who desire to know Spain better'.

Walking is probably the most popular recreation on the Costa Blanca, and mountain walking is the quintessence of this pastime. Although we are the oldest-established walking group in this area, there are now many more informal groups, some founded by our own members who were dissatisfied with only one walk in the mountains per week. Costa Blanca News (Friday) and the Weekly Post (Sunday) are published weekly, and The Entertainer (Fridays) is available free at supermarkets and some newsagents. All these publications give details of walks by Costa Blanca Mountain Walkers and other walking groups.

The walking season starts at the end of September, and usually over 50 walks are provided before the season ends, with our AGM on the last Wednesday in May. During the summer months, leaders meet once each month for lunch, sometimes including a short stroll, and those members who are still in Spain are more than welcome to join them.

The Publications Secretary of the group provides members with updates and booklets.

Anyone who completes the first five sections of the Costa Blanca Way is entitled to become a compañero. Certificates and badges are available at a modest charge, on submission of a suitable log. Information is available from the Secretary of the group (see local press for information) or through Cicerone Press.

2. Useful Reading

Recommended Guidebooks in English

Michelin Guide to Spain
Berlitz Guide to the Costa Blanca
Guide to Costa Blanca (Alicante Tourist Board)
Alicante & Costa Blanca Guide (ANAY Touring Publications)

Recommended Rock Climbing Guides

Rock Climbing Guide to the Peñon d'Ifach by Juan Antonio Andres Martinez (published by the author in Spanish, English, French and German): lavishly illustrated in colour, but no written descriptions of the routes.

Costa Blanca Climbs by Chris Craggs (Cicerone Press): excellent guidebook in the traditional English style and gradings.

Topo guides to one of the most popular rock climbing locations in the area, Sella, can be purchased at the bar in the village square, or up the valley at a climbers' refuge below the crags.

Geology

The Geological Field Guide to the Costa Blanca by C.B. Moseley (Geologists' Association)

Ornithology

Country Life Guide to the Birds of Britain and Europe by Bertel Bruun (Country Life)

Botany

Flowers of South-West Europe by Oleg Polunin and B.G. Smythes (Oxford)

Flowers of the Mediterranean by Oleg Polunin and Anthony Huxley (Chatto and Windus)

Wild flowers of Spain (3 booklets) by Clive Innes (Cockatrice)

Wild flowers of Southern Spain by Betty Molesworth Allen (Mirador Books, Malaga, 1993): covers Andalucia but applicable to Costa Blanca area.

Wildlife

Wildlife in Spain by John Measures (Crowood Press)

General Reading

Iberia by James Michener (Fawcett)

Spain by Jan Morris (Penguin)

As I walked out one Midsummer Morning by Laurie Lee (Penguin)

The Spaniards by John Hooper (Penguin)

The Spaniard and the Seven Deadly Sins by Fernando Diaz Plaja (Pan)

Culture Shock Spain by Marie L. Grafe (Kupera)

Spain by Dominique Aubler and Manuel Tunon de la Lara (Vista Books Longmans)

Marching Spain by V.S. Prichett (Hogarth Press)

The Face of Spain by Gerald Brenan (Penguin)

Lookout Magazine: publishes handy books on many topics relating to living in Spain, from cooking to the law, but most of the guidebooks relate to Andalucia.

The Story of Spain by Mark Williams: covers the whole country.

3. Glossary

The Mapas Militar normally use Castellano as their language, except for some place names which are in the Valenciano language. In recent editions of the maps, however, there is an increasing tendency to replace Castellano with Valenciano, no doubt in sympathy with the revival of this ancient language. This short glossary includes those terms which occur most often on maps and in guides.

Castellano	Valenciano	English
Alto/Collado	Alt	High Place
Arroyo	Rierra	Stream
Bancal	Bancal	Terrace
Barranco	Canal	Gully or ravine
Camino	Cami	Road
Casa	Casa	House
Casa de la Branza	-	Farmhouse
Casa de Molino	Moli	Mill
Cascada	Cascada	Waterfall
Castillo	Castell	Castle
Cauce Seco	Caixer Sec	Dry river bed
Cima/Cumbre	Cim	Summit
Colina	Tossal	Hill
Collado	Col	Col
Cordillera/Sierra/Cadena	Serra	Mountain range
Corral	Corral	Cattle pen/small farm/hamlet
Embalse	Embassament	Reservoir
Finca	Finca	Country house/ Farm
Fuente	Font	Fountain or spring
Hoyo	Forat	Hole
Lago	Llac	Lake
Lomo	Llom	Shoulder
Montana	Muntanya	Mountain
Nevera	Nevera	Ice-pit
Paso/Puerta	Pass/Port	Pass
Penn/Peñon	Penja/Penyal	Cliff, crag, or mass of rock
Pennaco	Penyal	Crag
Pozo	Pou	Well
Presa	Presa	Dam
Punta/Pico	Punta/Punuxa/Pic	Peak
Rio	Riu	River
Ruinas	Ruinas	Ruins
Senda	Sender	Footpath
Simas	Avenc	Pot-holes & fissures
Valle	Val	Valley

4. The Countryside

One of the main differences between the countryside and that of Britain is the almost total absence of manor houses and stately homes, set in parkland. Throughout its history, Valencia has never been a particularly wealthy province, and the Senorios (feudal landlords, tenants of the king), were usually absentees, preferring to live in their palacios in the cities. There were, however, one or two exceptions: at Alcalali, Penaguilla, Calpe, for example, the remains of fortified palacios can still be seen. Most mountain villages seem to have been left to themselves to scratch a meagre living from a poor soil and a harsh climate. It is remarkable how little the life of the campesino has changed whilst his children go on to become computer analysts, bankers, and public relations advisers, leaving most villages solely occupied by the very young and the very old.

You will find that, many of the villages have strange sounding names, a reminder of the long centuries of Moorish occupation.

Fuentes (Springs)

In ancient times, a good and reliable water supply was essential for survival in this arid region, and the site of a farm or a village depended on the springs issuing from subterranean reservoirs. These village *fuentes* were well maintained, and usually included a lavadero (wash-house) for the housewives. Surprisingly, many are still in use, and not only by the older ladies. Nearby can sometimes be found the remains of old watermills, especially where a reliable flow of water existed (Bolulla). At Font Moli, above the village of Benimantell, however, the *fuente* feeds a reservoir which once provided a head of water for the mill. Today, many villages have refurbished their *fuentes*, embellishing them with ceramics, and providing shade trees, barbecues and picnic sites, much loved by the Spaniards at weekends and fiestas for holding paella parties. Don't be surprised if you find people filling the boots of their cars with plastic bottles of the spring water. Spaniards and others seem to have a distinct distrust of the public water supply, despite the fact that most coastal resorts have a reliable supply of excellent water.

Irrigation

The regulation and allocation of water to those landowners whose deeds give them the right to irrigation is vested in a committee of landowners in each village. Each farmer is annually allocated a time when he may open the sluice gates, and allow the precious water to flow on to his land. This, if he is unlucky, could be in the middle of the night, nevertheless, at the exact time when his allotted period expires, you may rest assured that his neighbour will be waiting to ensure that the sluice gates are closed, ready for him to get his share of the water. Serious disputes concerning water rights are settled by an ancient court, which sits on the steps of the cathedral in Valencia.

When the A150 between Altea la Vieja and Callosa d'Ensarria was widened, it was necessary to reconstruct the water conduits alongside it, and this is a good place for those who wish to study these irrigation systems, which nourish the extensive crops of nispero and citrus fruits. The Moors seem to be credited with the introduction of irrigation during their occupation of the area.

The Huerta

This means, literally, irrigated land, used for vegetables. Huerto means an orchard of citrus fruit, and, where the land levels out on the coastal plain, vast areas of rich soil have been irrigated all along the coast of Valencia, diverting the water of the rivers by means of pumps and irrigation channels since Moorish times. The huerta inland from Denia is particularly interesting. Rising from the vast sea of orange and lemon trees the tall chimneys of the old steam pumping stations can still be seen. Further north, near Sagra, can be found an old Moorish water mill, still in reasonable condition.

Fincas And Casitas

The ruins of these farms and cottages are to be found high in the mountains, and show how hard these farmers had to work to wrest a living from this harsh land. You will hardly find any dressed wood, except perhaps, the door. All beams and lintels are rough-hewn. Windows are usually small and unglazed, and generally only on the north side. Roofs were lined with bamboo from the river, and then tiled. The space was then filled with almond shells to provide insulation; sometimes the traditional Valencian arches between the beams are plastered. Not far from the back door you will find the housewife's beehive-shaped oven, which was heated with brushwood until a sufficient temperature had been reached then sealed with a stone. The nearby well, with its lavadero, and troughs for the animals, completed the facilities available.

Not all these remote fincas were occupied the whole year. Some, like the old village under the crags of Bolulla Castle, were used as shelters when the herdsmen and shepherds took their animals to summer pasture. Others were used by the family when it was necessary to work on the land. Today, with the advantage of motor transport, the land is cultivated on a daily basis, with the farmer living in his village house.

Riu-Raus

This is a distinctive type of architecture, to be found only where the Muscatel grape is cultivated for the manufacture of raisins. They are long, arched porches along the wall of a single-storey building, and are so attractive that they have been incorporated in many modern villas. Their purpose, however, is strictly practical, in that the long loggia provides shelter from the weather for the trays of ripening raisins.

Village Bars

Sadly I have recently noticed a change in attitude amongst a small minority of bar owners, no doubt inspired by tales of a quick fortune to be made by adopting the inflated prices of the coast. They seem to treat all foreigners as eccentric millionaires, who do not know the value of Spanish money, and don't care if they don't get any change. It is not my intention to suggest that you spoil your holiday by haggling over every drink, but it might be prudent to learn a few Spanish phrases to use in the situations outlined above, such as:

Cuanto es?	How much is it?
Es muy caro	It's very expensive
A donde es mi cambio?	Where is my change?
Madre mia, caramba	(shrug shoulders, beat forehead, stamp feet) My goodness, tut-tut, general displeasure
Yo no estoy contento	I am not happy
Vamonos	We are leaving

Village Houses

As might be expected, these are a little grander, with tiled balconies and rejas (grilles) over the windows, a left-over from the Moorish preoccupation with protecting the female members of the family. Note the large double doors, which allowed horses, mules and carts, to be taken through the house to the courtyard at the rear. Even today, in the villages and larger towns, you can still see the ruts in some of the doorsteps, worn by the cartwheels, and the small stone pillars placed on each side of the door arch, to protect the masonry from damage from the cartwheels. The stone used in town and village houses is a coloured limestone called 'tosca', and very attractive it is, when carved to form arches and doorways.

Churches

Mountain villages are usually poor, without benefactors, and on the surface, the outside of the churches sometimes seem sadly neglected. There are, however, exceptions, and the beautiful domed church of Jalon has a Grandee of Spain for its benefactress, who, amongst her other titles, is Baroness of Jalon and Lliber. The insides of churches are usually particularly beautiful, but you will, except on Sundays and fiestas, have to seek out the guardian to obtain the key. They are all kept locked, due, no doubt, to the Spanish propensity for burning down churches in time of revolt. The tower of the church at Murla was built on the base of the old Moorish castle. It fell down during a recent storm, killing two elderly ladies.

In addition to the village church, there is usually a sanctuario, or a hermita, dramatically situated on the mountainside above the village.

Spanish village cemeteries are easily identified by an avenue of the tall Mediterranean cypress trees, and normally include a calvary (Stations of the Cross). Some are beautifully decorated with ceramics. The cemeteries are interesting places to study the history of the village, especially the names of the main families. It is traditional to place the dead in brick cubicles built into walls around the cemetery, rather than bury them in the earth. Only the very important families have vaults.

Crops

On the dry land, olives, vines, carobs and almonds prosper, often with a spring catch crop of vegetables sown between the lines of trees. The olives, almonds and carobs are harvested, as they were centuries ago, by spreading a net on the ground, and knocking the fruit down with a long bamboo pole. Green olives are picked first, then cured, a long and tedious process. Most of the olives sold in the shops are the produce of Andalucia, but in mountain restaurants, you will probably be served with a local product.

Ripe purple olives are crushed in an almazara (olive press). The oil extracted is usually for home consumption, or sold in village shops.

Almonds, for which the Jalon Valley is rightly famous, are grown in a great number of varieties. The blossom ranges in colour from white to deep purple, and this indicates whether the almond is sweet or bitter, and used either for eating, making turron (nougat), or for extracting oil. There are a number of cooperatives where the farmers can take their crops, and there are crushing plants in Altea, Fleix and Tormos, identified by the great mounds of almond shells in the factory yard. In remote villages, the mobile shelling machine is set up in the village square. You cannot miss it, the noise is ear-shattering.

The carob (locust bean) makes good animal fodder, and is useful for making chocolate substitute. Wherever the Muscatel grape is grown, eg., Calpe, Teulada and the Jalon Valley, some of the crop was made into raisins, by scalding with caustic soda, and leaving in the sun on wicker mats to dry. This practice is now only carried on in a few villages, eg., Lliber. The production of raisins gave rise to the distinctive architecture of Riu-Raus (see Fincas and Casitas).

Nature's Bounty

Mountain villagers have always been adept at living off the land. After rainfall, you may see groups of women and children foraging in the ditches by the roadside, seeking wild asparagus and snails. On the high mountains, the men will probably be collecting mushrooms, especially the large brown ones, a much sought-after delicacy.

Livestock

The further inland you go from the coast, the more chance there is that you will see long-legged mules, donkeys, and the lovely miniature shire horses, used by the farmers in cultivating their land. Although most farmers have turned to tractors, the mule and donkey have a distinct advantage when it comes to cultivating narrow terraces, or using the Mozarabic trails.

Cattle, including bulls, are often grazed in some valley bottoms, where there is a reliable water supply, eg., Maserof, Almadich and the Val de Infierno near Isbert's dam. Thankfully, they are always supervised by the vaquero (herdsman).

The mixed flocks of sheep and goats can still be seen grazing under the care of the pastor (shepherd), and his motley collection of dogs, whose purpose is to protect the flock against wolves! The shepherd guides his flock by throwing stones and shouting, but the lead ewe seems to decide where the flock will go, whilst the dogs mill about showing off. The flocks are corralled at night.

Other livestock, pigs, chicken, ducks, rabbits etc. are, it seems, raised in secret by the little old ladies you see returning home with baskets of grass and herbs.

5. Fiestas

Be prepared to find the village shop and even the bakery closed on fiesta days. The more local the fiesta, the less likely you are to find supplies, although the village bar will remain open as usual. The Patronal Festival is the most important. Village fiestas are modest, intimate affairs, unlike the more affluent towns where impressive processions, concerts, bull-running and extensive sports pro-grammes are the norm. Valencia was the last province to be reconquered by the Christian kings, so the fiestas of Moors and Christians are impressive sights. One of the most famous is in Alcoy, an industrial town some 40km inland, where in 1276 St George is alleged to have appeared to inspire the Christian troops, who then overcame the beseiging Moors led by Al Azraq. Since then they have celebrated their victory over the Moors. The museum has costumes and photographs dating from the 19th century. In recent times, the developing coastal resorts have followed this example, and there are spectacular celebrations in Villajoyosa, Benidorm, Altea, Callosa Ensarria, Calpe, Javea, Denia and Pego.

Volta En Carro

In Las Marinas in July each year, there is an unusual expedition through the mountains of old 'covered wagons' pulled by teams of mules or horses. Their owners are farmers or businessmen determined to keep up the old traditions, and each night they camp and accept the hospitality of a mountain village for a paella and a fiesta.

Tira Y Arrastre

This is a most unusual sport, a trial of strength, practised by Valencians. Each team of horses and men together pull a weighted cart along the shingle bed of a river in competition with each other. It is reported that it is only the men who need reviving after their exertions; apparently the horses take it in their stride!

El Bous

Bull-running is now not confined to Pamplona, but has been adopted as part of most fiestas. It seems, on the face of it, a harmless sport and an opportunity for the young to show their mettle. Whilst accepting that the Spaniards are not as sensitive as others about animals, this activity often gets out of hand with young people, sometimes the worse for drink, goading the frightened animals with sharp instruments, letting off fireworks and throwing bottles and cans at them. The Civil Governor has regularly threatened local mayors that if his local inspectors (retired matadors!) report any cruelty, he will ban the event in future (but he never does).

Bous a Carre

A street is closed off, stands erected for spectators, and boards behind which a hard-pressed 'torero' can hide.

Bous a Mar

The same, except that the event is held on the harbour wall, and refuge taken in the sea.

Bous Embolat

This is often the end of the event, with all lights being extinguished, and the poor animal, with flaming torches fixed to its horns, chased down the street.

Hogueras and Fallas

In Valencia, since the middle ages, carpenters have celebrated the day of St Joseph (19th March), their patron, by spring cleaning their workshops, and burning all the old wood and shavings, including the rough racks on which they hung their outdoor clothes. In later years crude effigies of local personalities were added, and today it has developed into a major art form. A huge industry exists in Valencia to produce giant displays of papier maché sculptures on wooden frames, often with a humorous or political message, as local personalities are mercilessly caricatured. All year round the Filas (clubs) of the various districts of the city work to raise funds so that they can commission the many artisans who will make the giant tableaux. With great festivity, a display of fireworks, and the many bands competing with each other, the whole lot goes up in flames at midnight, as the poor fireman try to prevent the nearby buildings from catching fire. Only one Falla, the one judged to be the best, is saved for display in the museum.

In Alicante, they celebrate the day of their patron St Juan (June) in a similar manner but the displays are called Hogueras, and many of the resorts along the Costa have added the Fallas to their lists of fiestas.

La Pilota Valenciana

This is a Valencian version of the Basque game of handball, but not using a basket, strapped to the hand to give velocity to the ball. There are two versions, Raspat, where the ball is skimmed over the surface of a street, and Llarges, where it is bounded off a high wall. The game is still played in Calle Garcia Ortiz at Calpe every Sunday afternoon, but even small mountain villages have their purpose-built court, recognised by its high, green painted walls set at 90 degrees.

Tourist offices will supply full details of local fiestas, and publish a monthly leaflet for the whole of the province. Details of all local events appear in the three English-language newspapers.

Religious Fiestas

Spaniards observe many more religious holidays than we do in the UK. In addition to the Patronal fiestas of villages and towns the main ones are:

6th January	Epiphany. Known as the Three Kings, when children receive their presents. Normally lasts for a whole week.
March	San Jose, patron saint of carpenters. Burning of Fallas in Valencia. Wooden and papier maché effigies burned are sometimes 15m high.
March/April	Semana Santa (Holy week). Very important in Spain.
May	Ascension, Pentecost and Corpus Christi.
June	St Juan – burning of Fallas – Alicante and Costa
25th July	Santiago.
August	Assumption of the Virgin Mary.
November	All Saints.
8th December	Immaculate Conception.
25th December	Christmas Day (one day only).

In addition, the following secular fiestas are held:

1st January	New Year's Day. Traditional to eat one grape for each chime as midnight sounds.
1st May	Labour Day.
9th October	Valencian Day.
12th October	Columbus Day (Dia de la Hispanidad).
6th December	Spanish Constitutional Day.

6. Relics of the Past

Castles

Valencia is rich in castles, and there are many ruins in the mountains, not all of them marked on maps. 'Castle' is rather a grand name, as some of them were only fortified lookouts. All date from the Moorish occupation and Reconquest in the 13th century, and whilst some of them are in reasonable repair (ie. Forna), others are just a few dressed stones or a single wall. Serrella has a cistern which still holds water, and in which mountain toads breed each year.

Eras

Where there is an extensive farmhouse, you will always find a well, an oven, and an *era*. This last is a flat surface for threshing and crushing cereals, by means of a metre-long tapered stone with a metal rod running through it. The stone was pulled over the grain by man or mule. When I first started walking in the area, most eras had at least one stone, left after the last harvest some hundred years ago. Sadly, most of them have now been taken away as souvenirs.

There is a gigantic *era* stone at the entrance to the village of Guadalest, and the Ponsoda restaurant on the road from Benimantell to Polop has lined the edge of the car park with them. At the Jami restaurant in Confrides, there is another good specimen, and you will park on what was once the *era* of an old *finca* (now the restaurant).

Almazeras

These are the old presses, normally used for crushing olives, but occasionally used for grapes. One or sometimes two conical stones ran in a circular stone trough, and were powered by mule or donkey. The stones were supported by a metal frame and cogwheel, and a good example can be seen at Km 169.7 next to the old venta (inn) on the CN332 at Calpe. The old inn is now a disco. There was another one in working order in the Val de Gallinera, in the remote village of Lombay, but this year, the roof fell in and buried it. The stones, along with millstones and old wine presses, are much sought after to decorate *fuentes* and glorietas in the villages, eg. Lorcha and Cuatretondeta.

Mozarabic Trails

'Mozarabic' is a term reserved for those Christians who accepted Moorish rule, and were allowed to follow their religion. Moors who, after the reconquest, were baptised were known as Mudejars.

The Spaniards use the term 'Mozarabic' to describe the narrow stepped trails which cross our mountains, zig-zagging down into the depths of the deepest ravines, and up the other side. They are truly marvels of engineering, with revetments used to support the trail in desperate places. Surprisingly, many of them have withstood the ravages of time, nature, and lack of maintenance. They are best seen in the Val de Laguart, where the Camino de Juvias first descends the sheer sides of the Barranco del Infierno, and then climbs out of the valley on the other side, towards the Val d'Ebo.

Neveras

These are deep cylindrical ice-pits, usually constructed on the northern slopes of the high mountains, for the purpose of making ice from snow. They are normally about 15m deep, and 10m in diameter. The larger ones had supporting stone beams, and a wooden roof which was tiled. Smaller ones were corbelled, built up in steps from bricks and stones, to make a dome. They were mainly used during the 17th and 18th centuries, and fell into decay with the introduction of refrigeration by electricity.

In winter, the pits were filled with snow, sometimes in sacks, and sometimes layered in straw. During the summer men with mules spent the night at the *nevera* cutting the ice into blocks, insulating it with straw, and transporting it by mule down the hazardous trails to the villages before the sun rose. Whether it is true or not I do not know, but an old villager in Fachega told me that his father remembered seeing the fires lit by the ice-cutters on the mountain Pla de la Casa, and could describe to me the route taken back to the village down the Barranco del Moro.

There is an excellent example of an arched *nevera* above Agres on the Moro del Contador, near the Refugio Santiago Reig del Mural, on the way to climb Monte Cabrer. Next to the Refugio is a small corbelled *nevera*, with the roof intact. There are also good examples on the Peña Mulero route and the biggest, deepest and highest is a few metres below the summit of Pla de la Casa.

Salinas (salt pans)

The only place in the area where salt was produced by evaporation are the salinas on the isthmus, under the Peñon d'Ifach at Calpe. Salt was last produced here in 1988, by pumping sea water from a point near the Queen's Baths (Roman remains) on the Arenal beach. The area of the salinas has now turned into a freshwater lake, and attracts a great many water birds, including the colourful flamingos from the Camargue in France, who winter here. One day, it is hoped that plans to turn the area into a Natural Park may soon materialise. Salt is still produced commercially further south in Torrevieja and Santa Pola.

Mountain Crosses

On a prominent crag above many mountain villages can be found a stone or metal cross, which protects the village, from Moors, lightning and tempests. In 1952, the cross on top of Perereta (826m) above the tiny village of Benimaurell, was restored by the young men of the village, no doubt at the instigation of the old people, who felt they still needed the protection of the old cross, which had disintegrated.

Windmills

Water mills, mentioned in the section 'Springs', needed to be near a reliable source of water. Windmills, which were more numerous, needed the best possible position to tap their power source, the wind. You will find them on any piece of high ground near a village, on the coast (Calpe) and even the top of cliffs (Javea). They are gregarious, like the company of other mills, and on Cabo St Antonio, near Javea, there are over ten of them on the cliff edge. They were used to grind wheat and indicate the amount of cereals which were grown on the narrow terraces in ancient times. Many of the mills, date from pre-Moorish times but today only the ruined towers remain, unused for over 100 years. When in use the mill had a conical cap, which could be rotated to catch the wind, and which accommodated the sails which were sometimes of wood, but more often of canvas. Wooden shafts and gears drove the large grinding stones on the ground floor. Some mills were also used as early lookout towers.

Watch Towers

These round lookouts were built in the 16th century on the coast to provide an early warning of raids by pirates. Piracy had always been rife in this part of the Mediterranean, even in the 14th century. Raids by ships from Africa and even from the one remaining Moorish kingdom, Granada, were quite common. After the final expulsion of the Moors in 1609, the raids became more frequent and the authorities had to take steps to combat them by building the towers and by providing a fleet of defensive ships. The costal towns were, of course, the most vulnerable to attack. In 1636, the pirates, after pillaging the village of Calpe, took nearly all the population back to Algiers as slaves. They were released many years later, when a ransom had been paid. We even know the names of some of these desperados: Dragut, Barberroja (red beard) and Picelilli Pacha. Moraira has restored its tower on the beach, and one of the many windmills on Cabo St Antonio near Javea, was also used as a lookout.

LISTING OF CICERONE GUIDES

LISTING OF CICERONE GUIDES

THE WEALDWAY & VANGUARD WAY

SCOTLAND

WALKING IN THE ISLE OF ARRAN
THE BORDER COUNTRY -
  A WALKERS GUIDE
BORDER COUNTRY CYCLE
  ROUTES
BORDER PUBS & INNS -
  A WALKERS' GUIDE
CAIRNGORMS, Winter Climbs
  5th Edition
CENTRAL HIGHLANDS
  6 LONG DISTANCE WALKS
WALKING THE GALLOWAY HILLS
WALKING IN THE HEBRIDES
NORTH TO THE CAPE
THE ISLAND OF RHUM
THE ISLE OF SKYE A Walker's Guide
WALKS IN THE LAMMERMUIRS
WALKING IN THE LOWTHER HILLS
THE SCOTTISH GLENS SERIES
  1 - CAIRNGORM GLENS
  2 - ATHOLL GLENS
  3 - GLENS OF RANNOCH
  4 - GLENS OF TROSSACH
  5 - GLENS OF ARGYLL
  6 - THE GREAT GLEN
  7 - THE ANGUS GLENS
  8 - KNOYDART TO MORVERN
  9 - THE GLENS OF ROSS-SHIRE
SCOTTISH RAILWAY WALKS
SCRAMBLES IN LOCHABER
SCRAMBLES IN SKYE
SKI TOURING IN SCOTLAND
THE SPEYSIDE WAY
TORRIDON - A Walker's Guide
WALKS FROM THE WEST
  HIGHLAND RAILWAY
THE WEST HIGHLAND WAY
WINTER CLIMBS NEVIS &
  GLENCOE

IRELAND

IRISH COASTAL WALKS
THE IRISH COAST TO COAST
THE MOUNTAINS OF IRELAND

WALKING AND TREKKING IN THE ALPS

WALKING IN THE ALPS
100 HUT WALKS IN THE ALPS
CHAMONIX to ZERMATT
GRAND TOUR OF MONTE ROSA
  Vol. 1 and Vol. 2
TOUR OF MONT BLANC

FRANCE, BELGIUM AND LUXEMBOURG

WALKING IN THE ARDENNES
ROCK CLIMBS BELGIUM & LUX.
THE BRITTANY COASTAL PATH
CHAMONIX - MONT BLANC
  Walking Guide
WALKING IN THE CEVENNES

CORSICAN HIGH LEVEL ROUTE:
  GR20
THE ECRINS NATIONAL PARK
WALKING THE FRENCH ALPS: GR5
WALKING THE FRENCH GORGES
FRENCH ROCK
WALKING IN THE HAUTE SAVOIE
WALKING IN THE LANGUEDOC
TOUR OF THE OISANS: GR54
WALKING IN PROVENCE
THE PYRENEAN TRAIL: GR10
THE TOUR OF THE QUEYRAS
ROBERT LOUIS STEVENSON TRAIL
WALKING IN TARENTAISE &
  BEAUFORTAIN ALPS
ROCK CLIMBS IN THE VERDON
TOUR OF THE VANOISE
WALKS IN VOLCANO COUNTRY

FRANCE/SPAIN

ROCK CLIMBS IN THE PYRENEES
WALKS & CLIMBS IN THE
  PYRENEES
THE WAY OF ST JAMES
  Le Puy to Santiago - Walker's
THE WAY OF ST JAMES
  Le Puy to Santiago - Cyclist's

SPAIN AND PORTUGAL

WALKING IN THE ALGARVE
ANDALUSIAN ROCK CLIMBS
BIRDWATCHING IN MALLORCA
COSTA BLANCA ROCK
COSTA BLANCA WALKS VOL 1
COSTA BLANCA WALKS VOL 2
WALKING IN MALLORCA
ROCK CLIMBS IN MAJORCA, IBIZA
  & TENERIFE
WALKING IN MADEIRA
THE MOUNTAINS OF CENTRAL
  SPAIN
THE SPANISH PYRENEES GR11 2nd
  Ed.
WALKING IN THE SIERRA NEVADA
WALKS & CLIMBS IN THE PICOS
  DE EUROPA
VIA DE LA PLATA

SWITZERLAND

ALPINE PASS ROUTE,
  SWITZERLAND
THE BERNESE ALPS A Walking
  Guide
CENTRAL SWITZERLAND
THE JURA: HIGH ROUTE & SKI
  TRAVERSES
WALKING IN TICINO,
  SWITZERLAND
THE VALAIS, SWITZERLAND.
  A Walking Guide

GERMANY, AUSTRIA AND EASTERN EUROPE

MOUNTAIN WALKING IN AUSTRIA
WALKING IN THE BAVARIAN ALPS
WALKING IN THE BLACK FOREST

THE DANUBE CYCLE WAY
GERMANY'S ROMANTIC ROAD
WALKING IN THE HARZ
  MOUNTAINS
KING LUDWIG WAY
KLETTERSTEIG Northern Limestone
  Alps
WALKING THE RIVER RHINE TRAIL
THE MOUNTAINS OF ROMANIA
WALKING IN THE SALZKAM-
  MERGUT
HUT-TO-HUT IN THE STUBAI ALPS
THE HIGH TATRAS

SCANDANAVIA

WALKING IN NORWAY
ST OLAV'S WAY

ITALY AND SLOVENIA

ALTA VIA - HIGH LEVEL WALKS
  DOLOMITES
CENTRAL APENNINES OF ITALY
WALKING CENTRAL ITALIAN ALPS
WALKING IN THE DOLOMITES
SHORTER WALKS IN THE
  DOLOMITES
WALKING ITALY'S GRAN
  PARADISO
LONG DISTANCE WALKS IN
  ITALY'S GRAN PARADISO
ITALIAN ROCK
WALKS IN THE JULIAN ALPS
WALKING IN SICILY
WALKING IN TUSCANY
VIA FERRATA SCRAMBLES IN THE
  DOLOMITES

OTHER MEDITERRANEAN COUNTRIES

THE ATLAS MOUNTAINS
WALKING IN CYPRUS
CRETE - THE WHITE MOUNTAINS
THE MOUNTAINS OF GREECE
JORDAN - Walks, Treks, Caves etc.
THE MOUNTAINS OF TURKEY
TREKS & CLIMBS WADI RUM
  JORDAN
CLIMBS & TREKS IN THE ALA DAG
WALKING IN PALESTINE

HIMALAYA

ADVENTURE TREKS IN NEPAL
ANNAPURNA - A TREKKER'S
  GUIDE
EVEREST - A TREKKERS' GUIDE
GARHWAL & KUMAON - A
  Trekker's Guide
KANGCHENJUNGA - A Trekker's
  Guide
LANGTANG, GOSAINKUND &
  HELAMBU Trekkers Guide
MANASLU - A trekker's guide

Cicerone's mission is to inform and inspire by providing the best guides to exploring the world

Since its foundation over 30 years ago, Cicerone has specialised in publishing guidebooks and has built a reputation for quality and reliability. It now publishes nearly 300 guides to the major destinations for outdoor enthusiasts, including Europe, UK and the rest of the world.

Written by leading and committed specialists, Cicerone guides are recognised as the most authoritative. They are full of information, maps and illustrations so that the user can plan and complete a successful and safe trip or expedition – be it a long face climb, a walk over Lakeland fells, an alpine traverse, a Himalayan trek or a ramble in the countryside.

With a thorough introduction to assist planning, clear diagrams, maps and colour photographs to illustrate the terrain and route, and accurate and detailed text, Cicerone guides are designed for ease of use and access to the information.

If the facts on the ground change, or there is any aspect of a guide that you think we can improve, we are always delighted to hear from you.

Cicerone Press, 2 Police Square, Milnthorpe, Cumbria LA7 7PY

Tel 01539 562 069   Fax 01539 563 417
email info@cicerone.co.uk   web: www.cicerone.co.uk

CICERONE